Stagecoach East

Stagecoach Days in the East from the Colonial Period to the Civil War

OLIVER W. HOLMES
PETER T. ROHRBACH

SMITHSONIAN INSTITUTION PRESS
Washington, D.C.   1983

Library of Congress Cataloging in Publication Data
Holmes, Oliver Wendell, 1902–1981
    Stagecoach East.
    Bibliography: p.
    Includes index.
    Supt. of Docs. no.: SI 1.2:St 1
    1. Coaching—United States—History—18th century. 2. Coaching—
United States—History—19th century. I. Rohrbach, Peter T. II. Title.

HE5747.H64 1983   388.3′228′0973   82-600375
ISBN 0-87474-522-5

Uncredited illustrations are from the collections of the
Smithsonian Institution's National Museum of American History.

Contents

Acknowledgments

 SEVERAL PEOPLE are owed a debt of gratitude for their invaluable assistance in producing this volume. Felix C. Lowe, director of the Smithsonian Institution Press, brought together and encouraged all the people involved in the project. Edward F. Rivinus, director emeritus of the Smithsonian Institution Press, was enthusiastic about it from the beginning; he served as editor of the volume and guided it through to publication. Lowell Newman and Roger White, both of the Smithsonian's National Museum of American History, offered valued advice and opened the treasures of their museums collections. Calvet M. Hahn was kind enough to review the completed manuscript and offer some important suggestions. Special thanks are due to Sheila Ann Sheehan, who typed the manuscript. Bradley Rymph did a truly splendid job of copy-editing the text. Finally, eternal gratitude goes to my collaborator, Dr. Oliver W. Holmes, who passed away on November 25, 1981, just after the major research for the book had been completed.   P.T.R.

Introduction: Stagecoach East

 *"The finest vehicles in the world without any dispute."*

WHEN THAT PROUD and enthusiastic statement about the stagecoach appeared in the Boston *American Traveller* in July of 1825, staging in the East was in its golden age. More than seventy different stagecoach lines serviced Boston alone in 1826, and that number was almost to double during the following decade. The stagecoach owned the American roads in the East during the first half of the nineteenth century, providing a vast network of transportation for citizens in the young Republic. But the stagecoach was much more than a mere mode of transportation; indeed, the eastern stage set the very tempo of American life in that period. It carried the mail and thus became the country's major communications network in those pre-telegraph days. The stagecoach also delivered the newspapers, thereby increasing literacy and disseminating vital information to the public.

When the American stagecoach is mentioned, the immediate image is of the stage of the Far West, the romantic inspiration of so much drama and fiction. But that is another and later story of a frontier period after the Civil War. Unfortunately, little has been written of the important earlier chapter of staging in the East prior to the Civil War, when the stagecoach played a critical role in forming the social and political climate of the new Republic. And a full understanding of how the nation developed during those pre–Civil War years requires a recognition of the unique role the stage played in that development.

Stagecoach service started in the colonies in the early eighteenth century, and there was a modest amount of staging in the East during the fifty years before the Revolution. Service was largely disrupted during the war, but as the British began to retreat and withdraw from various areas, a renewed and expanding stagecoach industry started to appear up and down the eastern seaboard.

In 1785, Congress voted to employ stagecoaches to carry the mail on established stage routes, thereby giving them a quasi-public character as an arm of the General Post Office. For the next sixty years, the stage-coach was the main carrier of the mail in the United States, and until telegraph lines in the 1840s it was the nation's principal communications mode. Its contributions to the fledgling Republic in its often uncertain days were therefore enormous.

Furthermore, the stages in the East had a generous policy toward the newspapers, allowing them low rates and free printers' exchanges. This encouraged a healthy and burgeoning newspaper industry, and thanks in large part to the stages, the American people of the nineteenth century became the largest newspaper-reading population in history up to that point. Again, that contribution to molding the thinking of the Republic is almost incalculable.

The stagecoach network—with its special *culture* of stagecoach taverns and stagecoach customs—continued to develop through the early nineteenth century, reaching its golden years in the East during the two decades from 1820 to 1840. The railroads of the 1830s and the telegraph of the 1840s began to make inroads on the old stage lines; yet the stage's decline was so gradual that in 1860 on the eve of the Civil War there were still more miles of stagecoach mail lines than of railroad mail lines. But the final outcome was inevitable: The age of eastern staging was just about over, and after the Civil War, the railroads would virtually drive the stagecoach off the main eastern roads they once traveled in such great numbers. However, by the time of the Civil War, the eastern stage lines had also been extended to the Mississippi, and a new romantic period for the stage was about to develop across the Mississippi during the Reconstruction period.

This chronicle is derived in large part from primary sources—such as government records, personal narratives by people who built and rode the stages, and contemporary newspapers—and many of them have never been published in book form before. The book is therefore a story of how the eastern stagecoach was constructed and developed, culminating in that pre-eminent stagecoach of the 1830s, the Concord coach, but it is also the story of the people involved in that unique and now long-gone stagecoach culture: the proprietors who established and expanded the stage lines, the stagecoach makers, the colorful stage drivers, the stagecoach travelers, and the postmasters general who supervised the vast stage network. It is a chronicle of a time when the nation was very young, and when the stagecoach was king.

I

Colonial Stage Lines

 IN THE BEGINNING, they came by water, and for many years afterward they continued to travel the waters of their new home.

Those colonists of the seventeenth century, like almost all the early settlers of a new continent throughout history, had used the ocean waters to carry them to the Atlantic seaboard of North America, and during the early colonial period, their main avenues of travel were those other waters discovered on the new continent: the ocean inlets and the inland waterways. The choice of the waterways was a pragmatic one determined by the characteristics of the land and the demands placed upon them as settlers and colonists. For one thing, the waterways were already there and waiting to be used. And they were extremely navigable and required no maintenance. Furthermore, along that eastern North American seaboard, the harbors were many and good, and timber for shipbuilding was plentiful and conveniently located.

The development of land travel in a new country, however, is a more time-consuming and arduous process. Carriages, carts, and, in forested regions, even horses must be left behind at first; the settlers, of necessity, must return to the primitive foot travel of the natives. To improve the condition of land travel, roads must be constructed, bridges built, and ferries maintained. If the land is rough and heavily wooded, as it was along the Atlantic seaboard, the difficulties are greater. In addition, settlers have other more pressing tasks to claim their time and energy—cabins to be constructed, fields to be cleared, food and clothing to be somehow secured in an inhospitable wilderness. Roads are not vitally necessary for a time. A pathway to the nearest landing will suffice. Only when the pressure of immigration forces a penetration of the interior to a point where waterways cannot serve will roads become a matter of public concern.

Such penetration was long postponed in a country so well provided with deep bays, estuaries, and navigable rivers as the eastern coast of North America was. With numerous indentations stretching far back into the interior, the normal shore line was multiplied many times, and plantations and settlements had access to the sea.[1] Indeed, these waterways served so effectively that few inland trade centers of importance developed during colonial days that were not served by water.

TRAVEL in colonial days in North America, when not by water, was chiefly on horseback. Even when carriages of various sorts were introduced, the countryfolk continued to use horse and saddle for their pleasure trips, and travelers preferred them for long journeys. Outside the towns, the roads were practically impassable for carriages during a great part of the year. Horse and rider, encountering unexpected obstructions, could act with more freedom and therefore move with greater speed and certainty than a vehicle could. Also, horseback travel was less expensive—a weighty consideration for ordinary farmers and townsmen of the time.

During the colonial period, the mail was originally carried by postriders on horseback. In England, the Post Office already supervised a highly organized system of postriders in which postmasters maintained fresh horses for the riders, allowing them to change mounts at each posting station along the route.[2] In the colonies, there were both "official" and "private" postriders, the former paid by the Post Office establishment and the latter paid by the patrons they served.[3]

Before 1700 in the colonies, few carriages were used expressly for the conveyance of persons. Colonial governors owned some coaches, but their use was confined to a half-dozen principal towns and to state occasions. The earliest mention of coaches seems to be in 1674 when Governor Anthony Colve of New Netherland presented his coach with horses to his successor, Sir Edmund Andros.[4] Governor William Berkeley of Virginia possessed a coach of which mention was made in 1677.[5] Samuel Sewall in his diary frequently mentioned meeting the Massachusetts governor in his coach, and in 1699 when that official dined at Roxbury, there were four coaches in attendance.[6] However, coaches were regarded as a prerogative of the official class, and possession of them by anyone else was frowned upon as vanity and pretension. The only other riding carriage to make its appearance in the seventeenth century was the calash, a two-wheeled, one-seated vehicle, with collapsible hood, pulled by two horses and used for hard travel rather than for display.[7]

The tendency in New England was toward lighter vehicles. The English chaise, introduced between 1710 and 1730, when modified and simplified became the Yankee "shay." A similar vehicle without a hood was called a chair. These, together with calashes, became the popular vehicles for the city gentry by 1730, and soon afterwards, they were appearing in the smaller towns. They were still regarded as an indulgence, however, and a good Puritan would think seriously before buying one. The Reverend Joseph Emerson of Malden, Massachusetts, wrote in his diary, January 24, 1735; "Some talk about my buying a Shay. How much reason have I to watch and pray and strive against inordinate affection for the Things of the World." Nevertheless, on January 31, he entered, "Bought a Shay, £27 10s. The Lord grant it may be a comfort and blessing to my family."[8]

By 1740, a traveler in New England was able to write, "There are several families in Boston that keep a coach, and pair of horses, and some few drive with four horses; but for chaises and saddlehorses, considering the bulk of the place, they outdo London."[9] The tax list for 1753 gives more definite information: The entire province of Massachusetts returned 6 coaches, 18 chariots, 339 chaises, and 992 chairs and calashes.[10] Of these, so many were in Boston that a committee was appointed at a town meeting to draw up a memorial to the General Court protesting against the tax since Boston "will pay much more than all the Province beside."[11]

In New York, the number of carrages similarly increased. Newspaper notices of coaches, chaises, and chairs for sale became frequent after 1730.[12] By 1750, a newspaper item mentioned that a horse race on "Hampstead Plains" engaged the attention of so many New Yorkers that "upwards of 70 Chairs and Chaises were carried over the ferry from hence the Day before."[13] The artist Pierre Eugene Du Simitiere, visiting New York in 1770, listed the owners of the more aristrocratic four-wheeled carriages in the city. He found that sixty-two individuals owned eighty-five vehicles, of which twenty-six were coaches, thirty-three chariots or post-chaises, and twenty-six phaetons.[14]

In Virginia in the eighteenth century, the coach became the fashionable vehicle of the planter. However, chairs and chaises also were frequently found, especially in the towns.[15] Hugh Jones, as early as 1724, observed that most families of note in Williamsburg had a coach, chariot, berlin, or chaise,[16] and an anonymous writer in the *London Magazine* in 1746 noticed in Yorktown "the prodigious Number of Coaches that crowd the deep, sandy Streets of this little City."[17]

However, a rough estimate of the available statistics indicates scarcely more than one pleasure vehicle for every fifty families in the years just before the American Revolution. The working class in towns and cities had no carriages at all. Except for a few southern planters, the country people, who overwhelmingly predominated the population, did not purchase them until after 1800, and even then they did not own carriages in significant numbers until the mass-produced vehicle was introduced in the 1870s. During the colonial period, they still made their excursions in carts and wagons, putting hay or straw in the bottom of the box if the family were to be taken along.

What those English colonists of the eighteenth century obviously needed was some form of land transport upon which they could rely with some regularity. They needed a vehicle that could carry them on a scheduled basis with relative comfort and reliability and that could also transport the mail and colonial newspapers. Furthermore, the vehicle would have to be available to the common man, not just the privileged few.

And so, gradually, the stagecoach developed in the colonies, becoming an institution that would play a vital role in bringing the new country to maturity.

STAGECOACH SERVICE began in the colonies during the early eighteenth century. For instance, the state of New Jersey awarded a patent to Hugh Huddy, a member of the New Jersey Council, allowing him to establish a stagecoach line between Burlington and Perth Amboy in 1706. The patent gave him full power to "employ one or more stage coach or stage coaches and one or more waggon or waggons or any other and as many carriages as he shall see convenient for the carrying or transportation of goods and passengers."[18] However, whether Huddy was actually able to make the route operational is unclear, and although the patent uses the word *coach*, purists might object that those vehicles and the others of the period were in reality wagons (as is discussed in chapter 5).

One of the earliest intercity stage services for which we have good documentation was advertised on the back page of the *Boston News-Letter* for October 15, 1716, in these words:

These are to give Notice, That a Stagecoach will set out from the Orange-Tree in Boston, to Newport in Rhode-Island, and back again, once a Fortnight, while the Ways are passable: To be performed at Reasonable Rates, by Jonathan Wardall [properly Wardell] of Boston and John Franklin of Newport.

Jonathan Wardell had already served for four years as Boston's first hackney coachman. Mrs. Wardell attended to the Orange Tree, one of the city's better taverns. She had inherited it from her father, had managed it herself long before she married Wardell, and was to manage it long after his death.[19] Jonathan was free to devote his energies to the extension of that important adjunct of every tavern, the stable. As a hackney coachman, he received occasional calls for a carriage to Rhode Island, since Newport was then the point of embarkation for New York and points south. Except for the existence of Bristol Channel between the mainland and the island, Wardell might have handled these calls himself as they came to him. Hence, an associate was needed on the other side of the waterway to meet all passengers brought from Boston. Had it not been for Bristol Channel, New England might well have waited another generation for its first stagecoach service.

As it turned out, the Boston-Newport line was short-lived. Contemporary references show that it continued to run in 1717 and 1718, but no trace of its existence in 1719 has been found.[20] In 1720, an advertisement appeared by a new proprietor, John Blake, who seems to have taken over both Wardell's hackney business and the stage line. His announcement went into considerable detail and mentioned the transfer at Bristol Ferry.[21] However, Blake's service fades from sight; no later notice of the venture seems to exist.

Not until 1767 was regular stage service between Boston and Rhode Island permanently established. Permanent stage lines, meanwhile, had been running between New York and Philadelphia for many years.

THE MOST IMPORTANT lane of land travel and traffic in colonial times was across New Jersey.[22] If the first stagecoach service in New England was given by innkeepers and hackney coachmen, the first in New Jersey was offered by wagoners whose chief business was conveying goods back and forth between depots at New Brunswick or Perth Amboy on the eastern waters and Trenton, Bordentown, or Burlington on the Delaware River. In New England, a "stage-coach" was used at the very beginning, and there were also to be "stage-chaises" and "stage-chairs." In New Jersey, however, there was to be a long period of "stage-waggons"—partly, no doubt, because it was a Dutch region where coaches were rarely seen and wagons were plentiful, but also because passengers were, at first, only incidental to the carrying of freight. As passengers increased in number, staging freed itself from the freighting business; innkeepers along the route united their resources to form lines and managed them in a manner that became typical of later staging.

The road between Perth Amboy and Burlington, opened in 1634, was the earliest land route in America upon which provision was made for public transportation.[23] About the turn of the century, a man named Dell received from Governor Andrew Hamilton the privilege of driving a wagon between these terminal ports to convey public goods.[24] He inaugurated land commerce between New York and Philadelphia, and he may be considered the first of the professional "waggoners" who, before the day of railroads, carried the overland freight of the country. When Lord Cornbury, who succeeded Hamilton as governor in 1702, gave Hugh Huddy the exclusive right to convey goods on this route, the legislature angrily condemned the grant as a monopoly.[25] The business was becoming important, or it would scarcely have excited such controversy.

These early wagoners gladly added to their income by carrying travelers who applied for transportation. Apparently, however, no definite bid for passengers appeared until 1729, when a newspaper advertisement of Redford's Ferry over the Raritan River at Perth Amboy mentioned "a Stage Waggon kept at the Said Ferry, for Transporting of Passengers and Goods from thence to Burlington, when ever Freight presents."[26] Business seemingly improved, for the next advertisement, placed by Solomon Smith and James Moon of Burlington in 1733, gave notice to "Gentlemen, Merchant[s], Tradesmen, Travellers, and others" that they kept two stage wagons and made the round trip "Once every Week or offt'er if that Business presents."[27]

The first stage on the more northerly route, between Trenton and New Brunswick, was established in 1734 to run twice a week. Its advertisement made its major appeal to travelers, for the wagon "will be fitted up with Benches, and Cover'd over, so that Passengers may sit Easy and Dry."[28] The service lapsed in 1739 but was renewed in 1740.[29]

Also in 1740, service across New Jersey by a third route was begun by Joseph Borden, promoter of Bordentown. He hoped that by establishing a line from Amboy Ferry to Bordentown he might head off Burlington and Trenton as depots on the Delaware for the New York trade. His stage went only once a week at first, but it prospered, and under Borden and his son, Joseph, Jr., it was continued without lapse until the Revolution.[30]

Sloops and shallops probably attended frequently at the terminals of all these lines from the first, but the earliest known announcement of a definite schedule from both ends of the land route, thus providing through service from New York to Philadelphia, appeared in 1750 in connection with Borden's line. At the New York end, Daniel O'Brien announced that "there is now a Stage-Boat, well fitted for that Purpose, kept, and if Wind and Weather permit, shall attend at the late Col. Moore's Wharf in New York every Wednesday in every Week, (and at other times if Occasion) and to proceed to the Ferry at Amboy on Thursday, where on Friday Morning a Stage Wagon, well fitted, shall be ready to receive them and proceed directly to Philadelphia." Borden placed a connecting stage boat on the Delaware River that docked at Philadelphia at the well-known Crooked Billet wharf. Competition had become a factor because the advertisement promised that "all Passengers and Merchandize shall be transported at the same Rates as are customary from New Brunswick to Trenton."[31] The time required between New York and Philadelphia was ordinarily three days, but there was always the qualification "if wind and weather permit."

As roads were now becoming more comfortably passable, there was indeed reason for avoiding water travel. It was difficult by ice in winter; it was hazardous at all seasons whenever the wind was high; and as for speed, it was always uncertain, depending upon the whim of the breeze. The scanty news items of the old newspapers listed numerous ferry and stage-boat accidents. For example: "About two miles from Burlington... a Shallop in which were seven Persons going from this city (Philadelphia) was overset by a violent Gale of Wind. All the Passengers got upon the Bottom of the Vessel; but before any Assistance could come to them 4 of them were drown'd."[32]

IN 1756, the New Brunswick–Trenton line advertised a land extension between Trenton and Philadelphia to replace the slow passage up the Delaware, which had handicapped this route. In the following year, the land passage at the eastern end was extended from New Brunswick through Woodbridge to the New Blazing Star Ferry on Arthur Kill. The advertisement of this route revealed an arrangement typical of the cooperative nature of the few longer stage enterprises of the colonial period:

PHILADELPHIA STAGE-WAGGON AND NEW-YORK STAGE BOAT, perform their Stages Twice a Week,—John Butler, with his Waggon, sets out on Tuesdays, from his House at the Sign of the Death of the Fox, in Strawberry Alley, and drives the same Day to Trenton Ferry, when Francis Holman meets him, and proceeds on Wednesdays to Brunswick, and the Passengers and Goods being shifted into the Waggon of Isaac Fitzrandolph's, the same Day, where

Reuben Fitzrandolph, with a boat well fitted, will receive them and take them to New York that night. John Butler returning to Philadelphia on Wednesdays, with the Passengers and Goods delivered to him by Francis Holman, will again set out for Trenton Ferry on Fridays, and Francis Holman, he, will carry his Passengers and Goods with the same expedition as above to New York.[33]

In 1769, the first Philadelphia stage to go by way of Newark and to use the new causeway across the Passaic and Hackensack marshes was established. In Philadelphia, the stage set out from the sign of the Bunch of Grapes, kept by Josiah Davenport, one of the proprietors of the line, and went to Coryell's Ferry, fifteen miles from Trenton, where the Delaware was crossed, and then through New Jersey by way of Flemington, Somerville, Bound Brook, Plainfield, and Newark to Powles Hook. The route was generally known as the Old York Road.[34] In the summers of 1771 and 1772, Charles Bessonet, a tavern keeper at Bristol, Pennsylvania, and John Mercereau, who had taken over the New Blazing Star tavern on Arthur Kill, provided service over this route three times a week. And in the spring of 1733, these same proprietors began service four times a week, dividing their stack and equipment into two separate lines—the "Flying Machine," which left Philadelphia and Powles Hook every Monday and Thursday, meeting at Princeton, and the "New Philadelphia and New York Stages," which left the same places every Tuesday and Friday to perform the same route.[35]

SOUTH OF PHILADELPHIA, the only route of travel important enough in colonial times to support an organized stage line for the use of the public was across Delaware to Chesapeake Bay. Annapolis was at first the southern terminal, but Baltimore, rising rapidly into importance, displaced it after 1763.

In 1761, a line was established that went from Philadelphia to Wilmington by stage boat, then by a stage wagon that left every Monday from the ferry over Christiana Creek, immediately south of Wilmington, "by New-Castle, the Red Lion, St. Georges', the Trap, Witherspoon's, Warwick, etc. all in one Day," to Fredericktown.[36]

A third line was inaugurated in 1762, by which the land carriage was from Newcastle to "the head of Elk River."[37] In 1763, another wagon attended the same stage boat from Philadelphia and passed from Newcastle to Chestertown, about forty-eight miles, and thence twelve miles to Rockhall "where there is a Stage Shallop well accommodated for Passengers, which will sail to Annapolis."[38]

The line to the head of Elk River in 1762 probably was intended chiefly to serve Baltimore, but that city was first mentioned in a 1764 communication for a route covered by William Galbraith's sloop from Baltimore to Frenchtown at the head of Elk, then by Robert Muir's wagon to Christiana Bridge, and finally from William Patterson's shallop to Philadelphia. The journey required four days. The line was continued by the proprietors until at least 1769, and probably longer.[39] In 1772, a stage from Philadelphia to Baltimore was advertised with land carriage from Wilmington to Charlestown on North-East River, eight miles west of Elk River,[40] and in 1774, a different land route was promoted, running from Port Penn on the Delaware to Cecil Court House "near the mouth of Elk."[41]

Thus, no single route was definitely preferred across this isthmus in the years preceding the Revolution. Each competing line took a different road and found in its selection certain alleged advantages that it could boast over its rivals.

BOTH THE New Jersey and the Delaware-Chesapeake lines were therefore active before the first successful staging enterprise in New England was finally set in motion in 1761. This was not between Boston and Rhode Island, as might have been expected, but between Boston and Portsmouth, New Hampshire. The initiative came from John Stavers of Portsmouth, and the handbill, dated April 1761, read, "a large stage chair, with two good horses well equipped, will be ready by Monday the 20th inst. to start out from Mr. Stavers, inn-holder, at the sign of the Earl of Halifax, in this town, for Boston, to perform once a week." The stage chair carried four persons besides the driver. Leaving Portsmouth, it lodged the first night at Ipswich and the next day went through Medford to Charlestown ferry, which it did not cross. The driver went into Boston to execute his commissions and make his purchases, then, for his return, set out for Portsmouth Thursday morning and arrived Friday evening. It was announced that in case the undertaking met with suitable encouragement "a Stage-Coach with four horses will also be in readiness a while hence."[42] This promise was fulfilled in the spring of 1763 when notice appeared that "The Portsmouth Flying Stage Coach is now finished."[43]

Though the Portsmouth stage ran through Salem, the latter town in the spring of 1766 announced its own "Stage Chaise with two able Horses" to run three times a week to Charlestown ferry.[44] Benjamin Coats, the proprietor, advertised in 1770 that he had purchased a new stage-chaise, which he intended to place on the route between Salem and Boston, and which "with the one now improved in that business" would enable him to "carry and bring passengers, bundles, etc.," every day in the week, except Sunday.[45] This line, probably the first in the country to run daily, was continued until the Revolution.

In 1770, an opposition line was placed on the route to Portsmouth, furnishing Stavers with more competition than he could endure with silence. He appealed to his record:

Staver's was the first Person that ever set up and regularly maintain'd a Stage Carriage in New-England the Utility of which at all Seasons has been abundantly experienced for Ten Years past; .... He therefore humbly hopes that his Carriages will still continue to be prefer'd to any other.[46]

After 1773, Stavers also met opposition on that portion of his route between Newburyport and Boston, for Ezra Lunt gave notice that he had "purchased the Newbury-Port Stage, which has been lately fixed on a new Construction, in which he intends to improve Four Horses, which he will drive himself."[47] Lunt continued the stage until the outbreak of the Revolution, when he sold his coaches and horses and joined the army.

Travel from Boston southward had so increased that a permanent stage to Rhode Island was finally established in 1767 by Thomas Sabin of Providence.[48] The Providence headquarters was at the Sign of the Crown—soon rechristened the Crown Coffee House to keep up with the fashion of the times in tavern names. In Boston, Sabin put up at the Sign of the Lamb, then kept by John Burrows. An important extension of stagecoach facilities took place in 1768 when a weekly line was established between Providence and Norwich, Connecticut, thereby shortening the water journey to New York.[49]

Two ambitious efforts to complete a stage connection between Boston and New York were made in 1772. The first was the establishment of a line from the Brooklyn ferry landing, opposite New York City, to Sag harbor at the eastern end of Long Island where "a Passage Boat will be ready to carry all Passengers to New-London; likewise Stages are established in the different Towns in Connecticut and Rhode-Island Governments to carry Travellers to Boston."[50]

The second Boston–New York attempt was over the Upper Post Road. "Whereas the Communication between the capital places of New-York and Boston, is of the greatest public concern," began the opening announcement,

the subscribers, living in Hartford, have projected a plan upon proper encouragement, for establishing a Stage-Coach, for the conveyance of passengers through that beautiful part of the country of the upper Post road, to and from these places.[51]

A notice in the *Boston Gazette* for Monday, June 1, 1772, stated that "The New-York stage is now in Town, and will go out on Wednesday morning." Service from New York commenced two weeks later, the first stage leaving on June 24 from Fowler's Sign of the Plough and the Harrow, at the corner of the Bowery and Doyers street, according to a notice in the *New York Journal* for June 25, 1772.[52]

NEW YORK CITY, in contrast to Boston and Philadelphia, offered little encouragement for local stage lines because of its excellent facilities for water transportation to nearly every neighboring settlement of importance. Several lines, however, radiated into northern New Jersey from Powles Hook on the opposite side of the Hudson from the metropolis. The completion in 1766 of the causeway across the Hackensack and Passaic marshes to Newark not only turned much of the Philadelphia travel to that route but also opened the way to the establishment in 1768 of a local stage to Newark under the proprietorship of Matthias Ward.[53] A stage to go from Powles Hook to Hackensack twice a week was commenced by Abraham Van Buskirk in 1768 and was continued by one proprietor or another until the Revolution.[54]

A more ambitious undertaking was that of Daniel Burnett of Morristown who, in 1772, started a weekly stage from there to Powles Hook. The journey was completed in a day, and the fare was only half a dollar either way, with four shillings a hundredweight charged "for any kind of lumber or produce, suitable for a stage to carry."[55]

Philadelphia rivaled Boston in the number of local stage lines that radiated from it in the late colonial period. Many of them set out from the New Jersey end of Cooper's Ferry, the present site of Camden. Salem, the oldest settlement in southern New Jersey, was connected with Philadelphia as early as 1767 by a stage driven weekly to Cooper's Ferry by Aaron Silver.[56] In 1768, a stage owned by William Shute commenced weekly from his tavern near Roadstown, in Cumberland County, to Cooper's Ferry; and in 1771, Michael Lee took the line over and extended it five miles to Greenwich.[57]

Carrying passengers was but a part, and perhaps even a minor part, of the business of some of these local stages. The drivers were mail carriers and general errand boys for the entire countryside. As one advertisement worded it, "The orders of any punctually obeyed."[58] Another advertisement, that of the stage from Great Egg Harbor, is more detailed: "for passage through, 10s . . . ; any shorter distance 2 d. each mile; for dead carriage 1 d. per mile per pound; by retail, 1 s. 8 d.

per pound; for letters, 4 d. to be paid with the letter; for newspaper, 5 s. per year."[59] Most of these local routes, of course, had no official mail service at the time. Every tavern keeper whose house was on the route was an agent and also received a commission. An advertisement of the Kings Arms in Princeton illustrated the normal procedure: "As the Stage-Waggons from New-York to Philadelphia, and back, put up at his House, any Person inclining to send Goods or Parcels by that Convey-ance, may depend on their being carefully forwarded."[60] A notice of a store for rent in Princeton suggested the value of the stages to the local merchants, boasting that "by their conveyance may be had a great number of articles, not commonly kept in a country store, on three days notice, to oblige a customer."[61] Thus, almost from the first, stages were performing all the services to the community that were generally asso-ciated with them in their heyday during the nineteenth century.

The pre-Revolutionary years, therefore, witnessed the beginning of a stage transportation system along the eastern seaboard, particularly dur-ing the period from the end of the French and Indian War in 1763 until the beginning of hostilities in 1776. Those routes mainly followed the busier lanes of colonial land commerce and travel, and they were, as we have seen, basically limited to four areas: the New Jersey routes, the Delaware-Maryland peninsula routes, the Boston to New York route, and the local lines radiating out from the three hub cities of Boston, New York, and Philadelphia. But the capture of those three pivotal cities by the British during the Revolution eliminated almost all of the regular stage routes for all practical purposes until the return of peace.

The early years of colonial staging were primitive in comparison with what would be developed during the eight decades after the Revolu-tion, but they were a beginning—and a promise of the golden years of eastern staging that were to come.

II

Revival after the Revolution

THE REVIVAL OF the stage lines during the latter stages of the Revolutionary War was gradual, depending upon the evacuation of British troops in a particular area, but soon staging lines expanded rapidly up and down the Atlantic seaboard.

The main arm of this expansion route during the Confederation period (1781–89) was what came to be known as the Main Post Road, a route extending southward from Wiscasset, Maine, through the leading seaboard cities to Savannah, Georgia. It was the pre-eminent route in the new Republic from the close of the Revolution until the opening of the National Road from Cumberland to Wheeling in 1818, and if nothing else, it symbolized the continued domination by the Atlantic seaboard in American affairs. Not only were passengers and freight carried along this route, but soon it became the main artery for the mail. By 1790 alone, some 51 of the country's then 200 post offices were situated along the route. Other roads that branched off from this north-south route became designated in Post Office legislation and popular usage as "crossroads."[1]

One of the earliest of the revived staging operations occurred in November 1778, shortly after the British evacuated Philadelphia, when Joseph Borden advertised stage service across New Jersey as far as New Brunswick. He offered service by his stage boat to Bordentown and then by wagon to New Brunswick.[2] In February 1779, John Wills announced that he "hath erected a stage for accommodation of travelers from Burlington to Brunswick."[3] And in 1780, service was renewed on the land route from Philadelphia through Trenton and Princeton to

Elizabeth, and a stage to Morristown was established to connect with this line at Princeton.[4]

The initiative for this Trenton-Princeton-Elizabeth line was taken by Gershom Johnson of Philadelphia, who during the time of military operations in the region had commanded several hundred New Jersey wagon teamsters and held the rank of deputy wagon-master general in the militia.[5] Johnson was also the Philadelphia entrepreneur in the establishment in 1781 of a line of land stages between Philadelphia and Baltimore. In 1783, he became landlord of the Bunch of Grapes tavern in Third Streets, Philadelphia, which he immediately made the connecting point and headquarters for his stage lines. His partner in New Jersey was James Drake, keeper for many years of the Indian Queen at New Brunswick and proprietor there of the ferry over the Raritan River. In 1780 and 1781, Johnson and Drake provided service on the Philadelphia-Elizabeth line twice a week. Early in 1781, their "commodious Stage-Waggon" was replaced by a "convenient Flying Stage Waggon" with "four horses at the end of every twenty miles."[6]

In April 1782, service was increased to three times a week by adding a "genteel coach," which left the Bunch of Grapes every Friday.[7] Another competing line, commenced that same year by Charles Bessonet of Bristol, a well-known pre-Revolutionary proprietor, was absorbed by taking in Bessonet as a partner.[8] By June 1783, Drake had retired in favor of John Mercereau, another pre-Revolutionary operator who was to remain in the staging business still another decade before he followed his family to the vicinity of Binghamton, New York, where they were pioneer settlers.[9]

The veterans, Bessonet and Mercereau, must have brought strength to the establishment, for in September 1783, under the heading "The New-York Flying Machine," service six times a week was advertised. The "Flying Stage Coach" and the "Flying Stage Waggon" traveled on alternate days through the week, both leaving Philadelphia at 4:00 A.M., stopping for breakfast in Bristol and for dinner in Princeton, and covering the entire distance to Elizabeth in one day.[10]

In the spring of 1783, they raised the fare for passage between Philadelphia and Elizabeth from four dollars to six "as Oats and Hay are exceedingly high".[11] Soon there appeared an advertisement of a rival line with the fares set at the old rates. "The discerning Public," the announcement read, "will easily perceive the advantage of making use of this Conveyance in preference to any other, because it is equally convenient and less expensive."[12] Since the new line evidently had no suspended coaches or wagons it could not advertise them as "Flying

Machines" but was content to refer to its vehicles as "The Excellent Philadelphia and New-York Running Machines."[13] They, too, went through in one day, not to Elizabeth but, for the first time since the Revolution, to Newark, where they stopped to lodge at Kenney's tavern. Early the next morning, a stage carried the passengers over the marshes to Communipaw ferry, where a boat waited to take them across the Hudson to the city so that "A passenger from Philadelphia on Monday morning, may certainly breakfast in New York on Tuesday morning at eight o'clock, without danger from wind and weather."[14]

It is unnecessary to follow in detail the shifts in proprietorship and changes in the character of service on this busy sector of the Main Post Road. The business appeared to be lucrative from the first, and all the tavern keepers along the way were eager to share in it. When competition began to cut into profits too deeply, some working arrangement to share the business and maintain rates would be perfected; this would last until some entrepreneurs grew dissatisfied and united to form an aggressive new line.

A stage line between Baltimore and Annapolis, which ran three times a week, was started in 1783 by Nathaniel Twining and Gabriel Van Horne.[15] Twining had been a lieutenant in the Fourth Maryland Regiment during the war and was now the keeper of a tavern on the south bank of the Susquehanna River. Van Horne, the proprietor of a line of Revolutionary express riders between the Susquehanna and Baltimore during the hostilities, was now a tavern keeper in Baltimore. That same spring, the two men also opened a pioneer line on the road between Baltimore and Alexandria, the first to enter Virginia.[16] In 1785, Van Horne fortified his interests by securing from the Maryland legislature an exclusive right for three years to run stages between the Susquehanna and Potomac rivers.[17] Henceforth, his only competition came from land and water stage lines that had been re-established across Delaware. Retracing colonial routes, these lines employed stage boats on the Delaware and Chesapeake bays, and their land carriage was reduced to a minimum because their emphasis was upon freight, not passengers.

The next southward advance occurred in May 1784, when the Virginia legislature granted Twining the exclusive right for three years to run stages between Alexandria and Richmond, it being represented that he "hath laid out a considerable sum of money in the purchase of stage coaches and horses, for the purpose of conveying persons and their baggage" over that route.[18] His associate was John Hoomes, innkeeper and plantation owner of Bowling Green, who in October secured a similar exclusive privilege for conveying persons between Richmond and Petersburg and between Petersburg and Norfolk and Portsmouth. Certain conditions were attached to these grants, including minimum requirements about the quality and frequency of service. Five pence per mile was named as the maximum rate of fare. The grantees were required to give bond of £100 for violation of any of them. Twining was granted an extension of time in which to find his security "from his being a stranger in the state," since he had otherwise faithfully performed his obligations.[19] By the end of 1784, stages were running a long distance below Baltimore and Annapolis. From Richmond, Virginia, there was now an unbroken line of communication to the northern cities, even to Boston, because the gap between New York and Boston was closed in the autumn of the same year.

THE FIRST MOVE in the establishment of a stage line between New York and Boston was made by Jacob Brown, an innkeeper of Hartford, Connecticut, who early in the season of 1783 began running a stage between New Haven and Springfield. He stopped overnight going and coming at his own house in Hartford.[20] But if the distance between the Connecticut Valley and Boston could be bridged, a new passenger route between the two chief northern cities would be opened. Later, the stages could be extended from New Haven along the shore of Long Island Sound and eventually an all-land route to New York would be completed. The man who first conceived this idea was Levi Pease, a tavern keeper at Somers, some miles northeast of Hartford.[21] To his contemporaries, Pease's proposal seemed fantastic, and he could get no support or encouragement. In later life, he told how he had applied to John Ballard, the chief hackney coachman of Boston, to join him in the scheme and received the reply that a time might come when a stage between Boston and Hartford would support itself, "but not in your day or mine."[22] Rebuffed in his hope of finding an influential Boston confederate, Pease persuaded Reuben Sikes, a young blacksmith in his own village, to drive the stage out of Hartford, while he went to Boston to drive the eastern stage. In their first advertisement, published in the *Connecticut Courant*, October 14, 1783, they announced that they would commence service on Monday, October 20, 1783, and that the stages would travel every Monday from both Hartford and Boston and complete their journeys in four days. On the fifth day, passengers from Boston could take passage in Jacob Brown's stage for New Haven, and on the sixth day, wind and weather permitting, they would reach New York by sailing packet.

The publisher of the Worcester *Massachusetts Spy*, Isaiah Thomas, wrote in a gratuitous notice: "Should these carriages be encouraged, it will be of great advantages to the public, as persons who have occasion to travel between, or to or from either of these places, may be accommodated on very reasonable terms, and will not have the trouble and expense of furnishing themselves with horses".[23] He also arranged to have the stages carry the *Spy* from Worcester to Boston. At first, Pease and Sikes often would not have a passenger in the entire course of the journey. The perseverance of the proprietors kept the stages in motion all through the first winter, when both temperature and income must have been, to say the least, discouraging. In the spring of 1784, the running time between Boston and Hartford was reduced to three days and the route was changed from the shorter road through Somers to the more settled and vastly better one by way of Springfield, Massachusetts. The stages met to exchange passengers at Capt. Ebenezer Mason's tavern in Spencer, about halfway, at noon on the second day. The New Haven stage continued its connection, and in an announcement, Pease stated that "the Stage will be opened from New-Haven to New York as soon as possible."[24]

The line was completed to New York in October 1784, by enlisting the interest of Talmadge Hall, tavern keeper of Norwalk, Connecticut. Under the new arrangement, Brown was to extend his stage along the shore from New Haven to the ferry over the Housatonic River at Stratford. There, Hall's stage from New York was to meet him to exchange passengers. Hall advertised in the *New-York Packet* "that he had erected a genteel stage waggon with four good Horses, in order to convey ladies and gentlemen and their baggage, in one day and a half, from New York to Stratford Ferry, 74 miles, which compleats the whole line from Richmond in Virginia to Boston as there are stage waggons erected on every other part of the road."[25]

Pease, meanwhile, had moved to Boston and had opened a tavern opposite the Mall "at the sign of the New York Stage."[26] Sikes moved to Hartford, and Brown, probably at this time, moved to New Haven, where he took a tavern opposite the college green. Hall, with the most magnificent flourish of all, moved to New York, where he leased the Roger Morris mansion on Washington Heights, then about ten miles north of the city. This spacious home, with one of the best views on Manhattan Island, was made the breakfasting place for passengers on the stages to Boston and Albany.[27] When all was ready, an announcement signed by all four proprietors informed the public that "Stages leave New-York, Hartford, and Boston, every Monday and Thursday morning, precisely at five o'clock; the New York, and one of the Hartford Stages meet at Stratford ferry on Tuesdays and Fridays, exchange passengers at twelve o'clock; at the same time the Boston, and the other Hartford Stage meet at Colonel Reed's, in Brookfield, and exchange passengers. All the stages return to the places they left on Wednesdays and Saturdays."[28] According to this schedule, the traveler leaving Boston on Monday morning would lodge on successive nights at Worchester, Palmer, Hartford, New Haven, and Norwalk, and reach New York on Saturday night for what was probably a most welcome seventh day's rest.

Service on the Main Post Road was continued from Boston north to Portsmouth, New Hampshire, by John Stavers, the colonial entrepreneur on this route, and his younger associate, John Greenleaf. It is not known at what precise date they renewed service after the Revolution, but their stage was in motion in 1784 and quite possibly had been running for several years.[29]

CONNECTING STAGECOACH LINES operated over nearly 800 miles of the Main Post Road of the country by 1785. There were also, by this same year, two branch road establishments that deserve atttention because they represent, in each case, the commencement of great routes to the West. On one of these branches, that from Philadelphia to Lancaster, stages had operated in colonial times with seeming profit, and as on other pre-Revolutionary lines, the resumption of service did not wait until a peace treaty had been signed but took place as soon as danger from the enemy was removed. In March 1781, there appeared in the *Pennsylvania Gazette* an announcement that "The Lancaster Stage, established by Weaver and Schaffer, will set out from Adam Weaver's, at the sign of the Black-Horse, in Donnegall-street, in Lancaster, on Monday the 16th of April, and come in to Philadelphia on Tuesday; set out again from the sign of the King of Prussia, in Market-street, Philadelphia, on Friday, and return to Lancaster on Saturday. Mr. Schaffer will drive himself...and supply any person with the English and German News-papers."[30]

The second road to the West led up the Hudson and west by the Mohawk valley. Between New York and Albany, there had been no colonial stage service. The Hudson River, penetrating far into the interior of New York, afforded an excellent water highway that had served the settled area of colonial times well enough. Yet the Hudson usually froze in winter above Poughkeepsie, and travelers and the mail had to be forwarded by land. Even when the river was open, the sailing sloops were slow, small, and uncomfortable, and not always safe. With luck, the passage to Albany might be made in two days, but the average was four, and at times it might be extended to more than a week. Passengers paid extra for bed and board, which in the cramped quarters of the little vessels could hardly equal the same accommodations in the better taverns. Nor was the trip without its dangers when squalls suddenly caught the heavily laden little craft. Newspapers carried frequent accounts of overturned sloops and fatalities. All of these circumstances doubtless encouraged the establishment of a stage line to parallel the river. They were not in themselves enough, however, and the state of New York added the incentive of a ten-year grant of exclusive right to Isaac Van Wyck, John Kinney, and the previously mentioned Talmadge Hall, tavern keepers of Fishkill, Kinderhook, and New York, respectively.[31]

Van Wyck, Kinney, and Hall exercised their privilege in June 1785. Stages traveled twice a week at first, going through in three days, but they were soon pushed through in two, and the schedule was increased to three times a week. Additional partners were taken in along the line, most of them tavern keepers who furnished teams for a section of the route. Arrangements were ordinarily made so that a partner's tavern would be reached for either meals or lodging. When on the two-day schedule, the stages left their respective terminals at five o'clock in the morning, the one setting out from the ferry landing that was opposite the city of Albany and the other from Cape's Tavern, New York City. Passengers from Albany stopped for breakfast at ten o'clock at Kinney's tavern in Kinderhook, reached Rhinebeck about two o'clock for dinner, and passed on in the afternoon through Poughkeepsie to Fishkill, where Van Wyck gave them supper and lodging. Passengers from New York, meanwhile, had breakfasted at Hall's tavern on Washington Heights, where passengers in the Boston stage also breakfasted, dined at Mandeville's in Peekskill, and also arrived to sup and lodge at Van Wyck's. The stages exchanged passengers the next morning, and each traveled back over the road it came, observing the same stops.[32]

The natural increase of trade and travel formed the sole incentive to the establishment of all these stage lines, except where state governments indulged the entrepreneurs by granting monopoly privileges. Connecticut made several such grants before 1786, but instead of being for terms of specified lengths they were to last only "during the Pleasure of this Assembly," and the practice was soon abandoned. Later, New Hampshire, Vermont, South Carolina, and Georgia were to encourage their pioneer stages in the same manner. The usual rationale for these grants was that they brought about the establishment of stage lines before routes were normally profitable. Proprietors were willing to run them at some early sacrifice if they were guaranteed the total income from the road for enough years to return a profit. John Hoomes, petitioning the Virginia legislature in 1787 for an extension of his monopoly, wrote that "if no exclusive right is established, sundry adventures will set up temporary carriages at those seasons only when most business of that kind is to be had and which alone produce a profit to a standing line of stages."[33]

CORNWALLIS had been defeated at Yorktown in 1781, but the peace treaty with the British that formally ended the Revolutionary War was not signed until 1783 or ratified by Congress until January 14, 1784. By then, the process of revival after the upheavals of the war years had already begun, and by the end of the 1780s there was a brisk traffic of stagecoaches carrying passengers and freight up and down the 800 miles of the Main Post Road and over its various crossroads. But the stage was also beginning to perform one of its most critically important tasks during those years of its dominance in the East from the Revolution to the Civil War—carrying the mail.

III

Stagecoaches and the Mail —
A Debate of the
Confederation Period

PRIOR TO the invention of the telegraph line in 1844, communications and transportation were inextricably connected; all correspondence, both official and private, had to be delivered manually.

During the stagecoach's period of dominance in the East until the Civil War, those horse-drawn vehicles literally set the tempo of the nation's life. Business could move no faster than it received the reports upon which its decisions were based. A democratic government could not act with confidence before the response of its citizens to events and circumstances was registered. The speed of this shuttle, as it passed back and forth between communities, binding them together with its news and messages, was, for eighty years after the Revolution, a major factor in the pattern of American civilization.

It was not obvious in the beginning, however, that stagecoaches should be employed by the General Post Office to carry the mails. New circumstances, only half realized at first, were bringing new pressures upon Congress, and Congress, after significant debate, transmitted the pressures in the form of orders to Postmaster General Ebenezer Hazard to employ the stages, which he did with skepticism and compromises that eventually cost him his job. The story is important not only as a key event in the development of stagecoaching, but also as a forecast of basic policy debates in American politics.

In colonial times, only one American stage line, which ran between Boston and Portsmouth, is known to have officially carried the mail. His

Majesty's inspector of the colonial Post Office, Hugh Finlay, who toured the colonies in 1773, told the story:

One Stavers some years ago began to drive a stage coach between Portsmouth and Boston; his drivers hurt the office very much by carrying letters, and they are so artful that the postmaster cou'd not detect them; it was therefore judged proper to take this man into the pay of the office, and to give two mails weekly between Boston and Portsmouth. This was of no disadvantage to the Post Office because the mails brought by the Stage Coach did rather more than pay the £10 Str. Staver's yearly salary.[1]

Other stage drivers, however, carried the mail unofficially. The postmaster of Salem reported to Fanily that "the drivers take many letters so that but few are forwarded by Post." He added that "an informer wou'd get tar'd and feather'd."[2]

The practice of carrying letters for pay was quietly resumed by stagecoaches when lines were re-established after the Revolution, despite the fact that the Post Office Ordinance of 1782 specified that the postmaster general, his deputies and agents, "and no other person whatsoever, shall have the receiving, taking up, ordering, despatching, sending post or with speed, carrying and delivering of any letters, packets or other despatches from any place within these United States for hire, reward, or other profit or advantage."[3] Stagecoach proprietors, who remembered pre-Revolutionary precedent, and who had done much as they liked on the fragmentary lines established in the closing years of the Revolution, were not disposed at first to conform with the new post office law.

In December 1784 (during the period of the Confederation, 1781–89), Postmaster General Hazard instituted a suit against Gershom Johnson of Philadelphia. Johnson's practices were typical of all the stage proprietors, but he was probably selected for prosecution because he was on the route between New York and Philadelphia, where the evasions were most numerous.[4]

The question was also brought to the attention of Congress from another source when Nathaniel Twining, in a memorial read to that body on April 4, 1785, offered to contract to carry the mail by stages from New York to Norfolk, Virginia. In reciting the circumstances that induced him to make the proposal, he described how the merchants offered:

their annual Subscriptions, by which means your Memorialist was under obligation to convey all Packages and Letters which were offered by the said Subscribers.—That your Memorialist in a short period became sensible those engagements counteracted the Ordinance of Congress, and greatly injured the revenue of the Post Office—That under this Consideration he was stimulated to set forth to your Honbl Body a proposition for conveying the Mail by Post Stages. . . .[5]

Twining's petition was referred to a committee that had been appointed in March to prepare an additional ordinance for better regulating the Post Office.[6] It precipitated discussion of whether the stages were suitable as mail carriers. On June 30, 1785, Congress passed a resolution, introduced by one of the committee, William Houstoun of Georgia, "That the postmaster general make enquiry, and report the best terms upon which contracts may be entered into, for the transportation of the several Mails, in the stage carriages on the different roads, where such stage carriages are or may be established."[7]

Eleven months earlier, on August 2, 1784, the mail had begun to be carried by stage in England on the London to Bristol route. This fact has led English historians to contend that the American mail stagecoach system was an imitation of the English. However, for some time American historians have felt that the situation may actually have been the reverse, despite the chronological factors. The key in the story is Bartholomew Stavers, brother of the aforementioned John Stavers, who had received that initial stagecoach mail contract in 1773. Stavers, an Englishman, spent only about twenty years in the colonies and was a noted Tory. When the Revolution began, he fled to England, leaving behind his wife and unborn son. Home in England, he became engaged in the stagecoach business again, and there are strong indications that he encouraged his countrymen to adopt a stagecoach mail system similar to the one he had established in the colonies.[8]

At any rate, there is no evidence that the American post office committee was influenced by the English experiment. Conditions in America were themselves ripe for the idea of employing the stages as mail carriers. Indeed, there were a number of stages that already carried the mail unofficially. Furthermore, the increased weight of the mails on the main routes had required the use of second horses led by the post-rider and must have suggested the need for some kind of relief vehicle as soon as the roads were sufficiently improved. Letters and papers, which overflowed the saddlebags, could not be properly protected from inclement weather or from the hazards of the trail. A number of riders had been robbed at lonely spots and, as money was increasingly being sent by post, this gave the authorities much concern. Mail carried inside a stage and protected by passengers as well as by a driver would be much more secure. Also, it seemed reasonable that stages might carry the mail at less expense, since they were already sustained by their passenger and express business, whereas a system of postriders had to be wholly supported by the government.

Upon this last account, however, the postmaster general was to be disappointed. When, in obedience to the resolution of Congress, he forwarded to that body the bids of the stage proprietors, he observed, "Considering that the Proprietors of the Stages will be put to no additional Expense, or at most a very trifling one, their demands appear to me to be exorbitant, although, in some Instances, they will carry the Mails for less than it now costs."[9] The postmaster general failed to consider that he was cutting off a considerable revenue that had accrued to the stage proprietors as private carriers of the mail, whether or not their action had been legal. Talmadge Hall in bidding for the New York–Boston line asked £750 for mail conveyance that would have cost but £275 by postriders.

Another problem appeared when it was discovered that the hours of arrival and departure of the stages on the New York–Philadelphia route were extremely inconvenient for the "mercantile Interest, from whence the Post Office Establishment derives its principal Support."[10] Stagecoach proprietors always thought first of the convenience of passengers, and consequently, they refused to depart from their custom of arriving late at night and setting out early in the morning. Merchants had no opportunity to answer letters and fulfill demands by return mail, unless they wanted to do business at night. Furthermore, the post office clerks would have had to work at night to sort and make up the mails, whereby "the Expense of extraordinary Firewood and Candles must be superadded."[11]

FOR THE REGION south of Philadelphia, Postmaster General Hazard was more optimistic. Twining's proposal for the route between Philadelphia and Petersburg, though about £400 per annum more, would supply an additional mail delivery weekly between those two cities. The additional expense, Hazard felt, would be counterbalanced "by the additional Number of Letters thrown into the Office, which are now carried by Mr. Twining's Stage, and for Pay, too, but in such a way as to elude the Ordinance of Congress, and guard against the Consequences of a Prosecution." Also, "as Mr. Twining does not appear to insist upon the Stages arriving at any capital Office *at Night*, the Inconvenience arising from transacting Business at unseasonable Hours may be avoided."[12]

Hazard was to remain skeptical about the suitability of the stage for transporting the mail. Despite the doubts expressed in his reports, Congress took favorable action on September 7, 1785, on a motion proposed by Houstoun, "That the Postmaster General be, and he is hereby authorized and instructed, under the direction of the board of treasury to enter into Contracts under good and sufficient security, for the conveyance of the different mails by the stage carriages, from Portsmouth in the State of New Hampshire, to the town of Savannah, in the State of Georgia, and from the city of New York, to the city of Albany in the State of New York, according to the accustomed route."[13] Hazard accordingly arranged a single contract for the roads specified in the motion, and beginning on the first of January 1786, the mail was transmitted by stage from Portsmouth, New Hampshire, to Petersburg, Virginia, and from New York City to Albany, three times a week in summer and twice a week in winter.[14] South of Petersburg, however, Twining was not yet able to put his proposed stage line into operation.

It seems strange that Hazard should have united all the stagecoach interests on the route in a single contract with the government. The document was signed by four proprietors: John Greenleaf representing that part of the road from Portsmouth to Boston, Talmadge Hall from Boston to New York and New York to Albany, Matthias Ogden from New York to Philadelphia, and Twining south of Philadelphia. What type of contracts these men had with their associates is not known, but it was Hazard's intention that "the Proprietors . . . who signed the Contract engaged not only for themselves, but for all the Proprietors of the Line of Stages in which they were concerned."[15] Ogden, however, seems to have come to very little understanding with his associates on the New York–Philadelphia route, for many complaints of irregularity and carelessness soon reached the Post Office.

The flaws in the agreement came rapidly to the surface. This was the first and last time a single contract for the entire stagecoach establishment was attempted. In subsequent arrangements, the contractor was held responsible for all proprietors in the line that he represented, and he was expected to protect both himself and the Post Office by making binding agreements with his associates.

Another problem cited by the postmaster general on the New York–Philadelphia route was that "as there was no person with the mail whose express Business it was to take Care of it, it was, of Course, but a secondary Object of Attention."[16] Thus, the question arose as to what constituted proper care, and Hazard wrote to Alexander Hamilton, then a practicing lawyer in New York: "Are the proprietors of the Stages obliged either to go with the mail themselves or to send with it a person whose express Business it shall be to take Care of it, as that their not doing it will work a Fortfeiture of their Bonds?"[17] Hamilton's answer, after a study of the contract and bond, was that no special guard was necessary.[18]

WHEN THE NEXT contracts were to be drawn, Hazard requested that each proposal state the terms on which the contractor would engage a man to go with the stage expressly to care for the mail. The resulting bids were so high that the plan of a guard was abandoned.[19] From time to time, the idea was revived in the Post Office Department and guards were actually employed at several different periods on some of the main routes, but the high cost of labor prevented the system from taking root in America.

Upon the New York–Boston route, Hazard was greatly disappointed in the results. In a letter to Congress in September 1786, he wrote:

The Eastern Mails . . . frequently are left at the Office as late as at Eleven and Twelve O'Clock at Night; and in a late Instance, have been carried about the City (and even past the Office) in the Waggon til the Passengers were set down at their respective houses, and then the Mail was left at the Stage-House, from whence it was sent to the Office.[20]

Despite these difficulties, Congress instructed the postmaster general to enter into contracts with the "stage carriages" again for the year 1787. Having been made painfully aware of the shortcomings of the stages as mail carriers, Hazard pleaded that more discretion be lodged with him in the making of contracts. If the power to do so were given him, he might, by threatening a return to postriders, coerce the stagecoach proprietors into rendering more satisfactory service under better terms, but Congress rejected his motion.

WHEN HAZARD received the bid in 1786 for the next year's contracts, he again complained to Congress about the high price and the nighttime delivery. And when the time came for reletting the contracts in 1788, Hazard returned to his old complaints once more in a letter to Congress: "At present he [the postmaster general] is obliged to contract with the Proprietors of the Stages, if it is practicable, without attending to any other Circumstances:—it was so last year; and the Proprietors made their Advantage of it; . . . I have Information upon which Dependence can be placed, that the Demands are now to be made still more encreased."[21] This time Congress agreed to his request and altered its instructions to read "that the Postmaster General be authorized to Contract for the transportation of the mail for the Year 88 by stage carriages or horses as he may judge most expedient and beneficial provided that preference is given to the transportation by stages to encourage this useful institution when it can be done without material injury to the public."[22] This discretionary power for which he had pleaded was, as it turned out, to prove unexpectedly embarrassing to Hazard and to result finally in his downfall.

The postmaster general had found that the stages were slower than riders, that they were unaccommodating in their hours of arrival and departure, that the mail was frequently neglected because they were only a secondary interest with the proprietors, and that proprietors in some quarters were quite ready to demand an exorbitant price since they were sure of their possession of the road without competition. Consequently, in 1788, using the freedom of decision that had been granted him, Hazard put the mails on the main route between Boston and Philadelphia back on horseback.

Immediately, the offended stagecoach proprietors took steps to embarrass the Post Office by offering to carry letters free of charge. This they possibly had a right to do since the Post Office Ordinance of 1782 reserved to the Government a monopoly only of the carrying of Letters "for hire, reward, or other profit or advantage."[23] Cumming, Ward and Company now appended to their advertisements a note that "Letters, Newspapers, etc. left at the New-York, Albany, and Philadelphia stage office, kept by Christopher Beekman, in Cortlandt-street, New York, and with Mr. Michael Dennison, at the George Inn, corner of Arch and Second Streets, Philadelphia, will be safely conveyed gratis."[24]

Hazard's refusal to renew the contract with the stages between New York and Boston was, almost certainly, the cause of the suspension of through stage service on the line between those two cities. Talmadge Hall's interests on the New York end had been overextended, it is true, but the real collapse came in November when Hall's stages were drawn off the road between New York and Fairfield, Connecticut, and until July 1788, the line operated only between Boston and New Haven.

Levi Pease, who took upon himself the task of rehabilitating the New York–Boston line, went over the postmaster general's head and addressed several petitions directly to Congress asking for the restoration of the mail contract. In addition to the friendly disposition of Congress toward stage lines, Pease profited from the wretched performance of the postriders who had replaced the stages on the Boston road, and

Congress late in the year, by special resolution, ordered the postmaster general to again place the mail in Pease's care.[25]

The situation had been complicated by the uncertain status of newspapers in the mails. Before the stages were employed by the Post Office, printers made their own arrangements for distributing their journals, hiring private riders on some routes, but usually making an agreement with the public rider on official post roads. The Ordinance of 1782 authorized the postmaster general to license all public riders to carry newspapers and establish rates for this service and directed that a proportion of the receipts was to be turned in to the Post Office.[26] But despite these regulations, Hazard did not consider the newspapers to be a part of the mail. It was merely that the riders upon payment of an established commission were allowed to carry newspapers as a side duty. The carrier, not the Post Office, was responsible for their safe delivery. "It is a matter merely between the printers and the riders," he insisted.[27]

The mail stages, however, having plenty of room, had fallen into the custom of carrying newspapers free between the cities as an accommodation to the printers. Consequently, when in 1788 the mail was put back on horseback, and the riders refused to burden themselves with newspapers unless paid extra, there was an immediate protest from newspaper editors, a group that had always been quick to defend its privileges. Protests were the louder because the state conventions to ratify the federal Constitution were then being held and the general public was highly excited. The editor of *The Independent Gazetteer* (Philadelphia) asserted that the "free and independent newspapers" (meaning the Anti-Federalist journals) were being discriminated against and asked, "What is the meaning of the new arrangement at the Post-Office which abridges the circulation of newspapers at this momentous crisis, when our every concern is dependent upon a proper decision of the subject in discussion?"[28]

Hazard branded this accusation an "Anti-federal manoevre," but the protest was not limited to those who opposed the Constitution. George Washington, waiting impatiently in 1788 at Mount Vernon for word from the Poughkeepsie Convention in New York, wrote to John Jay:

It is to be extremely lamented, that a new arrangement in the post-office, unfavorable to the circulation of intelligence, should have taken place at the instant when the momentous question of a general government was to come before the people. . . . I know it is said, that the irregularity or defect has happened accidently, in consequence of the contract for transporting the mail on horseback, instead of having it carried in the *stages*; but I must confess I could never account, upon any satisfactory principles, for the inveterate enmity with which the postmaster-general is asserted to be actuated against that valuable institution. It has often been understood by wise politicians and enlightened patriots, that giving a facility to the means of traveling for strangers, and of intercourse for citizens, was an object of legislative concern, and a circumstance highly beneficial to any country. . . . I am sorry to learn that the line of stages is at present interrupted in some parts of New England, and totally discontinued at the southward. I mention these suggestions only as my particular thoughts on an establishment, which I had conceived to be of great importance.[29]

With this unequivocal support for the stagecoach from George Washington, the incoming president, it is not surprising that Hazard's days as postmaster general were numbered. Hazard's problem was that he wanted to administer the Post Office from a business point of view, each year turning a profit into the Treasury. But a surplus for the Treasury was not what the people necessarily wanted. The crying need of the newborn Republic was the improvement and extension of communication facilities, and at this time, the greatest hope seemed to lie in supporting the infant stagecoach establishments. The people saw the stage's theoretical benefits, but they were generally unaware of the practical administrative difficulties that so discouraged Hazard. Nevertheless, administrative problems had to be grappled with when a change was clearly necessary. This was to be one of the chief tasks of early postmasters general under the Constitution. Hazard was not destined to be one of them. With stage proprietors and newspaper publishers, Federalists and Anti-Federalists, and the incoming president all against him, he was marked for retirement. He was, as he admitted himself, a poor politician. No postmaster general during the next sixty years, whatever his difficulties at times with recalcitrant proprietors, would ever question the stagecoach as the principal carrier of the United States mail on the nation's leading post roads.

IV

The Stages Roll – 1790 to 1800

 GEORGE WASHINGTON was inaugurated as the nation's first president on August 30, 1789, and a new decade and whole new epoch was about to begin for the young Republic. Those ten years from 1790 to the turn of the century were also to be a period of enormous expansion for the fledgling stagecoach industry along the eastern seaboard from New England to the Potomac.

Massachusetts's Samuel Osgood, the first postmaster general under the federal Constitution, enthusiastically supported mail service by stagecoach, and soon a network of stagecoach postal service branched out. In 1790, for instance, stages carried the mail between New York and Philadelphia five times a week each way.[1] South of Philadelphia, they carried the mail three times a week, through Baltimore, Georgetown, Alexandria, and Fredericksburg, to Richmond.[2]

In New England, Jesse Brown of Norwich and Jacob Brown of New Haven started a stage line in 1792 to run twice a week along the north shore of Long Island Sound, following the old colonial post road east from New Haven through New London and Norwich to Providence.[3] This was the first stagecoach service along the Lower Post Road, which ran via Hartford, Springfield, and Worcester to Boston. In the summer of 1793, the postmaster general transferred to the shore road the two mails that had been sent over the Hartford-Norwich route, and the latter was abandoned as a stage road.[4] Not until the beginning of 1797 was six-times-a-week mail service inaugurated between New York and Boston. The mail was taken every weekday as far as New Haven and then sent alternately over the upper and lower post roads to Boston.[5]

In the spring of 1793, Levi Pease had established stagecoach service daily, except Sunday, between New York and Boston over the Upper Post Road. To his old line, which had been running three days a week, he had added a line of "small, genteel and easy" carriages "in which but four inside passengers will be admitted." These "limited" stages were to go through in three and one-half days, the fastest time yet attempted between these two major cities. The light stages carried the mail, while the older stages, continuing their usual four-day schedule, became accommodation lines concerned more with the comfort of the passengers than with the speed of the trip.[6]

During the previous summer, Pease had also extended his operations in the Connecticut Valley. He had successfully petitioned the New Hampshire legislature for the exclusive right to a stage from the southern line of the state up the Connecticut Valley as far as Haverhill for six years, provided " he shall run the same at least half the distance from Hanover to the South line of the state on the east side of Connecticut river."[7] From Vermont, he had received a similar privilege without any reservations.[8] Fortified with these grants and a mail contract for the route, Pease, in association with Beriah Willard, a Greenfield tavern keeper, had established a weekly stage from Springfield through Northampton, Greenfield, Brattleboro, Charlestown, and Windsor to Dartmouth College at Hanover.[9] This was the first line to run north into the Connecticut Valley districts of either Vermont or New Hampshire.

During the decade, Pease became the chief stagecoach entrepreneur in New England. There were opposition lines, of course, and in 1793 alone three new lines were established to run out of Boston. A shrewd businessman, Pease was usually able to underbid competitors and then construct mergers or arrangements with them for the routes. For instance, in 1794 he bid $200 less than John Greenleaf and William Stavers (the son whom Barthlolmew Stavers never saw) for the carriage of the mail in 1795 on their old route between Boston and Portsmouth, "the best road on the continent, or at least north of Virginia." Then instead of setting up an opposition line, he joined forces with them, the company becoming Pease, Greenleaf, and Stavers. Pease made a similar arrangement with Israel Hatch and Jesse Brown for the Boston, Providence, and New Haven road.[10] To care for his interests in Boston, he established a "General Stage Office," conveniently located in a room under the printing office of the *Columbian Centinel*, "for the accomodation of passengers, in the different Stages in which he is concerned, viz. from *Boston* to *New York*; from *Boston* to *Portsmouth*; from *Boston* to *Providence*; and from *Boston* to *Albany*—where will be kept regular

Books, and a person constantly to attend to take the names of Passengers; and to give the necessary information of the departure of the several stages."[11]

No other person in the nation before 1800 had stagecoach interests as extensive as those of Levi Pease. Pease who had been born in Enfield, Connecticut, in 1739, became a blacksmith by trade before the Revolution. During the war, he first served with the Third Hampshire County Regiment of Militia, marching in October 1776 to Ticonderoga for reinforcement purposes. Later, he was a dispatch carrier for the Army of General Thomas, and finally he became an aide to Jeremiah Wadsworth, commissary general, serving as the agent for purchasing horses for the French army, which he followed from its landing at Newport until the final campaign in Virginia.

Pease left the army with the rank of captain, and he settled down in Somers, Connecticut, where he opened a tavern. He began building his stagecoach empire in 1783, at the age of forty-four when (as was discussed in chapter 2) he entered the business with the Boston to New York run, part of which he drove himself. "Captain" Pease enjoyed the complete confidence of the General Post Office, and (as chapter 9 explains) he helped the Post Office establish the one federally owned stage line. In 1810, at the age of seventy-one, he sold his staging interests and retired to his farm at Shrewsbury. He died in 1824 at the age of eighty-four. But by the time of his death, he was able to look back over a remarkable period of growth and development in staging, an epoch when the time for carrying the mail between Boston and New York had been reduced from six days to thirty-six hours. Levi Pease was truly one of the great pioneers of American staging.[12]

THERE WERE other stagecoach entrepreneurs, of course, and stage lines began to proliferate during the last decade of the eighteenth century. By 1800, more than twenty-five separate stage lines were running out of Boston, and well over a hundred stages were arriving and departing each week. Also, they were moving further inland, first to Albany in New York, and then west of Albany.

The first stage service westward from Albany was inaugurated in May 1793 by a Schenectady innkeeper, Moses Beal. His weekly stage ran not only to Schenectady but also on up the Mohawk Valley to Canajoharie.[13] A few months later, John Hudson, a rival tavern keeper, put on the road between Albany and Schenectady a second line, which was advertised to run every weekday.[14] Instead of competing, Beal withdraw his stages from the Albany-Schenectady sector and confined his activities to the line up the Mohawk. In the summer of 1794, Jason Parker, postrider between Canajoharie and Whitestown under a sub-contract with Hugh White and others, began running a stage over his route.[15] Thus by the autumn of 1794, Hudson, Beal, and Parker were associated in giving service twice a week from Albany through Fort Schuyler (later Utica) to Whitestown, and, in Jason Parker's name, they had secured a direct contract from the Post Office for the carriage of the mail.[16]

There was also a demand for stage lines to run north and east of Albany to take care of increasing travel. In 1795, a stage commenced to run, in summer at least, from Albany through Troy, Lansingburg, Fort Edward, and Fort Ann to Skeensborough Landing at the south end of Lake Champlain. "This route runs through a populous and well settled part of the country a considerable distance and opens a communication to another part of it rapidly settling as well as to Canada by Lake Champlain," wrote the postmaster general to Chairman Thatcher of the House Committee on the Post Office as he urged that the route be made a post road so that official mail could be sent by stage.[17]

It is interesting to see the patterns of these regional networks emerging in this early period. All lines in New England, for example, seemed to run out from Boston (or into Boston, if one thinks with the country dweller). A map of these pioneer lines would show Boston truly becoming the hub of travel and communication in New England.

However, the busiest route in the young nation between 1790 and 1800 continued to be the one between New York and Philadelphia, successively the two capitals of federal government during that decade. The mail was first carried five times a week between these two cities in 1790, and the revenue was more than double that received the previous year from a triweekly service.[18] A similar schedule of service five times a week was inaugurated between Philadelphia and Baltimore in 1791, except that it was reduced to three times a week in winter. The postmaster at Baltimore protested against this reduction while the winter service to New York remained the same, but the postmaster general answered: "It is true that the mail is to be carried five times a week to New York: but there are two sets of Stages which run on those five days, and if the mail were not sent on the same days, multitudes of letters would be sent by them to the great injury of the revenue."[19] In other words, on this busy route stage service was ahead of a laggard postal service and was forcing the latter to perform better.

At that time, no stages left these cities on Saturday; to do so would have necessitated running on Sunday to complete the trip. In 1791, when service six days a week began between New York and Philadelphia, the sixth, or Saturday's stage, actually left each city on Friday afternoon (the regular starting time other days was 8:00 A.M.) in order to go through before Sunday.[20]

During the entire decade, 1790–1800, there were both morning and afternoon lines running each way between New York and Philadelphia. The running time between the two cities was usually one and one-half days, the passenger spending one night at a tavern on the road. Toward the end of the century, more night traveling became the rule, and the hours of rest grew shorter. In 1799, if speed were an object, a traveler could leave New York in the mail stage at 1:00 P.M. and be in Philadelphia by 7:00 A.M. the next day. The same schedule applied to a trip in the opposite direction.[21] During most of this decade, at least one rival association, which usually also ran morning and afternoon stages, was also on the road, making four lines daily. Local proprietors changed frequently, but several important proprietors generally remained the same from year to year and dominated their routes. Each line of stages was known by name. The Mail Diligence, the Despatch, the Industry, and the Federal lines all ran for the greater part of this decade. Their charge for passage between New York and Philadelphia was usually four dollars or, in times of spirited competition, three dollars.

In 1799, the Swiftsure line of stages was established to run over an entirely different road than the route through Trenton, Princeton, and New Brunswick that all the other lines used. The new line ran north through Jenkintown to Coryell's Ferry, fifteen miles above Trenton, where the Delaware River was crossed, and then passed through New Jersey by Somerville, Bound Brook, Scotch Plains, Springfield, and Newark.[22] Under this name, this line operated far into the next century.

The dominating figure in the stagecoach business across New Jersey at this time was John Noble Cumming of Newark. A graduate of the militia after the war, he was always addressed as General Cumming. A sister married Philip Stockton of Princeton, and her two sons later became associates of their uncle in the staging business. One of them, Richard Cumming Stockton, became the Stockton of Stockton and Stokes, the most famous stage company operating in the East during the "step-lively" period of staging. Two grand nephews carried on the family interest, with one of them, William Tennant Stockton, becoming a famous stage owner and mail contractor in the South. Some of Cumming's many business interests were naturally connected with his concern with transportation. He was a director of the Newark Turnpike Company, of the Passaic and Hackensack Bridge Company, and of the Steamboat Ferry Company, which, after 1812, ran the steam ferry between New York and Paulus Hook. He was also the largest stockholder in the Associates of the Jersey Company, which founded Jersey City. In connection with his stage line, he owned several taverns along the road.[23]

Cumming's partner in his first staging venture in 1789 was Michael Dennison, proprietor of the George Inn in Philadelphia, stopping place for both the New York and Baltimore stages. Dennison, a very popular landlord, decided at the end of the year to return to England, his native land.[24] His successor as landlord at the George Inn and as Cumming's partner was John Inskeep, a man who later was twice elected mayor of Philadelphia, and who was a founder and for twenty-five years president of the Insurance Company of North America. Cummings and Inskeep, in 1790, became the first men to carry the mail five times a week between New York and Philadelphia. Their pay for this service was $1,333 a year.[25] In 1793, the through mail between the two cities was sealed in what was usually called the "great Bag" and letters for intermediate offices were placed in the "way Bag." Before this, the stage waited while the postmaster in each post office examined all the letters in the single bag to find those addressed to his office. The new procedure sped up the service and increased the security of the mail.

IN A PERIOD when other states found it desirable to encourage the founding of stage lines by granting monopoly privileges for a period of years to the entrepreneurs, New Jersey found itself astride a busy highway upon the commerce of which it could levy tribute. By a law passed in 1786, the state exacted an annual tax of $400 from each line of stages carrying passengers between the Delaware and Hudson Rivers. This tax, although not prohibitive, did help to restrict competition to usually not more than two rival concerns, and it gave stagecoach operators an excuse to keep their mail bids high.[26] The statute, it would seem, contradicted the intention of the Constitution's framers to keep the mail free of the laws and regulations of lesser jurisdictions. Postmaster General Timothy Pickering (1791–95) did not say in so many words that the tax was a violation of the Constitution, but he did address a forceful letter to the speaker of the U.S. House of Representatives on the subject in February 1793. It was not until 1799 that the New Jersey General Assembly passed a bill exonerating all stage lines from the need to purchase licenses to travel across the state.[27]

Another state statute that acted to restrict the Post Office was the monopoly right to run stages between the Susquehanna and Potomac rivers granted by Maryland to Gabriel Van Horne. There may have been an excuse for the state's original three-year grant to Van Horne in 1785, but the privilege was twice renewed. Actually, Van Horne's grant gave him control of the Main Post Road all the way from Alexandria, Virginia, to Philadelphia because he could set his own price for cooperation at the Baltimore end of any proposed lines between these points.

Van Horne, secure in his monopoly, exasperated Postmaster General Pickering with repeated irregularities and failures. His carelessness affected all the mail south of the capital city of Philadelphia. His monopoly likewise allowed him to raise his bid to a sum just short of what it would require to place a line of carriages on the road to be used solely for the conveyance of the mail.

The situation prompted Representative Thomas Fitzsimmons of Philadelphia, when the permanent Post Office bill was being debated in 1792, to move "to allow the proprietors of stages employed in conveying the mail, to carry passengers also, without being liable to molestation of impediment, on any of the post roads." This innocent-appearing provision might have freed the Post Office from both the New Jersey and the Maryland restrictions had the states recognized this assertion of the post roads clause of the Constitution, but it was immediately challenged, thus provoking a lively two-day debate. The proposal was defeated by a vote of twenty-five to thirty-three.[28]

When Van Horne's contract with the Post Office expired at the end of June 1794, Pickering purchased horses and sulkies with public funds and carried the mail directly instead of through a contract. He did this "principally with a view to greater punctuality and earlier thimes of arrival; expecting at the same time that it will be done at an increased expense."[29] By 1795, Van Horne's name disappeared from the staging business. When his monopoly finally expired, the contract between Philadelphia and Baltimore was given by Postmaster General Joseph Habersham (1795–1801) to Dunnachey, Bicknell and Company, an inexperienced firm. It did not improve much on the quality of service rendered by Van Horne, except that in 1797 it began to run six times a week and to carry the mail that often between the two cities.[30] No solution to the difficulties on this route was found until, in 1799, Haber-

sham established a government-owned stage line run under the immediate direction of the Post Office.

IN ADDITION to the main routes from New York to the Potomac, a
number of small lines were established along the crossroads. By the
beginning of the decade, a weekly stage ran from Philadelphia through
Morristown and Pottstown to Reading.[31] In 1792, the Reading stage was
extended to Harrisburg.[32] That same year, the Philadelphia and Lancaster Turnpike was incorporated, making it the first important turnpike
road in the United States, and stages ran along the route.[33]

In 1797, stages continued to move westward with a route from Harrisburg to Shippensburg through Chambersburg, Greencastle, Hagerstown, Williamsport and Martinsburg to Winchester, Virginia.[34] The
Appalachian ridges were turning the lines southwesterly. The stagecoach was following the line of frontier migration into the Great Valley.

Thus, by the dawn of the nineteenth century, the stages were rolling
along a wide variety of routes from New England to the Potomac, and
the stagecoach had become a dominant force in the new Republic.

V

The Early Stagecoaches

THE STAGECOACH was now an increasingly important part of daily American life. Large numbers of people who previously had never been able to move far from their homes were traveling the roads from Maine to the Potomac. Commerce, too, benefited enormously, and there was a greater movement of goods and products. And, of course, the mail and the newspapers were carried rapidly by the stages. Furthermore, there was a certain prestige attached to riding the stages in the early nineteenth century: After all, the proprietors and drivers, with their mail contracts, were acting as agents of the government, and stagecoaches were given the right of way on bridges and ferries.

Unfortunately, no manuals about the actual construction of those early stagecoaches remain today. The skills used in early stagecoaches were learned arts of craftsmanship transmitted not by written word but by example and apprenticeship. However, a fairly clear picture of those early stages can be obtained by reading the accounts of some of the passengers who rode them. One thing is quite evident from those accounts—the early stage evolved from the original four-wheel freight wagons. In fact, in the late eighteenth century the vehicle was commonly called a stage wagon, and in that period the word was spelled "waggon."

The evolution from wagon to stagecoach is simple to follow. Benches or seats were first placed crosswise in the wagon box, and then a superstructure was constructed: The sides were made of either canvas or leather so they could be rolled up or down depending on the weather. As modifications were made, the superstructure was suspended upon stout leather thorough braces that permitted play between the body and the undercarriage, and the bottom of the body became slightly rounded in the manner of a coach.

Stage construction around the time of the Revolution seems largely to have been centered in New Jersey, and those early vehicles were frequently called "Jersey waggons."

Thomas Twining, who traveled over the Main Post Road from New York to Washington in 1795, described a ride in one of those stage wagons. The wagon-like box held four cross seats, he said:

Three of these in the interior held nine passengers, and a tenth passenger was seated by the side of the driver on the front bench. A light roof was supported by eight slender pillars, four on each side. Three large leather curtains suspended to the roof, one at each side and the third behind, were rolled up or lowered at the pleasure of the person being expected to stow his things as he could under the driver's bench. Of course the three passengers on the back seat were obliged to crawl across all the other benches to get to their places. There were no backs to the benches to support and relieve us during a rough fatiguing journey over a newly and ill made road. It would be unreasonable to expect perfection in the arrangements of a new country; but though this rude conveyance was not without its advantages, and was really more suitable to the existing state of American roads than an English stagecoach would have been, it might have been rendered more convenient in some respects without much additional expense. Thus a mere strap behind the seats would have been a great comfort, and the ponderous leather curtains which extended the whole length of the wagon, would have been much more convenient divided into two or three parts, and with a glass, however small in each division to give light to the passengers in bad weather, and to enable them to have a glimpse of the country. The disposal of the luggage was also extremely incommodious, not only to the owner, but to his neighbors.[1]

Another description, by Charles W. Janson, who passed over the same roads at about the same time, may aid in sharpening the picture. There was, wrote Janson for his English audience, "no such thing in the country as what we call a stage coach, or a post-chaise."[2] The American stage was "literally a kind of light waggon." This vehicle,

which is of the same construction throughout the country, is calculated to hold twelve persons, who all sit on benches placed across, with their faces towards the horses. The front seat also holds three, one of whom is the driver, and as there are no doors at the sides, the passengers get in over the front wheels, and take their seats as they enter; the first, of course, get seats behind the rest. This is the most esteemed seat, because you can rest your shaken frame against the back part of the waggon. Women are therefore generally indulged with it, and it is often laughable to see them crawling to their seats; and if they happen to be late, they have to straddle over the men, who are seated farther in front. It is covered with leather, and instead of windows, there are flaps of that article, which in bad weather are let down, and secured by buckles and straps. In summer these flaps are folded up, and this is some alleviation from the repeated shocks you receive in going over roads, many of which are never repaired.[3]

Many of these stages, even when Twining wrote, did have broad leather straps across the backs of the seats as supports for the passengers, and it was not long before the curtains were made in sections, though not with the glass windows for which Twining asked. In addition to the leather outside curtains, stages had baize or linen inside curtains, which were an additional fortification in cold weather.[4] Also, these stages soon had a flat platform behind, upon which trunks were tied.[5] "The heavier kinds of boxes and trunks are fastened behind, upon the frame of the carriage," wrote another traveler, "but the smaller articles and the mail bag are huddled under the seats in the inside, to the great annoyance of the passengers, who are frequently forced to sit with their knees up to their mouths, or with their feet insinuated between two trunks, where they are most lovingly compressed whenever the vehicle makes a lurch into a rut."[6] When the actor John Bernard and his wife were at last established in the rear seat of the stage between Boston and Newport, they discovered "that the floor was lumbered with a mail-bag and a valuable assortment of earthen and hardware jugs, kettles, fire-irons, and other articles consigned to a 'store' in the interior, which had the effect before the vehicle was ten minutes in motion, of dyeing our shins all the colours of the rainbow."[7]

Certainly, the clumsy way of entering at the front of the vehicle and having to step over the seats, and the shoulders of people who might occupy them, to reach seats in the rear was a serious handicap. It resulted in passengers having to keep their seats during brief stops when they might well prefer to stretch their legs. According to Twining, "the difficulty of getting in or out prevented our leaving these places on trifling occasions, such, as crossing a ferry, or stopping to change horses, or going up a hill."[8] Furthermore, it made escape almost impossible in case of danger. At this date, stagecoach builders seemingly did not dare weaken their heavily loaded vehicle by placing a door in the middle of one or both sides.

A LIGHTER VEHICLE than the regular stage wagon, with but two seats for passengers in addition to the driver's seat, became popular out from Philadelphia and Trenton before 1795. It was like the larger vehicle in almost all respects except that, being shorter, its bottom was more rounded like that of a coach, and it came to be referred to in handbills and newspaper notices as the "coachee." It seemed especially suited to the shorter lines. Isaac Weld, in his description of the coachee, noted that there was "a leathern curtain to hang occasionally between the driver and passengers."[9] This apparently was the first written mention of such a fixture, which probably could be found also in some of the regular stage wagons. It must have helped as a windbreak, and it gave the passengers a degree of privacy. The curtain represented the first step in the transition of the driver's seat from the inside to the outside of the coach. Once outside, the driver's seat could be raised gradually from the level at which the passengers sat, until it reached the level of the roof, as was the case with Concord coach of the 1830s (which is described in chapter 11).

Many of the features of the later American stagecoach were foreshadowed in a model developed in 1799 by the Post Office Department for use of the government stage line between Philadelphia and Baltimore (see chapter 9). Shortly after he made up his mind to establish this line as a model, Postmaster General Habersham ordered several stages to be made at Wilmington, Delaware, and others to be made in Newark, New Jersey. In each case, the postmaster of the city was his agent in arranging for, and supervising the construction of, the stages. To Postmaster John Burnet at Newark, he wrote:

I wish you to employ some carriage maker at Newark to build a four horse stage with harness and two Lamps complete as soon as possible. The stage is intended to carry two of our largest mails within its body and six passengers. At each end, within the body, is to be built a chest or box equal to 22 inches square and as long as the width of the stage will admit. The lids of the chest are to be covered in the same manner as the seats usually are, and it is intended they would be used for that purpose: the passengers who sit on the fore seat will set with their backs to the horses. An intermediate seat 18 inches high is to be placed between the chest seats.[10]

A few days later, Habersham wrote again asking Burnet to "enter into an agreement with Mr. Wade on my behalf to have three carriages made in the manner and at the times stipulated in his letter to you which I have returned for your information," the carriages to be made "in a workmanlike manner at £110, delivered at Elizabethtown."[11] These stages were revolutionary in that the passengers on the front seat were to ride facing backwards, and the driver was to be completely outside the body. They could now properly be called stage*coaches*. The concern for the mail was shown in the careful specifications for the mail boxes within the carriages, boxes that could, when necessary, be kept locked, and that were in all circumstances protected from the weather. The projection of the front box forward beyond the body of the coach formed a seat—usually termed the "box"—for the driver, who, though outside, was as yet placed very low behind his horses. Also, these stages were apparently the first in America to have lamps.

Another letter from Habersham to Burnet furnished details about the painting of the government stages:

By this post I send you a small piece of Board on which the intended colour of the carriage is painted and by which the painter is to be directed in the following manner. The body painted Green—colour formed of prussian blue and yellow ochre. Carriage and wheels red lead mixed to approach vermillion as near as may be. Octagon panel in the back—black. Octagon blind—green. Elbow piece on rail, front rail and back do red as above. All the beads and mouldings—Patent yellow *United States Mail Stage* and over those words a spread eagle of a size and colour to suit.[12]

The Wilmington coachmakers were soon making similar coaches for William Evans of Baltimore, proprietor of the stages between Baltimore and Alexandria, Virginia, which connected in Baltimore with the government line.[13] Later, the postmaster general wrote his Wilmington postmaster that Asa Potter, "the Contractor from New York to Albany wishes to have two stages made pretty much on the same construction as those in use on the public line between Baltimore and Philadelphia. He wishes them made by your best workmen, light in wood but heavy in Tire and to be constructed so as to admit of passengers sitting backwards on the Front seat. 'New York and Albany Mail Stage' in large letters on the middle panels—the mail box is to be constructed so as to admit the feet of the passengers on the middle seat under it."[14]

Meanwhile, less radical modification of the old stage wagon was winning favor. The body was made shorter and shallower, and the curve of the bottom was carried right to the roof, with the end posts at front and back slanting outwards. This made the body light and more like a coach in appearance, except that its roof remained very flat. The driver's seat was separated from the interior of the coach, though his head was still sheltered by the forward projection of the roof. In early representations of this type of coach, all passengers sat with their faces toward the horses, but in later illustrations, the passengers on the front seat faced backwards. Later models, especially in New England, often had a side door. Practically no information exists concerning the makers of this type of stage. The earliest ones seem to have been in use in the neighborhood of Philadelphia and in New Jersey, and were related in their origin, doubtless, to the light Jersey wagon. By 1805, they were on the main highways north of Virginia. In the South and toward the frontiers, the older, clumsier stage wagon continued to do service.

THE NEXT TYPE of stage to gain an ascendancy was the oval stage, dignified in all the literature of the day as the "post coach." It was the descendant of the type of coach encouraged by the Post Office Department at the turn of the century, and, like that coach, it was originally made chiefly in Newark, New Jersey. It was also the immediate ancestor of the famous Troy and Concord stagecoaches. The roof and ends were rounded, so that the coach presented a continuous elliptical curve, not unlike a blunt-nosed football, when viewed from the side. The paneling of the top was continued down the front and back of the body leaving only the sides open. There was a side door, albeit on one side only. The driver was forced outside the body of the coach and was unprotected from the weather, because the top sloped away from, instead of over, his head, as it had done in earlier types. He still sat on the same level as the passengers, his seat being formed by the box that extended through the body and served as the front seat of the interior of the coach. In the rear, the baggage rack was enclosed for the first time with leather curtains, the top cover sloping down on a tangent from the roof.

These post coaches were put into use on both main lines between New York and Philadelphia in 1817, the first noticed instance of their employment.[15] By 1818, they were found on Thomas Powell's lines running out of Albany and Schenectady. In January 1819, a new line between Albany and New York advertised itself as "the only complete line of Post Coaches" between those two cities.[16] The terms "post coach" and "post chaise" were emphasized in advertisements, and the word "stage" was scornfully referred to as the equivalent of stage wagon.[17] John Duncan, who traveled widely in this country in 1818 and 1819, gave in his *Travels* the following description of types of stages then on the road:

The American stages are of three kinds. The old fashioned stage-waggons, which have been described in the letter from Buffalo: an improved construction of these, with doors, and three seats instead of four, which are chiefly found in Massachusetts; and post coaches, as they are called, which have been recently introduced on the roads between New York and Baltimore, and are beginning to make their appearance in some other places. The post coaches are something like one of our six-seated stages, but with an additional seat in the center which enables them with close packing to contain nine inside; the roof in place of being flat is quite round, of course nothing can rest upon it; the luggage is contained in a kind of bag behind, and the driver sits on a low seat in front; one passenger may sit beside him but there are no others outside.[18]

In the early 1820s, newly manufactured post coaches were driven south from Trenton and Philadelphia for service in south Carolina and

Georgia. By 1825, the post coach had crossed the Appalachian ridges. It was found on the National Road as far west as Wheeling.[19] The best contemporary description of this stagecoach in the 1820s was given by Captain Basil Hall, in his *Travels*:

An American stage is more like a French diligance than anything else. Like that vehicle it carries no outside passengers, except one or two on the box beside the driver. It has three seats inside, two of which are similar to the front and back seats of an English coach, while the third is placed across the middle from window to window, or I might say, from door to door, only these stages very seldom have more than one door. Instead of panels, there hung from the roof leather curtains, which, when buttoned down, render it a close carriage; or when rolled up and fastened by straps and buttons to the roof, leave it open all around. This for summer travelling is agreeable enough; but how the passengers manage in the severe winters of the north, I do not know; for certainly we found it on many occasions, even in the south, uncomfortably cold. The middle seat is moveable on a sort of hinge, that it may be turned, horizontally, out of the way when the door is opened. The three passengers who sit upon it, rest their backs upon a stuffed leather strap, permanently buckled to one side of the carriage, and attached to the other side by means of a stout iron hook. These ponderous stages are supported on strong hide straps, in place of steel springs, and all parts are made of great strength, which is absolutely necessary to enable them to bear the dreadful joltings on the miserable roads they have too frequently the fate to travel over.[20]

Those early stagecoaches were decidely primitive and often onerous by any standards of later-day travel, but for the citizens of the early nineteenth century, the advantages the stages supplied seem to have more than compensated for the difficulties of travel by them. In 1825, the Boston *American Traveller*, in the quotation that opens this book's introduction, proudly called the stagecoach "the finest vehicle in the world." The writer of that statement went on to make another important point about those early stagecoaches:

The finest vehicles in the world without any dispute, are stage-coaches. Your sulkeys were made for physicians or single gentlemen; your carriages for old maids (or, to be fashionable, 'for single ladies advanced,') and old women; your carioles for young children and their nurses; and your gigs, your landaus, and your curricles, for fops, dandies and exquisites of both sexes; but your stage-coaches—your downright, modern, well-built stage-coaches—were made for no particular class in society, but for the young and the old, the rich and the poor, the great and small, male and female, of all ranks and conditions; and whether we ride for health, for pleasure, or for business, we almost invariably prefer one of these carry-alls to any other travelling machine now in vogue.[21]

In other words the stagecoach was a democratic vehicle, something for all people. In that new democratic age, the American people now had a vehicle that was truly *for* the people.

VI

Perils of the Road

 THE ENTHUSIAM of Americans in the nineteenth century for the growing stagecoach network had to be tempered against some very real perils of the road—principally, stagecoach breakdowns, accidents, and robberies.

The breakdown most frequently recorded by stage travelers was the snapping of one of the thorough braces. The thorough brace was one of several leather bands that passed under the rounded bottom of the carriage, supporting it and serving as a spring. An English traveler in 1842 wrote that the experience of riding on these thorough braces made the coach "dance in the air like a balloon," swinging forward or backward or sideways as the wheels passed over obstructions or dropped into ruts.[1] The thorough braces permitted the body of the coach to swing to counteract the jolting of the undercarriage, but in performing this function on the notoriously rough American roads, they were subjected to continuous stresses, which varied according to the weight of the driver, passengers, and baggage. Even though the thorough braces were made of many thicknesses of heavy leather, they did wear down, and on occasions of sudden or unusual stress they simply gave way.

But there seemed to be an almost universal remedy for the situation when a thorough brace gave way. John Melish, an English traveler writing in 1812, said that "the defect was supplied by braking down an honest man's fence, and thrusting a rail under the carriage, while the passengers stood almost up to the ankles in the mud, holding it up."[2] Another English traveler in 1819, John Duncan, described this rescue operation:

The roads through which we drove (it was literally through) had shaken our wagon, that after nine hours of jolting one of the straps gave way, and we were brought to a stand by the carriage sinking down upon the pole. Americans are not easily disconcerted. There was a rail fence by the road side, from which the driver selected a stout rafter long enough to reach from the footboard in front to the after axle, the body of the waggon was hove up by our united efforts, and the wooden substitute was thrust under it. We then resumed our seats and jolted on, quite unconscious of any additional inconvenience from riding on a rail.[3]

Only when no suitable rails were available, or a coach was in an unsettled area where there were no fences, was there a variation to the story. It was described in the picturesque language of the Irish actor Tyrone Power in 1836:

We broke by a sudden plump, into a hole, that would have shaken a broad-wheeled wagon into shavings. Our driver did not approve of any of the fence-rails in the vicinity, so plunged into the wood, accompanied by one of my western companions; and in ten minutes they returned, bearing a young hickory pole, that the driver assured us was "as tough as Andrew Jackson himself, and as hard to break, though it might give a little under a heavy load." This was shoved under the body of the carriage, and rested on the fore and hind axles; it was lashed fast, and the spare part of the spar was left sticking out behind, like the end of the main boom of a smack. The coach body when rested upon this, was found to have a considerable list to port . . . [but] the driver was enabled by this ingenious substitute for a carriage spring to "go ahead."[4]

Fence rails and the muscles of the passengers were also called into service when the pivot bolt of the front axletree broke, provided the driver was fortunate enough to have along a substitute bolt. The rails were thrust under the body, which was then raised off its bolster so that the new bolt could be inserted.[5]

Next to the thorough braces, the wheels bore the greatest strains. The constant jolting sometimes loosened the tires until the entire woodwork collapsed, often causing extremely dangerous accidents. Charles J. Latrobe related an instance in 1835 when at the top of a hill "a fore-wheel broke, and an instant overturn followed, at the head of a fearful chasm . . . [Passengers] had toes, ribs, and noses damaged, and one poor fellow a fearful wound in the forehead."[6] Captain Frederick Marryat testified to the Americans' resourcefulness in making temporary repairs to wheels: "the Americans are never at a loss when they are in a *fix*. The passengers borrowed an axe; and in a short time wedges were cut from one of the trees at the road-side, and the wheel was so well repaired that it lasted us the remainder of the journey."[7]

Despite their ingenuity, American drivers were not able to repair all types of breakdowns, and many times passengers had to walk to the next town.[8]

NOTICES of stagecoaches overturning appeared frequently in the newspapers of the time. Apparently few persons who traveled to any extent went through life without meeting with one or more stagecoach overturnings, and few also went on any long journey without some such experience. In 1828, Bernhard, Duke of Saxe-Weimar-Eisenach, recorded being overturned eight times in two years of travel in this country, though his stage journeys did not exceed four thousand miles.[9] Another traveler in that same year protested publicly in a New York newspaper against the nine upsets he had received in a journey from New York to Cincinnati and back to Philadelphia. Six of them were on the way to Cincinnati, a trip of scarcely a thousand miles.[10] A fellow passenger in Ohio informed the geologist Sir Charles Lyell during the 1840s that "in the course of the last three years he had been overturned thirteen times between Cincinnati and Cleveland."[11] Much depended on what time of the year one traveled, since the likelihood of an accident increased in the spring when frost on the roads was thawing and watercourses were overflowing. Analysis of several travelers' narratives yields the rough conclusion that, taking all seasons and all types of roads into consideration, one might expect an upset or worse accident about once in 1,200 miles of staging.

One reason for these accidents was the primitive character of all but the best roads over which the stages passed. "The drivers are very skillful . . . and if you are upset, it is generally more the fault of the road than of the driver," wrote Captain Marryat in 1839. He added, "No one thinks anything of an upset in America . . . these mischances must be expected in a new country."[12] Wrote the Duc de La Rochefoucauld-Liancourt, "The roads are very bad, and no attempts are made to repair them; we cannot, therefore, be surprised at hearing, that so many stagecoaches are overturned."[13] The highways of that day were narrow and hilly with many sharp curves, soft-bottomed and without proper drainage, and with dangerous stream crossings. Stages were frequently overturned after dark by striking stumps and ends of fallen logs either on or close to the edge of the track. Even skillful drivers could hardly expect to take a heavy coach and four-horse team, day in and day out, in all seasons, over such roads without occasional accidents.

The driver needed cooperation from his passengers to prevent overturnings, just as he needed it in getting out of a mudhole or in repairing a breakdown. Isaac Weld, who traveled the Main Post Road about 1796, wrote:

The driver frequently had to call to the passengers in the stage, to lean out of the carriage first at one side, then at the other, to prevent it from oversetting in the deep ruts with which the road abounds: "Now, gentlemen, to the left," and so on. This was found absolutely necessary at least a dozen times in half the number of miles.[14]

This practice continued through all the years of staging. As late as 1855, Amelia Murray wrote that the driver in a bad place called "to us to throw our weight now upon one side, now on the other, to keep a ballance."[15] Adam Hodgson in 1824 gratefully recorded a journey's end at Newport, Rhode Island, "where we arrived safe at last, after many 'alarms', and two or three times bringing the vehicle to the ground again by hanging to the windward, as the captain termed it."[16]

Next to poor roads, the chief cause of accidents was frightened and unmanageable horses. Frequently, driver carelessness was an element, since an alert reinsman was less likely to lose control when a team suddenly shied at objects along the road. A driver might also be careless by leaving a team unattended with passengers in the stage; he often had to leave his box to water his horses, chain the rear wheels, adjust the baggage, or ascertain the nature of obstruction ahead—without there being a passenger beside him to whom he could pass the reins. His team was usually well trained, so that there was little danger; yet sooner or later something might frighten the horses so that they would start forward driverless, leaving passengers in the coach entirely to the mercy of chance. Accidents of this kind occurred so often that most states found it necessary to pass laws prohibiting the leaving of horses attached to a stage without tying them or passing the reins to some suitable person.[17]

Occasionally, accidents were due almost wholly to negligence. Inexperienced drivers, reckless drivers, and drunken drivers were sometimes found on all lines, although they were a minority and were carefully weeded out by most proprietors. If the reputation of their lines and the value of their coaches and horses were not sufficient incentives for proprietors to select their drivers with care, cumulative court decisions making them liable for passengers' personal injuries caused by driver carelessness or neglect proved effective.

THE NINETEENTH CENTURY period of staging in populous regions witnessed a new cause of accidents—racing between stages of opposition lines. Drivers usually shared their employers' bitter antagonisms, especially when a route was not likely to support two competing lines and one was doomed to fail. Their jobs depended on victory for their line. If one believed the rival advertisements in the newspapers, the stages of each line arrived at their destination before those of the other. To fit into the elaborate connection arrangements for cross lines and continuing lines, starting times for the rival stages had to be at about the same hour, thus bringing them into competition along the way. One stage was not likely to be permitted to pass another without a dangerous race on the narrow highways. Occasionally, locked wheels resulted, and instances occurred when wheels were struck off the fast-traveling coaches.[18] Sometimes, the driver of the winning coach, as it drew ahead, swung too rapidly into the single-tracked road, whether deliberately or in his eagerness to gain safer ground, and thus forced the losing team to the side of the road and into a ditch.

On one typical occasion, in Rockland County, west of the Hudson in New York, the driver of the Albany mail stage in passing a rival vehicle excited the horses of the other coach so that their driver was unable to hold them. As the driver of the mail drew ahead, he reined his horses in so rapidly that he crowded the other team to the side of the road and upset the stage. The racing team dragged the overturned coach along and was stopped only by the fall of one of the wheel horses, "while the other coach passed ahead on the full run and in triumph." Five of the eight passengers who were overturned were seriously hurt, and the competing line's new coach, which had been "built in the modern style," was so completely "shattered to pieces that, not a particle of the body could be used in [the] repairing of it."[19]

Races between rival coaches sometimes took place on city streets, to the great danger of other persons as well as to the passengers on the stages.[20] Frequently, public indignation found vent in the newspapers, while many states found it necessary to enact laws against such racing. Eventually, proprietors found it necessary to reassure the public in their advertisements. "On account of the contention between the Union and Exchange lines, the proprietors are induced to change the hour of leaving the city of 5:30, in order to avoid that opposition, so disagreeable to passengers," read an 1825 advertisement of the Exchange line operating between New York and Philadelphia.[21]

IN THE earlier decades of staging in the eighteenth century, when roads were at their worst, the number of overturned stagecoaches was small. The lumbering stage wagons of that era had a low center of gravity and were extremely difficult to overturn. Also, the roads were so bad that no attempts at regular night traveling were made. Upsets, when they happened, were less likely to cause serious injury because the distance to the ground was not great. Neither did the improved turnpike roads of the nineteenth century lead to fewer accidents. This was because the roads permitted greater speed and higher hung stages, with outside seats for passengers. Any accident after the 1820s in the Atlantic states, and after the 1840s west of the Allegheny Mountains, was liable to be much more serious because of the greater speed of the coach and of the greater height from which passengers were thrown to the ground.

Stagecoach upsets were of many kinds, varying in seriousness from a gentle easing over into mud puddles to being thrown over precipices while descending hills at high speeds. Alexander Mackey in his 1849 travel narrative, *The Western World*, gave an amusing account of one overturned stagecoach. The road over which he was riding between Macon and Columbus, Georgia, was so wretchedly churned up after heavy rains that even though the coach proceeded at a painfully slow rate, its passengers were

so often threatened with an upset, that at last I came almost to wish for one . . . that we might be relieved from our anxiety. It was not long before I was gratified. Giving a tremendous lurch to the side at which I was seated, the coach seemed for a moment to poise iteself upon the two side wheels as if deliberating . . . I looked at the judge, and shuddered at the idea of the "fourteen stun," so, pressing towards the left, I called upon the rest to lean to the weather side. This they did but too effectually, for on the coach righting, the opposite wheels plunged into another hole, with such violence as to carry over the whole concern. It went gently enough, and I felt an inward satisfaction, as we were falling, that my weight was to come on the judge. I regretted it afterwards, on account of the rather severe contusions which together we occasioned the commissioner.

For a moment after the vehicle was fairly on its side there was neither motion nor sound within. Everyone seemed to be collecting his thoughts. At length, the lady in the back seat found courage to scream. . . . There was accordingly a general movement of arms and legs; an operation which, unless checked, might have led to rather serious results, as heads and heels were in awkward juxtaposition.

"Lie still all 'cept them as are at the top," said the judge in a muffled voice, "and let the topmost git at oncet, so that the rest can foller."[22]

There were occasions, however, when a driver might deliberately elect to turn a coach over to prevent what threatened to be a worse accident. David Gordon, a driver on the National Road, won a reputation for coolness when, with a coach full of passengers behind a runaway team that he could not check, he pulled the racing horses off the road and overturned the coach against a high bank. The passengers were badly frightened but not hurt, and the coach was little damaged.[23]

The most dangerous accidents were those in which a stage traveling at high speed was thrown over an enbankment. Rarely were the outer precipices of mountain roads in America guarded by rails, and if they were, the rails were almost certain to be too weak to hold a stagecoach in the road. Edward Coke graphically described in 1833 an upset that might have had a more tragic result. The coach party was crossing a mountain west of Pittsfield on the way to Albany

and having a heavy load on the coach, and as usual in America, no slipper of the wheel, we descended the hill with such frightful speed, that whirling around a sharp turn (where the road too had a sharp inclination outwards) the vehicle lost its equilibrium, the passengers screamed out and over it went. I would not at that moment have given half a dollar to insure all our lives. I saw the tops of the trees far below, and thought nothing could save us from perching among their boughs. The rails gave way with a crash, when I was surprised by a sudden and violent shock, occasioned by the coach falling on the friendly stump of a tree which checked us in our course. The vehicle in part overhanging the precipice, carpet bags and mail bags, trunks and hat boxes were to be seen rolling down the hill to the depth of 150 feet. Regulus of old could not have had a more uncomfortable descent in his barrel than we should have had, if the coach had been two or three feet farther on either side of the stump . . .

We had just raised the shattered coach again, when some people who had seen it upset from the Lebanon Springs galloped up, expecting to find half the passengers killed.[24]

In another instance, a Boston-Albany coach overturned crossing the Berkshires, throwing the driver and nine passengers with much violence among the rocks. The driver and one passenger were instantly killed. Another died a day or two later and several others received broken limbs. All were so badly hurt that they were unable to give any account of the accident. Nor could they be taken the seven miles to Northampton, but had to be left at houses near the scene of the accident to recover.[25]

Distinguished public characters of the day were, of course, no less exposed to the hazards of the road than were their less prominent companions. Indeed, since they probably traveled much more than the average citizen, their chances of such unpleasant experiences were the greater. "We regret to state," wrote the editor of the *City of Washington Gazette* on January 2, 1818, "that the Hon. Mr. Dana, Senator of the United States from Connecticut, while on his way to this place, was upset in the mail coach at Elizabethtown, New Jersey, and his left shoulder joint dislocated and his right leg broken." Another news item reported that "Gen. Root of New York was overturned in a stage when proceeding from Washington to Baltimore, a short time since, and had one of his arms broken."[26] Even the postmaster general, Gideon Granger, was upset on one occasion when traveling to Baltimore.

Although Granger escaped unhurt, the postmaster of Baltimore, who was with him, "sustained considerable injury."[27]

Henry Clay was a veteran of a number of stage upsets. In 1834, he was unhurt in a serious overturn between Harpers Ferry and Winchester that proved fatal to a fellow passenger.[28] On another occasion when proceeding to Washington over the National Road, the coach in which he was riding was upset on a pile of limestone in the main street of Uniontown. According to tradition, Clay was still puffing his cigar upon being extricated from the wreck and remarked facetiously: "This is mixing the Clay of Kentucky with the limestone of Pennsylvania."[29]

Martin Van Buren, while on a political trip through the Old Northwest the year after he left the presidency in 1842, was upset on the National Road a few miles west of Indianapolis but escaped injury when the coach landed in a convenient mudhole. "Sorry for it. Mr. Van Buren was always such a special friend of good roads, and particularly of this same National Road," acidly commented the editor of the *Ohio State Journal*, referring to Van Buren's veto of the bill to extend the National Road.[30] The *Sangamo Journal* at Springfield, Illinois, remarked: "He was always opposed to that road, but we were not aware that the road held a grudge against him! He fell very handsomely into a very soft place."[31]

ANOTHER serious cause of accidents in America, following poor roads and frightened horses, was the primitive nature of the stream crossings, both large and small. Small streams even on main highways were, until fairly late in the stagecoach era, crossed by fording. The only real reason for a bridge was to permit passage during high water, and the building of the bridge was usually delayed until a road became so busy that it was a serious inconvenience to wait for the water to subside. The first streams to be bridged were those over which simple bridges could be thrown. For wider and deeper rivers, the stagecoach generation relied chiefly upon ferries.

A newspaper account of an accident that occurred while crossing a swollen run on the Main Post Road as early as 1784 may be recorded as typical of many that occurred later:

The stage attempting to cross, the current was so violent, that it overturned with eight passengers in it, some of whom like to have been drowned; all the baggage with the bed of the waggon and the hind wheels were taken down stream some distance . . . the horses with the fore wheels got out . . . the passengers being under water some time disengaged themselves of the waggon, and got out with a great deal of difficulty; a log which lay across the run, some distance below, brought up the remains of the waggon. A few things were found in the creek this morning, chiefly belonging to the passengers. . . The mail was taken up a mile and a half below the ford.[32]

One of the more dramatic adventures incurred in crossing a swollen stream was that of Theodore Weld, famed reformer and abolitionist, who was touring Ohio in 1832 as an agent for the Society for the Promotion of Manual Labor Institutions. An attempt was made about midnight to cross a flooded creek a few miles east of Columbus. The horses were forced to begin swimming almost at once. Two drivers who were on the stage and the only other passenger were thrown out of the tilted vehicle and washed ashore, but Weld became entangled in the harness of the struggling horses as they drifted rapidly below the landing on the opposite bank. When, after much straining, he finally freed himself, he swam and floated in the dark, past banks too steep to allow him to climb out. Finally, a mile below the crossing, he reached some bushes and, holding to them, eventually pulled himself safely out of the stream. He could not climb the bank, but managed to shout before he sank unconscious to the ground. The cry was heard in a nearby cabin, whose occupants searched the bank until they found him and after an hour of rubbing brought him back to life.[33]

The earliest bridges were generally constructed by laying loose poles across two or three logs that had been thrown across the stream. They were usually intended to serve only in cases of high water. Consequently, they were often neglected and therefore out of repair when high water came. A stage driver would often have to halt to rearrange or replace the poles before he could take his team and coach across. Passengers usually preferred to get out and walk while the driver cautiously led his team across, fearful that one of the sixteen hooves might get caught between the treacherous poles. Even when planks came to be used as bridge floors, they were left unnailed and floated away with the first flood unless they had been previously removed. James Silk Buckingham mentioned in his *America* that as late as 1838 in traveling through Vermont his coach came to many bridges from which the loose planks had been removed, "but the driver, with great humour and alacrity, set to work himself to place the planks across again in their proper places."[34]

Ferries, although they usually represented a welcome interlude in a journey, were time-consuming, and they took a toll from the travelers. Furthermore, during storms and high water, it was often impossible or dangerous for them to run. Some were little more than narrow scows barely wide enough to receive the stage, so that there was an element of risk in driving onto them after dark.[35]

American ingenuity eventually met the challenge of these wider rivers by building such wooden bridges as the world had never seen before. Timber was cheap and conveniently at hand, and American carpenters became experts in throwing long wooden arch and truss combination spans across the rivers. Theodore Burr, who built the most remarkable of these structures and made the greatest contributions to their accepted design, began building his bridges in the first decade of the nineteenth century. By 1839, there were many wooden bridges where trunk highways crossed large coastal rivers. It was not until the period between 1830 and the Civil War, however, that they were built in great quantity throughout the Atlantic states. The old wooden bridges were thus associated with the stagecoach when its glory was on the wane.[36]

ROBBERIES were more rare than accidents along the stagecoach routes of the nineteenth century, but they were a more fearsome peril of the road for the travelers of the day.

One of the lesser types of robberies of that time was the very pretty and undramatic theft of baggage from the rear trunk of the stage. There was comparatively little danger of detection if a robber crept up behind a coach as it was proceeding slowly through sand or climbing a hill and quickly cut the straps that held a trunk or two to the small rear platform. The ordinary rumble of a vehicle moving over the road usually covered any small noise that the robbers made, and the discovery that the baggage was missing might not take place until the stage halted at the next station. Very rarely were the perpetrators of this crime caught. Since the mail was seldom involved, the power of the federal government was not thrown into the chase. Only if there were repeated robberies along some stretch of road would efforts be made to discover the thieves.[37]

Since large sums of money regularly passed over the road in unprotected stagecoaches, it is surprising that there were relatively few holdups. Not until 1864 did the Post Office establish the money order system that eliminated "money" letters from the mails. The "great Mail" pouches often contained between $50,000 and $100,000 in bank notes and other transferable paper, particularly on roads that led into important commercial and financial centers. In addition, the passengers usually carried substantial sums. There were no modern facilities where passengers could renew their supplies of cash or credit at intervals along the way. The amount of money necessary for the entire trip had to be carried from the beginning. Most passengers, too, were businessmen— merchants, attorneys, land buyers, speculators—who had with them the funds needed for their activities. A pioneer Cincinnati businessman, Gorham Worth, wrote about setting off in the mail stage for Pittsburgh in 1817:

I had with me a large sum of money, too large indeed to be mentioned with prudence even now, and which in those days, when human habitations and mile stones were wide apart, it was desirable to keep as much in the shade and as far from the eye of suspicion as possible.[38]

The harsh Post Office law was possibly a deterrent to stage holdups. The Act of 1792 made robbery of the mail punishable by death. The Act of 1799 modified the sentence to forty lashes plus imprisonment not exceeding ten years for the first offense but retained the death penalty either for a second offense or for cases where, in effecting the robbery, the life of the driver was jeopardized by the use of dangerous weapons.[39] Actually, few highway robberies could be committed without the display of weapons since such threats were necessary to bring the coach to a stop.

A favorite stretch for mail robberies along the Main Post Road seemed to be within twenty miles either way of the Susquehanna River on the route between Baltimore and Philadelphia. This was a sparsely settled and heavily wooded region, with stops few and far between. Practically no vehicles but the mail stages traveled the route at night, and the mails from the South presented a tempting prize.

About two miles south of Havre de Grace, Maryland, on the night of March 12, 1818, three men with blackened faces held up the Great Eastern mail coach proceeding toward Philadelphia. They had erected a barrier across the road, and as the driver and a single passenger tried to clear the obstruction, the robbers rushed upon them with pistols and took them into the woods. There, while their prisoners were tied to trees, the robbers spent some three hours going through the mail, then they mounted the stage horses and rode off toward Baltimore.

As soon as the robbery was discovered, notices were sent to the banks and lending merchants of Philadelphia and Baltimore, and an express was dispatched to New York to guard against the payment or acceptance of any of the notes, drafts, or checks. Within a few days, two of the robbers were caught while attempting to pass a bank note in a Baltimore clothing shop. The third was caught in Philadelphia within ten days. Over $90,000 worth of bank notes, post notes, drafts, bills of exchange, and checks were recovered from the robbers. So lucrative had been their haul that they had not troubled to rob the driver and passengers who reputedly carried considerable sums of money themselves. Post Office representatives carefully saved the mutilated envelopes and letters of transmittal, and as soon as the fragments could be pieced together and associated with their proper contents they were forwarded by mail as originally directed. "This daring robbery affords another strong proof of the necessity of having an armed guard attached to the mail coaches, as is the case in England and other countries," commented the editor of the *City of Washington Gazette*.[40]

Two of the robbers were sentenced to hanging; the third, who was barely twenty years of age, was given a ten-year prison term. The newspapers gave much attention both to the robbery itself and to the court proceedings. Joseph T. Hare, the leader of the trio, had a long career of crime, beginning on the Natchez Trace in the first decade of the century. As was the custom with condemned men in those days, he wrote his "Confession," an interesting and straightforward narrative, supposedly intended as a "warning" to others who might be tempted. It served as a form of "escape" literature and was widely reprinted.[41] The two men were hung on September 10, 1818, at Baltimore in the presence of a crowd reported by newspapers to number 15,000 persons.[42] (Interestingly, in 1818 less than six months passed from their actual crime until their capture, trial, and execution.)

Neither the "Confession" nor the hanging served sufficiently as a deterrent, however. Five months later, at about 4:00 A.M., a stage carrying the Great Eastern mail from Philadelphia to New York was held up by three masked highwaymen near Elizabethtown, New Jersey. As one man ran before the horses to stop them, the other two armed with pistols presented themselves at the side of the driver and took him from his seat. They forced the passengers, four men and a woman, to descend from the stage and robbed them of watches and money. Then they cut open the leather pouch containing the mails and after selecting the packages likely to contain the most lucrative "money" mails they made off. A Philadelphia merchant sitting in the back seat had managed to conceal in the straw on the floor $33,000 that he was carrying to a Manhattan bank, and another passenger had secreted a large amount in bills in a hole in the stage lining. Again, editorials appeared in the newspapers: "We cannot but believe that this circumstance will quicken the government to adopt the measure which has often been urged, of providing the mail with a guard."[43]

When the stage reached New York, the mail was immediately checked, and the missing packages were listed together with an offer of $1,000 reward for information leading to the capture of the robbers. A few days later, two of the robbers were captured in New York with much of the money still in their possession. After making a full confession, they led the officers to a cache under a tree in New Jersey where they had concealed $25,000 more of their loot. The third robber was caught within two weeks in Lancaster, Pennsylvania. Three months later, the jury brought in a verdict of guilty of robbing the mail but not guilty of jeopardizing the life of the driver—the latter decision saving the robbers from the death penalty. The judge sentenced each of the prisoners to the maximum term of ten years solitary confinement.[44]

In 1821, a different method of stage theft was used. A person who had taken his seat as an only passenger at Havre de Grace struck the driver from behind when the coach was near Elkton, stunning him with the heavy blow. The robber then drove the coach off the road and rifled the mail. Reported the *Niles Weekly Register* this time, "We learn that for this desolate part of the mail route a regular guard will be established."[45]

Even a guard did not save the coach from attack. In July 1823, after guards were provided, the stage was again, on a dark night near the Gunpowder River in Maryland, stopped by a fence-like obstruction thrown across the road. The guard said that in the dim light of the coach lamps he saw four men and fired his blunderbuss among them. He then drew his pistols and discharged them. When the guard was through shooting, the robbers advanced to the coach and seized both guard and driver and then stole the mail. The next day, the contractor, a Mr. Stokes of Baltimore, led a party that traced the highwaymen to the iron forges on the Gunpowder, where they were found and captured and the mail recovered. Although the robbers had guns in their hands when they held up the coach, they had not fired them. The jury again refused to find them guilty of more than simple robbery, and their sentence was only ten years' imprisonment.[46]

One or two spectacular robberies each year along trunk lines in the East continued to furnish excitement until the railroads replaced the coaches as carriers of the mail. The full course of a cycle had been run in the fifty years since it had been argued that a stagecoach and passengers would provide greater security for carrying the mail than would the lone postrider on his horse. Nevertheless, the Post Office Department established an excellent record in capturing highwaymen who robbed the stages. The postmaster general from 1814 to 1823, a gentleman with the unusual name of Return J. Meigs, Jr., was able to boast in 1818 that "since I have been at the head of this Department not one instance of a violent robbery of the mail has occurred, where the perpetrators have escaped apprehension, conviction, and punishment."[47] Meigs had advised Congress against the employment of guards because the expense was too great to permit their employment on even all of the important roads. To employ them on some and not on other, he said, would seem only to expose the others even more. However, a series of robberies induced the department in 1823 to provide guards along the Main Post Road by requiring as a condition of the contract that the proprietors of the stages furnish them. They were soon, however, abandoned.[48]

ONE CELEBRATED attempted robbery occurred as stagecoach driver Samuel Luman from Cumberland, Maryland, was driving a mail and passenger stage one night in the mountains near Frostburg in 1834. His passengers that night were a group of western merchants who were traveling east to buy goods, and among them they had about $60,000 in cash. Luman had just come around a bend in the road when he confronted a barricade of wood and brush thrown across the road. He reined in his horses, and a group of five highwaymen wearing masks jumped out of the woods. Luman yelled to his passengers to help him, but as he later said, they only crouched on the floor of the coach.

One of the highwaymen held the bridle of the lead horse, while another approached Luman, pistol in hand, and told him to climb down. Luman refused, and the robber leveled the pistol and pulled the trigger. Only a snap was heard, because the powder had failed to explode in the damp night air. Luman was unarmed, but he grabbed his whip and flayed at the robber who was holding his horse. In the face of the stinging lashes, the robber fell back, and Luman whipped his horses, sending them toward the barricade. They crashed through, and although the coach almost capsized, he managed to keep it upright and dashed toward Frostburg.

When they arrived at the Highland House in Frostburg, the grateful passengers took up a collection for Luman, but he refused it. He later said that the sum was "ludicrously small," and he also remembered their unwillingness to help him out on the road. Whenever Samuel Luman told the story after that, he always called his passengers that night "a mean set." And he told it often, particularly when he retired from driving in 1839 and became a popular tavern keeper at the National House in Cumberland.[49]

There were therefore very real perils of the road along the stagecoach routes of the nineteenth century, but they seemed to be accepted as almost inevitable travel adversities of the era, occasional occurrences that did not dampen the growing enthusiasm of Americans for stagecoach travel.

VII

The Stage Driver

 THE DRIVERS of those nineteenth-century stage-coaches were true American originals, colorful characters of the road who exuded an air of daring, bravery, and authority.

As English travelers in the states soon discovered, the American stagecoach driver was quite different than the "coachman" of England, who tended to be viewed as a lackey or servant. Here, the driver ruled—it was his coach, his route, and his passengers. Many Englishmen, accustomed to the servility of their coachmen, considered these American drivers to be astonishingly independent and sometimes even surly.

One factor that contributed to the independent attitude of the American driver was the common practice in the nineteenth century of not accepting tips or gratuities from the stagecoach passengers. And despite the independent spirit it created for the stage driver, the English did find this one aspect of an American journey quite pleasing, and in the journals of the day we find frequent expressions of relief at not having "to remember the coachman" at every stage of the journey. In England, there was also a guard who looked after the baggage who expected a fee, and so wonderfully had the system of petty exaction developed that at many of the principal coach offices there were men who made it their sole business merely to hand the baggage to the top of the coaches, for which they expected a few half-pence. In America, English travelers missed the constant attendance that the expectation of a reward led the English guard to give. "As the driver never expects or demands a fee from the passengers, they or their comforts are no concern of his," wrote one traveler in the 1830s, and "they throw up the reins and the passengers together, and as they get nothing from the passengers, they do nothing for them." [1]

In the eastern United States, the stage driver was seldom aided by a guard, or conductor, who had as his special concern the care of the passengers and their baggage. The price of labor was too high. For a while, the Post Office Department put guards on the routes of the great mails from Washington to New York, and from Washington west over the National Road, but they were paid by the department, and their services were confined to caring for the mail and giving it added protection. Even they were soon abandoned, following the postmaster general's recommendation. [2] In the West in later days, guards were employed by the express companies who owned the more important lines to give added security to their valuable shipments of gold and goods, but that is a later story. The greater responsibility that, in the absence of guards, fell upon the eastern drivers is perhaps one reason for their generally higher standing in American communities, compared with the station of their English colleagues. An American driver had to be something more than a horseman.

An Englishman's view of the American stagecoach driver was contained in the very popular nineteenth-century memoirs, *Retrospections of America*, written by John Bernard, who traveled the new Republic from 1797 to 1811. After describing the stout, well-bundled and muffled, reticent coach driver of his native England, he went on to say:

The very opposite of all this was the New England "driver." He was usually a thin, wiry, long-backed, leather-skinned fellow, sharing the front seat with the company, and flying in and out of the vehicle with the crack of a harlequin. No one more abhorred a superfluity of clothes. A straw hat was his creed, and he would often wear nankeens and shoes in frosty weather. I can remember one—a tall Vermonter, in an village where I resided some time—who, when winter was whistling his sharpest airs, would stand up amid a well-clad undergrowth of travelers, lank as a leafless elm. Placed upon their level, he sympathized with all his company, yet not intrusively. He was a general book of reference, almanac, market list, and farmer's journal; a daily paper published every morning, a focus; which, by some peculiar centralpetality, drew all things toward it. [3]

There is no indication that a uniform or even typical stage driver's costume existed in America. Drivers used the garments they had at hand, with the weather probably having more to do with their choices than their tastes had. Few took any particular care in the matter, for a storm, a breakdown, or even routine duties soon made all clothes look the same. "The coachman, or driver, as he is here universally called, is generally very ill-dressed, though civil and well qualified for his duty," noted James Silk Buckingham, an experienced traveler, in the 1840s.[4] In the South, according to the same writer, "the greater number went without neckclothes, some without coats, and a good hat was a rarity. Instead of woolen clothes, a kind of grey, or blue and white cotton cloth of domestic manufacture, was used for coat and trousers."[5]

Though he may have been careless in his dress and inattentive at times to his passengers, the American driver won nothing but praise for his skill in driving. Bad roads only served the more to bring it to attention. "The road is execrable," wrote J. R. Godley of the route from Saratoga to Lake George, "nothing but the most wonderful dexterity on the part of the driver, and the strength and steadiness of a team that would have done no dishonor to the Tantivy in the days when England was a coach country could have brought us through."[6] Going from Albany to Utica over "rocky and uneven" roads, John Fowler related, "we reached Utica about twelve o'clock in the evening, having travelled during the day, though at grievous bodily expense, at the rate of six miles an hour including stoppages; a feat which I will venture to say would never have been performed by an English coachman."[7]

Few American drivers handled the reins like the "scientific" regulations of the English coaching era. Little style in driving made its appearance upon the National Road, and most drivers were satisfied with the careful, yet common and unpretentious, sort of driving. Their chief regard for appearance was to keep their teams together.[8] Their sole test of a driver's worth was the pragmatic one—did he come through in time, with passengers, horses, and stage all sound?

The word *execrable*, so frequently used by foreigners to describe American roads, was entirely proper for those roads not turnpiked. It was after 1800 before the turnpike movement gained momentum enough to count, and then it involved scarcely more than half the stage roads in the older regions and almost none on the frontiers. One could scarcely perform a major journey in America without spending much time on raw roads, which received a minimum of care. Frequently, these roads were cut through forests where the sun rarely penetrated to dry them. In the low places, the rich, vegetable mold soaked up and long retained water, creating mires in all but the driest seasons.

On the many hills of the eastern states, loose stones abounded, and not infrequently more permanent ribs of bedrock were encountered in the road bed. Brissot de Warville wrote that when he crossed Horseneck Hill near Rye, New York, in 1788 he "knew not which to admire most in the driver, his intrepidty or dexterity" and that he could not "conceive how he avoided twenty times dashing the carriage in pieces, or how his horses could retain themselves in descending the stair-cases of rocks."[9] James Dixon writing of a journey across Ohio to Sandusky, sixty years later, said:

Our course could not be called a road, in any sense, except from the mere fact that it had been traversed before, and we also were now passing over it. We made our way across gullies, rivulets, rising hillocks, and then again sunk up to our axles in bogs. We were roughly handled by great stones lying in our course, roots of trees projecting their fibres; and then again by pieces of timber put into soft places, by way of making a pavement for passengers to cross. Really this journeying of American stages, in the midst of a country such as we passed through this day, is a curiosity. It would be, indeed, extremely difficult, a priori, to imagine how the carriage was to escape being capsized many times told; how the horses were to keep their feet, and perform their task; and how the driver could possibly preserve his seat, and pilot his vehicle through so many shoals to a safe anchorage.[10]

Such descriptions were scarcely exaggerated. Under the American system of townships caring for their own roads, more mountainous regions and forested areas, where roadwork was most needed, received the least attention, because settlers were few and poor. Even in other districts where a frontier economy still prevailed, farmers were too busy to work on the road except in certain in-between seasons. But the stage driver had to cope with all conditions, and often he was forced to do the minimum repair work needed to get through.

It was at the driver's mastery of such situations and road conditions that foreign travelers marveled. Tyrone Power, seated upon the driver's box in the 1830s, felt certain upon seeing dismal mudholes ahead that the driver would back out:

But no such thing, faith! he steered round all impediments as cooly as the wind that whistled through the half-frozen reins he held. Finding one place in the road quite impassable, he cast his eyes about him for a moment and chose the best part of the right bank; when gathering up his leaders, he first vexed them a little with the whip, and then, putting them fairly at it, gaining its summit, a thick cover of shrubs growing breast high, when having thus turned the impracticable bit of highway, he cooly dropped down into it again.[11]

If the roads presented difficulties in the daytime, they must have furnished many hair-raising situations after dark. The dim candle-lantern lights of the stage, provided they were in working order, only served by their shadows to give the illusion of greater dangers, and the moon, if it came out, was as likely to confuse as to help. If the driver and his horses had not usually been familiar with every road of the route, the danger would have been too great to permit night travel. John Duncan told of coming after dark to a swamp in 1818 where the water, after much rain, had entirely covered the causeway:

Our charioteer, however, feeling secure in his knowledge of the channel drove dauntlessly forward, the horses dashed into the water, and very soon our bones bore testimony to the correctness of his pilotage. Well was it for us that the driver's skill was not inferior to his daring, for had he gone to either side of the proper line, horses and waggon, with all that it contained would probably have found in the marsh a last resting place.[12]

The charge most frequently cited against American drivers was that of recklessness. In the words of one traveler in the 1830s, "He drove most furiously over every thing, rough and smooth alike. Ravines and water-courses were no impediments; he dashed on at a surprising rate, over rough stones and tottering bridges that would have cracked every spring in an English carriage and caused its coachman to deliberate sometime before he even ventured over them at a foot pace."[13]

As a matter of fact, comfort and speed were irreconcilable on most American roads. The driver, especially if he drove the mail, had his schedule to meet, with a Post Office Department fine and a possible deduction from his own salary facing him if he caused the mail to miss connections. Doubtless, he became somewhat hardened to the complaints of travelers.

Indeed, the utmost exertions of the driver were frequently required to enable him to keep his seat. Passengers within the coach, at least, had four sides and the top to assist them in keeping their places while a companion passenger on the driver's box could grip tight with his hands. The driver relied chiefly on bracing his feet against the footboard and on balance. Occasionally, drivers were thrown from their seats.

Under the heading "Drivers, keep your seats," the *American Traveller* for February 3, 1826, carried the following item:

The western stage arrived at Caughnawaga, New York, the other night when to the surprise of the passengers no driver was to be found. After stamping and hallooing in vain for the driver to open the door, they, without ceremony, helped themselves out, and found that the horses had brought up regularly, except the leaders had been divided as to which route to take around the sign post. A man rode up at full speed to inform them that the driver had been picked up three miles back. He had fallen from his seat, and the rattling of the coach over the rough, frozen road had prevented his cries being heard by the passengers. He was considerably injured by his fall.

Almost all foreign travelers commented at the hair-raising custom of the American driver in giving rein to his horses going down hill. "The youth who drove us," wrote G. Combe, "ascended the numerous hills which we traversed very leisurely, but dashed down the other side with extraordinary rapidity. We allowed him to take his own way, judging that he and his horses best knew the practices of their own country, and we were not disappointed. They were steady and safe."[14] Thomas Twining, after mentioning that the stage was not provided with a drag, wrote that "at first our rapidity on these occasions, with a steep declivity, without rail or fence of any sort on one side, seemed to be attended with no trifling degree of danger; but I soon found that the driver managed his four active little horses with all the skill of an English coachman, although he had little appearance of one."[15]

Mechanical brakes were not yet in existence. A driver could get down and lock his rear wheels with a chain or place a drag under them, but it was tedious in hilly country and the act of descending from the box to do so was not in itself unaccompanied by danger, especially if the team was a spirited one. James Silk Buckingham wrote that in one instance: "The road was a series of ascents and descents, to each of which the driver had to adapt the coach, by locking or unlocking the wheels as required. For this purpose he was obliged to get off every time with the reins in his hand."[16]

Though such driving may seem excusable with hills of moderate size, it also was surprisingly common upon the long descents of the Allegheny ridges in western Pennsylvania and Maryland. Tyrone Power in the 1830s returned across the Alleghenies in the Good Intent line and subsequently wrote:

The practice is for the team to be put on a run the moment they gain the summit of a hill; and if all things hold out, this is kept up until the bottom be reached: the horses are excellent, and rarely fail. On my asking the coachman,—by whom I rode as much as possible,—what he did in the event of a wheelhorse coming down in a steep pass, he replied "Why, I keep driving ahead, and drag him along;"—an accident which he assured me had occurred more than once to himself when the roads were encrusted with ice and snow.[17]

The willingness with which the American driver forded swollen streams also made foreign travelers hold their breath. There were many fords in the West and South where bridges had not been erected. They presented slight obstacles except when raised by heavy rains. Charles Latrobe, describing his journey through Georgia, observed, "The coolness with which the coachman, after halting for a moment on the edge of the steep broken declivity, and craning forward to look at the stream in advance, broad, muddy, and rapid, running like a millrace, will then plunge into it with his horses, descending down till the water covers their backs, is admirable."[18]

In such instances, of course, the drivers were familiar with the fords. The four horses and heavily loaded coach would hold the bottom much better than, and could cross a stream that would be dangerous for, a light vehicle. Nevertheless, there were opportunities for misjudgment, and American newspapers of the time were filled with accounts of stage accidents, both in descending hills and fording streams.

ANOTHER CHARACTERISTIC of American driving that struck foreign observers was the directing of the horses more by the voice than, as in England, by the whip. "The main thing to be done in all kinds of hostlering here, is to make as much noise as possible," Charles Dickens sarcastically commented in his *American Notes*.[19] "It is more by the different noises which they make than by their reins, that they manage their horses," noted Isaac Weld in 1807.[20]

Captain Basil Hall also noted "how much more the drivers managed their horses by word of mouth, than by touch of the whip," and in remarking upon that fact to an American companion, received the reply that it showed "both intelligence in the men and sagacity in the animals."[21]

The American driver knew his horses well—knew each one's virtues, shortcomings, and peculiarities. The horses also knew their driver— knew by the tone of his voice what was expected of them. It is natural that in time the cooperation between man and beast reached a high degree of efficiency. In time, the driver knew just how to handle his team on every mile of the road in order to get the best results.

NO MATTER how slow a journey had been, the driver as he approached town, knowing all eyes were watching after his horn had sounded, gathered up the reins of his four-in-hand, cracked his long-lashed whip around the leader's ears, and with a jingle of chains and rattling of wheels, thundered down Main Street, halting sharply at the Post Office while he handed down the padlocked pouch and then, with a sweeping turn, bringing up at the tavern entrance. This turn was necessary when stages had only one side door in order to bring it properly adjacent to the tavern steps and was apparently continued by many drivers, even after two doors were common, as a final flourish at the end of a stage ride.

The stage driver's horn, imported into American staging from England, was useful on the winding hill roads of the East to warn unwary drivers of private carriages and cumbersome freight wagons that the stage was about to meet or overtake them. It was also brought into play when approaching a village to notify the population that their mail had come and that anyone expecting to take the stage must step lively. Frequently, the driver would by the number of short, sharp blasts notify the tavern keeper of the number of plates to set at his table for passengers.

This instrument seems to have fallen into disuse sometime after 1830, however. It may have survived on local routes in the East, but it was rarely heard in the West, perhaps because it was less needed on the comparatively straight roads of the prairies there. Possibly, the driver abandoned the horn on his own initiative, for it was rather bothersome to carry and take out of its sheath and seems to have been a difficult instrument to sound with dignity. Harriet Martineau wrote, "The driver announced our approach by a series of flourishes on one note of his common horn, which made the most ludicrous music I ever listened to . . . we were convulsed with laughter."[22]

MUCH OF THE PLEASURE of a journey depended upon the coachman's nature. His surliness might put the passengers out of humor, but a driver in high spirits provoked smiles in the sourest weather and on the roughest roads. John Lambert wrote in 1814 of his first trip in an American stage: "This tedious travelling was by no means to our taste, and we should possibly have lost our good humour, had not the arch whimsicality of our driver, who was called Captain White, furnished us with abundant matter for mirth. He entertained with many humorous stories, and had always something smart to say to every waggoner or person that passed us." Lambert, an English traveler, was having his eyes opened to the democracy of the New World when he added naively, "He spoke to several people of consequence with the utmost freedom."[23]

It was perfectly natural in America that the driver should eat his meals at the same table with his passengers. English commentators seldom failed to note this as one of the striking examples of American democracy. "The driver breakfasted with us," recorded James Stuart, "and was quite as free and easy with the whole party as if they had been his companions."[24] Indeed, the driver was apparently the autocrat of many tavern tables. James Silk Buckingham mentioned in 1842 an instance in which the driver "appeared to be the principal person at the table," and added, "it being the custom, we are told, throughout New England for the drivers to take their meals with the passengers." He noted, further that "they were often superior in appearance and manners to many of their passengers."[25]

Henry Tudor in his 1834 *Narrative* wrote, "Our amiable and facetious driver . . . on dinner being served up, stalked into the *salon à manger* with the careless nonchalance of a bidden guest—seated himself at the table with the ladies, whose elegant dresses presented rather a violent contrast to the grotesque habiliments of honest Jehu, and entered into conversation, and cracked his jokes, with all the agreeable and winning familiarity imaginable."[26]

Most of the important through lines were in the hands of companies, and the drivers were hired. A driver's wages included board, lodging, and washing, and an extra allowance was made if he boarded and lodged part of the time at home. When the Post Office was running its government-owned stage line between Baltimore and Philadelphia in 1799, it paid its drivers fourteen dollars a month, a rate the postmaster general considered generous.[27] John Palmer, crossing the Allegheny ridges of Pennsylvania in 1817, learned that the drivers in that section were then receiving from sixteen to twenty dollars a month, "according to their work."[28] A ledger of the Reesid-Slaymaker line between Philadelphia and Pittsburgh, with accounts of some seventy drivers on the western part of the road in 1831–35, showed the average monthly pay of drivers then to be back to twelve dollars a month, although some received fourteen dollars. A driver boarding himself two-thirds of time received seventeen dollars and thirty-three cents a month.[29] And according to the records of the Eastern Stage Company in New England for 1837, that company's drivers were then paid the large sum of twenty-eight dollars a month.[30]

Relay stations on the well-established eastern routes were between ten and fourteen miles apart, depending upon where satisfactory tavern arrangements could be made. In the South and on the western frontier, they were likely to be further apart. Drivers of mail coaches on the faster routes continued to drive for three or four relays. The minutes of the proprietors of the Boston–New York line for 1805 mentioned a vote "to lessen the number of drivers, each driver to drive forty miles in winter and sixty miles in summer."[31] The relay teams in these instances were in the charge of someone other than the drivers. Sometimes a regular stablehand connected with the tavern might be responsible for them, or at a larger stage tavern, the company might have its own stablehand. Frequently, the company kept extra hands at the larger centers who could help around the stables and, on occasion, act as extra drivers.

Drivers of accommodation coaches apparently changed, for the most part, at every relay and cared for their own teams.[32] In this case, after a rest and feed, the same team and driver would usually haul the coach coming from the opposite direction back to their home station. Thus, they did not have to spend a night away from home. Another advantage of this system was that each driver was made wholly responsible for the care of his team, for properly rubbing the horses down, feeding and currying them, doctoring their minor injuries, and keeping the harness in repair.

STAGE DRIVERS, as a class, saw much of life, and to some of our Puritan ancestors, they seemed a little rough. Occasionally, one heard offensive profanity, especially in western New York, where the manners of the frontier were overwhelming the New England heritage. Both profanity and drunkenness seemed less common over the whole North, however, than in the South. Laws of most northern states required the dismissal of drunken drivers and established fines. The Post Office Department stipulated that no drunken driver should be allowed to carry the mail, and there are numerous letters in the postmaster general's letterbooks ordering mail contractors to discharge anyone whom postmasters reported as intoxicated while on duty.[33] Many proprietors were exceedingly strict in this matter and, to protect themselves, secured pledges of abstinence or temperance from their men. Among the papers of Ginery Twichell was an agreement signed by nine of his drivers, reading "We the undersigned agree to abstain from the use of *Ardent Spirits as a Drink* while Engaged in Running Stages Between Norwich and Palmer Wharf During the Present Contract."[34]

Despite these strong deterrents, there were nevertheless guardians of morals who felt something should be done about the stage drivers. A correspondent wrote in 1816 to the Boston *Recorder and Telegraph* protesting against the drivers' profanity "which increases to an alarming degree. They spend their leisure time entirely in idleness, lounging in the bar-rooms of public houses, smoking or drinking. They generally shun the house of God on the sabbath and are out of the way of moral restraints. The number of drivers is increasing every year and it is time to attend to their moral interests."[35]

The same paper admitted that barring the custom of tipping, the only way a passenger "can strengthen his claim upon the attention of the driver, is by inviting him to drink." Of tipping, it added, "The nature, of our society, and the degree of pride which exists in the character of the American citizen, does and will forever prevent the introduction of this custom."[36]

The stage men won the day, it seems, in this skirmish over their character and social standing. The intemperate and unobliging were likely sooner or later to be weeded out of a profession that was highly selective. A stage company could not afford to trust any but responsible men with so much property. There was the coach and team, which the driver had to keep in good condition. His cargo was human life, where a slip might mean broken limbs and possibly death. It required a man of tact and diplomacy to deal with passengers, arbitrate their differences, and meet or resist their demands. In his hands were the mails—lifeblood of a nation—which he had sworn to protect not only against robbery but also against loss or damage by a dozen other dangers of the road. There was the passengers' baggage, perhaps not so valuable but the safety of which was necessary to insure in order to preserve good will for the company. There was express, forwarded by the stage company, whose safe arrival was guaranteed, or reimbursement had to be made for the loss. There were bank notes and other forms of money that the driver usually carried on his person. There were the mails to deliver at the local offices, newspapers to throw at the gates of farmhouses, messages to deliver, business directions to pass on.

All of these constituted the driver's everyday responsibilities. The real test came when the elements were contrary; when rain, darkness, and winter snows created their hazards; when washouts made the roads and bridges treacherous; when breakdowns taxed his ingenuity; when teams were frightened and unmanageable. Instant action in sudden emergency, infinite patience at other times, constant vigilance always, were requisite qualities of the ideal driver.

As STAGECOACH TRAVEL increased in the United States, some of those stage drivers became legendary figures along the well-traveled roads. One such figure was Montgomery Demming—known as "Old Mount"—who drove stages along the routes from Baltimore to Wheeling. Thomas Searight said that Old Mount was over six feet in height and about 400 pounds in weight, and it was a common remark along the National Road that "Old Mount on the front boot of a coach balanced all the trunks that could be put in the rear boot." He first appeared on the road in 1836 as a driver for the quaintly named June Bug Line, a line of brief existence. Later, he was a driver for the Express Line, a line of small, rapid coaches used to transport perishible goods and a few passengers quickly, which locals called "The Shake Gut Line." Old Mount continued to ride for a number of different lines until he retired from the road in 1851 and, like many other drivers, became a tavern owner. He ran the Eagle House in McKeesport, Pennsylvania, where he died in 1855.[37]

An even more legendary figure was Redding Bunting, a driver for the National Road Stage Company in the 1830s and 1840s and an independent tavern owner, who was described as a giant of a man, six and one half feet in height, with a florid complexion and a deep baritone voice. He is remembered chiefly for two famous stagecoach runs that became part of the lore of the National Road. The first was in 1838 when the government wanted quick dissemination of a message from President Martin Van Buren. The B & O Railroad at that time did not yet run west of Frederick City, Maryland; so Bunting made arrangements to pick up the message in Frederick and have a relay of stagecoaches carry it to Wheeling, West Virginia. Bunting did not drive the route, but he sat next to the driver all the way, supervising the operation as they changed horses and drivers periodically along the way. The trip was 222 miles, and Bunting arrived in Wheeling just twenty-three hours and thirty minutes after he had picked up the message in Frederick.

An even more famous run was his ride of 1846 when he did all the driving himself. This time the message was President James Knox Polk's official declaration that war existed with Mexico. By that time, the railroad had been completed to Cumberland, Maryland, and Bunting picked up the message at Cumberland at 2:00 A.M. He reached Uniontown, Pennsylvania, at 8:00 A.M., where he had breakfast at the National Tavern, and then he was back on the stage, clicking the reins again. Bunting reached Wheeling at 2:00 P.M. He had covered the 131 miles in twelve hours of magnificent stagecoach driving.[38]

To THE VILLAGERS of the nineteenth century, the stagecoach driver brought news and gossip from the big world without. He was a traveler when most people remained at home. He saw and heard things that were new to his hearers. If he possessed imagination, he almost certainly developed into a good storyteller. He could relate his adventures with the belles along his route. He could speak of the changes of the countryside, suiting his theme and manner to his audience and the occasion. No matter if he embroidered his tales a little; his listeners were in no position to dispute his facts.

Many responsible drivers were, as they grew older, given positions as line agents or managers, a step toward becoming proprietors themselves. Many looked forward to leasing or purchasing a tavern in some favored town along the way. They might possibly inherit their tavern from their father-in-law, for many married innkeeper's daughters. Allied so closely with the life of the old road, as they were, few drivers were able upon retiring to turn their back upon it. Instead, as the railroad came, they remained stranded upon the highway, their properties depreciating while they dreamed of the days that were gone. A few drivers, still unattached and willing to leave old associations, continued westward with the stagecoaches, and even in California we find New England, Pennsylvania, and Ohio drivers once more following their old profession.[39]

But there was a time during the first half of the nineteenth century in the eastern United States when the stagecoach driver occupied an important and even honored place in American society. Morris Schaff, who as a boy lived along the National Road, recalled in his memoir what it was like to see one of the stages passing by:

As for the driver, I honestly believe that had the choice been given me, or any other small boy, between taking his place and that of the President, we would not have hesitated a moment—the driver was the greatest, the most envied man in the world. I always thought that even my father felt deeply honored when anyone of them—he knew them all—would call out bluffly "Good Morning, Squire," or give a little friendly wave of his whip.[40]

By the second half of the nineteenth century in the East, those drivers had been largely replaced by railroad engineers riding in their enclosed metal engines. But it was not the same, and something quite colorful and unique had been lost on the American scene—those stage drivers, sitting perched on their drive-deck seats, snapping their whips, yelling at their passengers to lean this way and that, driving at high speeds over the eastern roads, and finally triumphantly blowing their horns as they approached the end of their journey. They were American originals.

VIII

The "Step-Lively Era" in the East

 THE FIRST two decades of the nineteenth cen-
tury were a period of phenomenal growth and
development for American stagecoaching in
the East, particularly north of the Potomac, and it can rightly be called
the "step-lively era" for the stage.

By 1801, the weekly transportation of the mail "in carriages furnishing accommodation for passengers" was 24,490 miles—almost triple
that for 1793 (8,567 miles).[1] The total length of stagecoach routes had
not been greatly extended; instead, much of the increase was caused by
the greater frequency of service each week over the older routes. The
increase to daily (except Sunday) service of the Main Post Road from
Portsmouth, New Hampshire, south to Petersburg, Virginia, especially
boosted the figure. South of Philadelphia this increased frequency had
been prompted chiefly by the transfer of the seat of government to
Washington.

The weekly transportation of the mail by stagecoach further
increased by 1803 to 30,172 miles.[2] A major reason was the recently
inaugurated triweekly stage service between Petersburg, Virginia, and
Charleston, South Carolina. By 1811, the figure had reached 45,380
miles; by 1816, 71,046 miles; and by 1820, it was close to 80,000 miles.[3]
This may be considered a slow and steady growth for the two decades,
1800 to 1820. The increase was built up by three factors: (a) the increased frequency of trips on the old routes; (b) the addition of routes
that made the network more intricate in the older, more settled areas,
and (c) the constant extension of routes on the frontiers.

Prior to 1800, few stages did not carry the mail; so for those years the

74.

Post Office figures were a fairly accurate index of the growth in all staging facilities. After 1800, however, as the mail coaches were sped up and the hours of travel extended far into the night, the mail coach proprietors were obliged to put on the road accommodation coach lines that gave their main attention to passengers' comforts and conveniences.

The growth of staging in these years was associated with and, to a considerable degree, dependent upon another conspicious contribution of this period—the turnpike. Turnpikes were built primarily to facilitate the movement of freight, rather than passengers and mail, but the latter benefited when the pikes were being promoted.

The turnpikes were built in response to insistent demands for better transportation facilities to rich, newly settled Piedmont and Appalachian valleys and growing inland towns. The water highways of the deeply indented coast could reach no further; their contribution had been made. The next one- to two-hundred miles inland needed well-constructed trunk highways that could serve as veins to a capillary system for gathering up the surplus produce of these fertile new areas and taking it to the growing ports on navigable rivers and bays. The turnpike was the answer of the age to the inadequacy of local road-building funds, the divided authority of local supervisors, and the amateurish engineering of local road supervisors. Even states could not levy taxes sufficient to meet demands from all quarters for adequate public roads. The federal government, with the important exception of the National Road, refused to enter the field. So private stock companies were chartered to borrow money to carry out these improvements, with the subscribers to be reimbursed from future toll receipts. Such was the theory, at least, and the public accepted it as the answer to its dilemma. The turnpike became one of the symbols of progress of the new century.[4]

The most important and best constructed turnpikes were those leading inland from important ports, beginning with the Lancaster Turnpike, which reached westward from Philadelphia and was completed in 1794—the success of which provided a great stimulant to the movement—and ending, so far as these decades are concerned, with the National Road, from Cumberland to Wheeling, completed to the Ohio River by 1818.[5] But in addition to the main roads, a whole network of turnpikes crisscrossed the nation, radiating mainly out of the major cities.

By 1820, almost 40,000 miles of turnpikes had been constructed. Toll-road construction was at its height and was soon to decline, as it was already being realized that dividends did not sufficiently attract further capital. Over most of these greatly improved roads, stages were being run by 1820. Over the Philadelphia and Lancaster Turnpike in 1814, for instance, passed and repassed the Baltimore Stage via Lancaster and York, the Carlisle Stage, the Columbia Stage, the daily stage to Harrisburg, the daily to Lancaster, the York Stage, the Juniata Valley Stage, and the Pittsburgh Stage.[6] The Trenton and New Brunswick Turnpike in New Jersey bore the heaviest stagecoach traffic in that state, and its receipts in tolls from stage operators amounted to some $2,500 annually.[7]

Stagecoaches almost never paid the full legal tolls. Instead, they received substantial discounts or commutation rates that varied widely but usually amounted to at least 30 percent.[8] In some cases, the owners of stage lines were stockholders in the turnpikes and presumably exercised their influence in behalf of their interests. In other instances, the stagecoach companies exhibited a good deal of bargaining power. At a meeting of the directors of New Hampshire's Eastern Stage Company in 1818, for example, it was voted that $700 a year be accepted as tolls by the Newburyport Turnpike or the stages would go by Old Town Bridge.[9] Payments were made annually or quarterly so that the stages were not required to halt at the turnpike gates. Since the stage proprietors, and not the passengers, paid the turnpike and bridge tolls on all their routes, it was in their interest to hold down these payments. Costs may have been passed on to the passengers through higher fares whenever it was possible during this period, but competition likewise exerted a constant pressure to hold the fares low.

Any increase in costs of operation because of the turnpikes and toll bridges was minor compared with the tremendous benefits these improvements brought to American staging. They lifted the stages out of the mud; made journeys possible at all seasons; made lighter, higher, and better hung carriages practicable; eliminated the hazards associated with fords, ferries, and primitive bridges; shortened distances; permitted much greater speed; and made night travel feasible. The turnpikes encouraged the development of stage lines and made possible many of the features that characterized American staging at its highest level of development.

IN THE YEAR 1816, a twenty-seven-year-old Scotsman who was to become a major figure in nineteenth-century American staging appeared on the stagecoach scene. James Reeside—whom the press would later call "the Land Admiral—had been born in Scotland and then brought to

America as an infant. He was raised in Baltimore, and before the War of 1812 he became a wagoner, hauling merchandise from Baltimore to Pittsburgh, and then west to Columbus, Ohio. Reeside served under General Winfield Scott during the war, and afterwards he settled in Hagerstown, Maryland. In 1816, he started his first staging venture with a stagecoach line that ran from Hagerstown to McConnellstown, and two years later, along with some partners, he opened the first regular stagecoach mail service from Baltimore to Wheeling. It was the beginning of his stagecoach empire.

In 1827, Reeside obtained the mail contract from Philadelphia to New York and moved to Philadelphia. He was a splendid organizer, and in the first year of the New York to Philadelphia mail run, he reduced the time from twenty-three hours to sixteen hours, and then to twelve hours. Soon he was the largest mail contractor in the United States, and he controlled most of the major lines between Philadelphia and New York. Reeside, at the height of his operations, employed over 400 men and owned over 1,000 horses. Unfortunately, his last years in staging were not particularly happy ones: He fell into a dispute with the Post Office over fees owed him, and he eventually had to sue the government in court. He won the case in 1841, but he refused any more mail contracts and abandoned staging. Then his health failed, and he died the following year.

But for a few years this immigrant's son, a former wagoner and stage driver, was the largest stagecoach mail entrepreneur in the nation.[10]

THE TWO greatest centers of staging activity in the two decades 1800 to 1820 were Philadelphia and Boston. New York might have been a rival had it not been for the Hudson River and its packet and steamboat facilities, which resulted in much of the travel passing up to Albany by water before the transfer to coaches. Albany and Baltimore, respectively, were the third- and fourth-largest staging centers of this period, but with scarcely one-third the number of lines that radiated from Philadelphia or Boston.

By 1810, there were listed in the *Philadelphia Directory* a total of thirty-eight different land stage lines operating out of the city, with 213 scheduled coaches departing each week and as many arriving. The number of coaches was swelled somewhat by the beginning of suburban coaching, with the lines to Chestnut Hill, Frankford, and Germantown running coaches twice a day, both morning and afternoon, each way. By 1819, there were seventy different coach lines out of Philadelphia listed, with 520 arrivals and as many departures scheduled each week.[11]

Aside from the heavy travel across New Jersey to New York, Philadelphia's main routes of travel in these decades led westward into Pennsylvania's own rich valleys and to the Ohio. There were lines to the towns closer in, such as dailies to Norristown and Downingtown and a triweekly to West Chester. There were three daily lines running to Pittsburgh, one via Harrisburg and one via York.

BOSTON OCCUPIED a similar position of pre-eminence as a hub of staging in New England. In 1800, there were twenty-seven different stage lines radiating from the city—perhaps as many as from Philadelphia in that year—with 119 scheduled arrivals and as many departures.[12] Growth was apparently slower for the decades 1800–20 than it was in Philadelphia, however, because *The Boston Directory* for 1820 listed only forty different lines with 165 scheduled arrivals and as many departures each week.[13] This would mean a weekly average of 1,155 travelers arriving—about 60,000 per year—and as many departing. But though Boston lagged behind Philadelphia before 1820, the New England city soon entered an era of rapid expansion in staging. By 1825, there were sixty-one different lines listed, and the *American Traveller* of Boston reported on June 30, 1826, that "we have more than 70 different lines of four and six horse stages, which regularly depart from the city in every direction." The *American Traveller's* figures should be reliable because in 1825 the publishers of this newspaper had commenced printing and distributing every three months *Badger and Porter's Stage Register*, which endeavored to list all stage lines in New England and New York. The first issue, for July 1825, listed about 150 different lines. At the end of its first year, this *Register* was being distributed to more than 600 stage houses and taverns.[14]

Boston was also beginning to have its suburban stages: for example, stages left for Cambridge daily, except Sunday, at noon and 5:00 P.M.; for Dorchester and Milton daily, except Sunday, at 4:00 P.M.; for Medford daily at 1:00 P.M., except Wednesdays and Saturdays, when it left both at noon and 6:00 P.M.; and for Watertown, Newton, and Needham Mondays, Wednesdays, and Saturdays at 4:00 P.M. Stages to towns a little further out included dailies, except Sunday, to Dedham, Gloucester, Marblehead, and Newburyport and three daily lines to Salem, one of them continuing to Beverly.

The New England frontier lay not to the west but to the north. In

1800, one did not go far north of the present Massachusetts boundary before encountering sparsely settled areas.[15] In that year, the only stage lines running into the northern states for certain were the line to Portland, then five years old; the line to Amherst in southern New Hampshire, established in 1794; and a line to Concord, New Hampshire, just inaugurated in 1800 (the original venture of 1794 having lapsed about 1796).

Portland, for many years the northernmost terminal of the only stage line in Maine, remained throughout the staging period the natural center for all travel from within the state and the distributing point for travel from without the state. It was also the distributing point for the mails coming from the south. The first important extension of staging north of Portland occurred in 1806 when Col. T. S. Estabrook of Brunswick, who had previously carried the mail by horse, began stage service between Portland and Augusta.[16] By 1810, this had become a daily line at least to Brunswick, from where a branch led eastward to Bath and Wiscasset, and, some years later, it was continued along the shore through Belfast to Bangor. A writer remarked of Brunswick in 1820 that "from the great eastern, western and northern routes the stages arrive at 12 o'clock, at noon, and so well are they regulated, that they often arrive at the same moment—From the east, west, and north, they arrive and depart every day in the week."[17]

The pattern of stage lines in southwest Maine was not fully established until about 1825, and the heyday of staging in the region continued from that date until about 1845, after which the stagecoach moved north and east in the state beyond the extending railheads. The Maine Stage Company, incorporated by the state in 1823, and the Portland Stage Company, incorporated the following year, dominated the staging in the older part of the state. The latter operated from the lines south and west to the New Hampshire boundary and the former controlled the lines from Portland eastward. Each owned over 200 horses, sleighs, and coaches, and were very profitable enterprises. Each had grown out of earlier unincorporated associations, with the Portland Stage Company representing the interests built up by Josiah Paine and the Maine Stage Company the network of lines that had come to be dominated by Samuel Hale and Israel Waterhouse.[18]

The stage service inaugurated to Concord, New Hampshire, in 1800 was pioneered by Joseph Wheat, tavern keeper at Nashua River Bridge, where the Nashua River entered the Merrimac, a location that in the future would develop into the city of Nashua. In April, Wheat had purchased from Dr. Samuel Curtis an older line that went from Amherst,

New Hampshire, to Boston and passed by his tavern. He arranged for the Concord stage to set off from his tavern every Friday morning, taking along any passengers that had arrived from Boston in the Amherst Stage the previous evening. It would then pass up the Merrimac valley and arrive in Concord that same evening to set them down at Benjamin Gales's tavern. Return trips began on Mondays from both Amherst and Concord; both stages met again for the night at Wheat's tavern, and the following day the passengers were carried on into Boston.[19]

By 1803, a line of stages was operating between Albany and Rutland, Vermont, where connections could be made after 1806 with the stage running from Walpole via Rutland to Burlington and thence to Montreal.[20] Doubtless, in summer most travelers preferred the more direct stage route from Albany to Whitehall at the southern end of Lake Champlain, where they boarded sailing packets to Burlington. By 1815, however, a stage line was running directly from Albany three times a week up the east side of Lake Champlain to Burlington, in addition to the triweekly line to Whitehall.[21] In December 1818, what apparently was the first line of stages to travel up the west side of Lake Champlain, between Albany and Montreal, was inaugurated. This line carried the mail through a rapidly developing region and, from the beginning, offered service three times a week.[22] After the War of 1812, staging activity throughout the whole upper Hudson area noticeably quickened, with Albany at its hub. By 1827, the *American Traveller* noted: "Probably there is no point in the United States where so many public stages meet and find employment as at Albany. They issue from thence upon every point in the compass, and it has become a business in which a very large amount of capital is invested, and much enterprise, vigilence, and competition enlisted—It is almost incredible how establishments so extensive and so expensive find maintenance; yet maintained they are and flourish."[23]

SOUTH OF the Potomac and Ohio rivers, stagecoach travel never acquired the vigor and bustle that characterized it in the North in the "step-lively" period; nor was it as efficiently organized. There was not enough patronage to stimulate improvements and not enough competition to force them. Little traveling was done by the poorer whites and the slaves, who together formed more than two-thirds of a generally sparse population. In the North, townsfolk were the chief patrons of the lines, but in the South there were few cities. Even villages were far apart. Planters of the tidewater districts, who might have afforded stagecoach journeys, possessed their own conveyances and used them on both long and short excursions. The farmers of the Piedmont area, for the most part, traveled by horseback until almost the middle of the nineteenth century. Since they owned their own mounts, it was economical to use them. Most of them had little money to pay out for hired facilities.

Geographical conditions also affected southern staging adversely. Running north and south and dividing three more favorable areas—the Tidewater, Piedmont, and Bluegrass—from each other were two barrier areas, the sandy pine barrens and the difficult Appalachian ranges. In these two areas, both the nature of the roads and the want of inhabitants discouraged staging enterprise. In the barrens, the roads were often so deep with churned sand that the stage teams could draw the heavy coaches no faster than a walk. In low and marshy stretches, rock was not available to give the roadbed a bottom. Raised causeways of brush, logs, and sod were built and surfaced in corduroy fashion across the frequent low areas. Seasonal flood waters, however, made these causeways boggy and washed away the surface poles of corduroy stretches, leaving a treacherous footing for straining horses. At the same time, these raised roads were so narrow that drivers could see no alternatives to the poor tracks. In mountain districts, coaches and passengers were shaken to pieces on the limestone ridges that the rains washed bare or by the infrequently mended ditches in the hilly roadways.

Throughout the South, prices for provisions were higher than they were in the North. In fertile areas, the land was more valuable for tobacco or cotton than for raising horse feed, while in barren areas, there was little farming of any kind. Consequently, the charges for keeping horses and boarding drivers were high, and this in turn resulted in high stage fares. Always to be added to high fares were high tavern rates, as guests paid dearly for dining on imported provisions. The slower progress of the stages also meant increased tavern expenses for a journey.

Had southern stage lines depended upon passengers for their support they would, previous to the boom 1830s, at least, have come to an abrupt halt. In practically all instances, southern lines were established only after the Post Office offered substantial financial encouragement, and usually they leaned heavily upon that agency for continued support. Whatever competition existed in later years manifested itself in bidding for the mail contracts every four years rather than in putting lines on the road to compete with the mail stages. Despite the competition for the contracts and the general light weight of the mail in the South, the expense of mail carriage per mile was considerably above the general average for the whole United States. Once they received the coveted contract, proprietors were so secure in their possession of the road that they had a virtual monopoly. Accordingly, a spirit of accommodating passengers was often little in evidence. Such special services of the business in the North as accommodation stages, extra stages, and chartered or exclusive stages were almost unknown in the South. One went through with the mail or did not go at all.

THE ROOTS of staging in the South extend back into the eighteenth century when Nathaniel Twining received his contract in 1786 to carry the mail by coach south of the Potomac. In October 1786, he announced in Maryland newspapers that "The Southern Stage is now in complete order, with four horses to each Stage, as far as Wilmington, in North Carolina, where there is a complete packet boat to carry passengers to Charleston, South Carolina. The causeways and bridges from Wilmington to Georgetown, are such as renders the passage of the Stage impracticable. The Stage begins again at Georgetown, and runs to Charlestown, and thence to Savannah, by way of Augusta in Georgia."[24] So ran the notice of the first staging in the lower South.

But Twining's optimistic announcement proved to be premature. He could not make a success of the southern line, falling into financial difficulties, and failing to deliver the regular promised service. In an attempt to protect his new line, he was obliged to dispose of his interests in the Philadelphia-Alexandria line, which he had helped to establish, and, soon afterwards, in the Alexandria-Pettersburg route, which he had pioneered. By 1787, he admitted his failure and informed Congress that he was abandoning his southern route.[25]

The control of the Alexandria-Petersburg sector of the Main Post Road fell into the hands of Twining's associate, Col. John Hoomes of Bowling Green. In 1787, Hoomes had Twining's exclusive privileges on the Alexandria-Richmond road extended for three years in his own name.[26] The privileges between Richmond and Petersburg and Norfolk, which had been in Hoomes's name, were extended in the names of his associates, Richard Townes and John G. Woolfolk.[27] Hoomes, however, held the mail contract for all these lines, and the three operated, apparently, under a well-understood working agreement. Possibly, Hoomes's membership in the Virginia House of Delegates from 1791 to 1795 and in the state Senate from 1796 to 1803 aided the associates in having their monopolies on all these routes renewed repeatedly until 1799.[28]

The only stage lines south of Petersburg, Virginia, in the eighteenth century were those in South Carolina and Georgia, which led out from the two great seaports, Charleston and Savannah. When these were founded in the last years of the century, Nathaniel Twining's name reappeared after nearly ten years in eclipse. Twining, in 1796, secured from the legislatures of South Carolina and Georgia the exclusive right to run stages between Charleston and Georgetown, South Carolina, and between Savannah and Augusta, Georgia.[29] In the last grant, Thomas Davis and Joseph Grant were associated with Twining. All these grants were for a ten-year period. The South Carolina assembly specified that Twining was to "keep fit, good and sufficient stagecoaches, and good strong able and proper horses, and suitable and capable drivers for the convenience and accommodation of travellers, and to be obliged to run a stage at least once in every week each way."[30] Failure to do this was to forfeit his privilege. However, this time Twining was successful in his southern venture, supplying regular and dependable stage service.

There was still no stage connection between Petersburg and the South in January 1802, when Gideon Granger, a New Yorker, assumed the duties of postmaster general for what proved to be a twelve-year period. One of his first letters was sent to Colonel Hoomes. "Feeling that the expediting of the mails as well as the introduction of Mail Coaches through Virginia, North and South Carolina are objects of great importance," he wrote, "I have taken the liberty to request of you what are the difficulties which may prevent these objects—expense? prospect of gaining any travellers? price of Horse feed—Obstructions by rivers, etc.?"[31]

In 1803, a mail contract was awarded to Hoomes for the distance between Petersburg and Fayetteville. From Fayetteville by Camden to Augusta and Louisville, there were no bidders. To effect a stagecoach connection of some kind between North and South, Granger concluded a contract with Robert Henderson to run from Fayetteville by Lumberton to Georgetown on the seaboard, where he would connect with the stage line already established to Charleston.[32] This line went into operation about the first of March, 1803. Henderson's carriages "were not such as to do justice to the public expectations or his interest" between Fayetteville and Georgetown, the passengers averaged only one for each stage, and an additional subsidy from Congress was later necessary to support the line. But, despite these problems, there seems to have been no cessation of stage service on the route, except in rainy seasons when horses were used temporarily.[33] At last, a connected line of stages ran along the Atlantic seaboard from Portland, Maine, to Savannah, Georgia.

THE SOUTHERN network continued to expand during the first two decades of the nineteenth century, and by 1820 the skeleton of the stagecoach pattern was fairly well completed. The backbone was the route of the "Great Southern Mail" running parallel to and 100 to 150 miles inland from the Atlantic Ocean, passing through the capital cities in each state and through other large cities located along the "fall line" of the rivers. It skirted the lower edge of the cultivated Piedmont lands. This stage line in 1820 ran from Washington on the Potomac south to Augusta on the Savannah River, and from there 86 miles further to Milledgeville, then the capital of Georgia. Beyond Milledgeville, to the southwest, the mail was still carried by postriders. That portion of the line from Fayetteville, North Carolina, to Augusta was still new in 1820, since it had been started only after the close of the War of 1812.[34] The old, or "lower," road, which branched off at Fayetteville and ran to the ocean at Georgetown, South Carolina, and thence along the coast to Charleston and Savannah, was at this date still much more important than the "upper" road and was to remain so until the establishment of the through mail to New Orleans over the upper road in 1827.[35]

There were several north and south lines of secondary importance. The newest of these left the main southern road at Fredericksburg, Virginia. It passed Cumberland Court House, Charlotte Court House, and Halifax, Virginia; Greensboro, Salisbury, and Charlotte, North Carolina; and York and Laurens, South Carolina, before arriving at Augusta. This was advertised as the "Upper Line of Stages" and still later as the Piedmont line. Not until 1820 was the southern end of this route placed in operation.[36]

Another north and south line was the Coast line, running from Norfolk into eastern North Carolina, passing through Elizabeth City, Edenton, and Washington to New Bern.[37] No evidence has been found to indicate that at this date it was being continued farther south to Wilmington or along the coast to Charleston. Apparently, travel further in that direction was slight, and water facilities were sufficient to care for it. The southbound traveler might reach Norfolk by the line down the peninsula from Richmond to Hampton Roads, by the line down the Eastern Shore, or, more likely in this period, by steamboat down Chesapeake Bay from either Washington or Baltimore.[38] The popularity of the steamboat was responsible for the establishment, in 1820, of another line from Norfolk to run southwest to Fayetteville, from where the traveler could either continue southwest on the "upper" line or take the "lower" road to Charleston. The stage left Norfolk immediately after the arrival of the Baltimore and Washington boats and reached Fayetteville sixty hours later. This line passed through few cities, or even villages, of consequence, except Tarboro, and depended for its income almost entirely on its being a shorter, faster, and more comfortable route to the South for passengers from north of Baltimore than was the Main Post Road.[39]

Crossing and connecting the north and south lines and usually forming a means of communication between populous Piedmont districts, "fall line" cities, and seaports were a number of important "crossroads" with mail stages operating over them. The most northerly and one of the oldest was the road between Alexandria on the Potomac and Winchester in the Shenandoah Valley.[40] A stage from Richmond to Charlottesville intersected this route into the Great Valley[41] but became somewhat less important after 1819 when the well-established Richmond-Lynchburg line was extended across the Blue Ridge to form a more direct connection with the Valley line near Fincastle.[42] The old Richmond-Hampton line, through Williamsburg and Yorktown, and the Petersburg-Norfolk line continued to operate in the 1820s much as they had about 1790, running three times a week each way.[43]

In North Carolina, the main crossroad passed east and west through Raleigh. To the west, stages on this line ran through Chapel Hill and Hillsboro as far as Winston-Salem;[44] to the east, one line ran through Tarsboro to Plymouth and a second line through Tarboro to Washington on the Pamlico River.[45] From Fayetteville, lines ran east to New Bern and southeast to Wilmington.[46] In South Carolina, the cross lines were from Charleston to Columbia and Charleston to Augusta.[47]

THE REGION west of the crest of the Alleghenies and south of the Ohio, which had its birth in the years of the Revolutionary struggle, was by the turn of the century growing vigorously but had yet to see its first stage lines. Both the federal government and the settlers were anxious to drive through a line of stage communication, but the unsettled mountain wilderness was a formidable barrier. In a situation more characteristic of a later day in the Far West, lines had to be maintained at high cost, and with no return in local patronage, through inhospitable areas where no one lived and roads were barely passable in order to reach and serve islands of settlement beyond. There were, in this instance, three such islands of settlement, namely eastern Tennessee with Knoxville as a center, central Tennessee with Nashville as the capital, and the Bluegrass region of Kentucky with Lexington, the "Athens of the West," as the leading city. The active agent in accomplishing this end was, of necessity, the Post Office Department.

The first mail service to these regions was provided in 1794 when a horse route was extended from Staunton, Virginia, southwest up the Great Valley, over the low divide to the Holston, and down this valley to Knoxville.[48] The mail route down the valley to Knoxville was extended westward in 1797 over the newly opened road to Nashville, reaching that capital the year after Tennessee had become a state.[49] The need for providing communication with Natchez, capital of the newly organized territory of Mississippi, led to a further extension of the service in January 1800 from Nashville over the Natchez Trace to that southwestern outpost. Service to Natchez was only monthly at first, and the road was "no other than an Indian footpath very devious and narrow."[50]

It was over these horse routes into the Southwest that, a decade later, stages entered the region. A series of crises, including the danger of a war with Spain and fears of separatist movements in the western settlements, increased the government's concern for the adequacy and safety of these mail lines. After the purchase of Louisiana, rapid communication with New Orleans, now the emporium of the New West, became so important that, in addition to the regular mail, an express mail was established. Its riders were to make 100 miles a day on that part of the route between Washington and Nashville and to reach New Orleans within seventeen days of leaving the national capital.[51]

Early in 1805, Postmaster General Granger wrote to Senator Andrew Moore: "I have been for this two years struggling to establish a respectable line of stages through West Virginia [i.e., western Virginia] to Tennessee for the better security of the mail and for the accommodation of the people of that part of the country. The little experience I have had since I have been in office has demonstrated the futility of a two horse stage and of every attempt to carry on that business otherwise than in the correct line of staging."[52]

Finally, in 1807, Granger contracted with Benjamin White for a stagecoach route between Knoxville and Nashville, offering an annual compensation of $2,375 for weekly trips each way over the 190-mile route.[53] Robert Hall, in 1809, secured the contract from Blountville to Knoxville.[54] The part of the line between Fincastle and Blountville remained in the capable hands of George Oury, postmaster at Wytheville, Virginia, and the pioneer stagecoach proprietor on this sector.[55] The long distance from Fredericksburg via Charlottesville and Staunton to Fincastle was in the hands of Jonathan Shoemaker and his sons, who also had the line from Richmond to Charlottesville.[56] The 1809 contracts called for service twice a week each way on that portion of the route from Staunton to Nashville in return for an annual compensation to the contractors from the Post Office of $15,100. The Valley line to the Southwest was at last firmly established.[57]

Although the Wilderness Road through Cumberland Gap in Kentucky was made passable for wagons, with "the stumps well rounded," as early as 1796, there was, apparently, even after the establishment of the Valley line, no thought of a branch stage line to travel this historic route to Kentucky. Instead, the first stage service into the Bluegrass region was to follow the postrider. The distance from Washington, D.C., to Kentucky by way of Pittsburgh and Zanesville was little greater than by the Wilderness Road, particularly since the leading settlements were in the northern part of the state and it was necessary to travel from Cumberland Gap northward nearly 150 miles to reach them. Stage service over Zane's Trace to Kentucky was firmly established in the same year as that down the Great Valley.

Further expansion of stagecoach facilities in the area was delayed by the War of 1812 and was to await the movement of population, following that struggle, to the newest frontiers of the South, the territories of Alabama and Mississippi.

No stagecoach entered Alabama until 1820, one year after it had become a state. The first line was not from Georgia, as one might expect, but an extension from the Tennessee network south to Huntsville in northern Alabama. It began as a weekly, branching from the main Knoxville-Nashville line at McMinnville.[58] Huntsville at this time was the most flourishing place in the northern part of the state, the location of the federal land office and of the first bank in Alabama. It had, in fact, in 1819 served as the first capital of the new state. Service was increased to twice a week by 1823 and to triweekly in 1825.[59] In the latter year, a line was put into operation from Huntsville west to Tuscumbia in northwest Alabama, where the Natchez Trace crossed the Tennessee River, and for the next two years the important Natchez--New Orleans mail was sent over these stage lines as far as Tuscumbia, passing thence down the Natchez Trace by horseback.[60] The mails to Natchez were so heavy that, after 1820, the riders led one, and frequently two, additional horses, but the Trace was not sufficiently improved to permit the use of stages beyond Tuscumbia until 1827.

Two experienced mail contractors, Lewis Calfrey and James W. Johnson, with substantial financial assistance from the Post Office, inaugurated stage service from Milledgeville to Montgomery in April

1821. Their stages were but two-horse carriages, accommodating only two passengers besides the driver.[61] To the frontier, however, this welcome enterprise was a symbol of advancing civilization. The *Montgomery Republican* in June reported that the stages had been regular despite an "unusually wet season" and that "the proprietors have been patronized beyond their anticipations."[62]

By 1820, however, the three southern states of New England and the middle states of the Atlantic seaboard, in a strip not more than 150 miles wide from the coast westward, contained well over half the country's staging activity. At the end of this period, staging was increasing more rapidly than ever and would continue to do so for over a decade. A faster pace was becoming noticeable in American life, especially along the seaboard. "The rapidity introduced into our travelling by stages and steamboats is such," exulted the editor of the *National Intelligencer* at the nation's capital, "that in these days a citizen in Vermont or Maine may leave snow on the ground at home, come here and find all nature verdant with exuberant foliage; travel halfway to Charleston, dine on green peas and sup on strawberries; and, returning home, arrive there before a flower opens or a leaf is displayed."[63]

It was new for the country to be thinking in terms of such distances as well as in terms of such speed. In 1819, one could travel by connected stage lines from Anson, Maine, via the nation's capital, to Nashville, Tennessee, a distance of 1,448 miles, or from Highgate, Vermont, to St. Mary's, Georgia, a distance of 1,396 miles.[64] Also, in the South and the West, staging was growing rapidly, doing its vital part to knit the country together.

From Chaise to Concord

The American Stagecoach in Illustration

An eighteenth-century chaise, a light and popular vehicle of the era, and a forerunner to the stagecoach. The English chaise, introduced in the colonies between 1710 and 1730, became the Yankee "shay" after it was modified and simplified. The chaise pictured here was probably built in Massachusetts about 1780. It is suspended on leather thorough braces and wooden cantilever springs.

Though this covered wagon is from the 1800s, its design is remarkably similar to wagons of the preceding century. Thus, it provides a view of how people traveled on the first public stages in the eighteenth century. Several unpadded, backless benches running across the body were placed in the wagon for passengers.

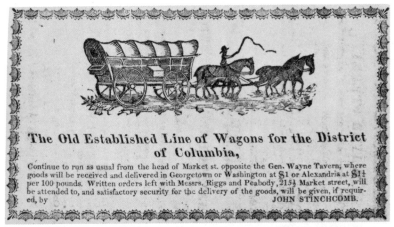

The first public stages in the colonies in pre-Revolutionary days were nothing more than primitive covered wagons, like the one pictured here. This advertisement is actually from a later period after the establishment of the District of Columbia, when the vehicle was used primarily for freight, but the wagon is from the old period. It gives an approximate idea of the style in which it was used to carry people.

A stage wagon on the road near Trenton, New Jersey (from a sketch by contemporary artist Paul Svinin). The eighteenth-century stage wagon was the next phase of what would eventually become the stagecoach as we know it. It had evolved from the old covered wagon and was basically a wagon with a superstructure added. Since it had no doors, the only entrance was from the front. Passengers still rode on benches, and women were usually allowed the rear seat because it was the only one with a back rest. Curtains could be rolled down over the side openings in foul weather. Suspension was on thorough braces carried by iron jacks.

Suter's Tavern in 1791. This famous stagecoach tavern in Georgetown had been established in 1783 by John Suter. George Washington frequented it and, while he was president, conducted some of his most important business there. In 1791, he completed the negotiations for the purchase of the site for the Federal City at the tavern.

A sketch of a 1795 New England stage wagon departing a tavern. The great network of stage taverns along the stage routes was an important part of the stagecoach culture. During the time when the stagecoach was dominant in the nineteenth century, there was apparently one tavern for every mile of stagecoach route. This sketch appeared in a memoir published in 1807 by the Englishman Isaac Weld describing his travels in America from 1795 to 1797.

A stage leaving the Waterloo Inn in Baltimore for the trip to Washington in the early nineteenth century. By this time, the stage had evolved so that passengers entered through a door on the side and sat so that they faced each other.

A stage wagon on High Street in Philadelphia in the late eighteenth Century. The illustration is from Charles Janson's *The Stranger in America*, published in London in 1807.

In 1785, Congress voted to employ stagecoaches to carry the mail on established stage routes. This handstamped letter was written on November 11, 1790, by Aaron Burr, and it was carried on the Van Wyck post line of stages operating out of Albany, New York. Postage stamps, which did not make their appearance in America until the 1840s, were not used, but Burr prepaid this letter, contrary to the usual custom at the time. More frequently, the postage was paid by the recipient. (From the private collection of Calvet M. Hahn.)

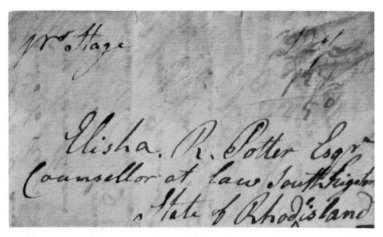

This letter, written on December 24, 1792, was sent from Rhinebeck, New York, "per stage," as noted in the upper left-hand corner. It was addressed to Elisha Potter, a lawyer in South Kingston, Rhode Island. (From the private collection of Calvet M. Hahn.)

Detail from an 1801 newspaper ad for the Union line of stages from Washington to Philadelphia.

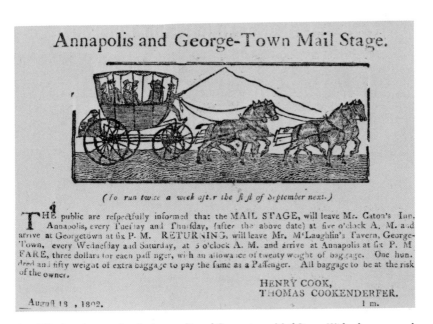

Annapolis and George-Town Mail Stage.

(To run twice a week after the first of September next.)

THE public are respectfully informed that the MAIL STAGE, will leave Mr. Caton's Inn, Annapolis, every Tuesday and Thursday, (after the above date) at five o'clock A. M. and arrive at Georgetown at six P. M. RETURNING, will leave Mr. M'Laughlin's Tavern, George-Town, every Wednesday and Saturday, at 5 o'clock A. M. and arrive at Annapolis at six P. M. FARE, three dollars for each passenger, with an allowance of twenty weight of baggage. One hundred and fifty weight of extra baggage to pay the same as a Passenger. All baggage to be at the risk of the owners.

HENRY COOK,
THOMAS COOKENDERFER.

August 18, 1802.   1 m.

An 1802 advertisement for the Annapolis and Georgetown Mail Stage. With a baggage rack added onto the rear of the stage, this vehicle could now properly be called a stagecoach.

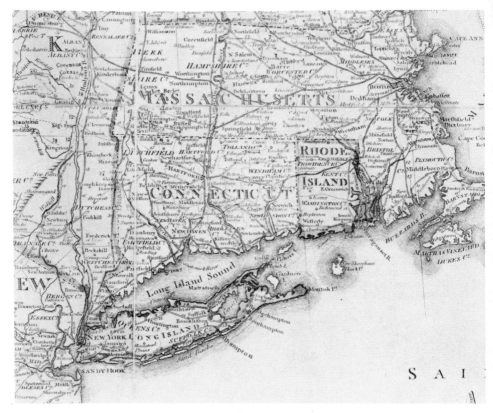

Detail of the classic 1804 Bradley map, showing the postal and stage routes of the era from Boston to New York. Abraham Bradley, Jr., had become first assistant postmaster general in 1799, and he issued these maps to all the postmasters. The official title of the map is "Map of the United States Exhibiting the Post Roads, the Situations, Connections & Distances of the Post-Offices, Stage Roads, Counties & Principal Rivers." The size of the original map is 38 x 53½ in. (Library of Congress.)

This print depicting "American friends going to meeting in summer" appears in Robert Sutcliff's book *Travels in Some Parts of North America in the Years 1804, 1805, and 1806.* In commenting on the picture, Sutcliff wrote: "The open carriages described in this plate are called wagons, and the very best of them Jersey Wagons. They are made very light, hung on springs with leather braces, and travel very pleasantly."

This letter, written on March 23, 1815, was carried from New York City to Flushing, Long Island, on the Flushing stage. (The Flushing mentioned here was not on the same site as the present city, where the post office was not established until 1829.) The message inside this cover, signed by Sarah Payne, encouraged her friend to attend the Peace Ball that was to be held in New York on April 4 to celebrate the end of the War of 1812. (Courtesy of Richard C. Frajola, Inc.)

Union Line of Stages

FOR PHILADELPHIA.

EIGHT DOLLARS.

The subscribers have connected their Line of Stages from WASHINGTON, to the *Union Line of Post Coaches* for PHILADELPHIA, and will commence this day to run from the Fountain Inn, Light street, and continue every day, leaving this at half after 2 o'clock, P. M. directly after the Mail and Expedition Stages arrive from Washington, (the passengers in those Stages having a preference.) It is intended that the shall arrive next day to dine at Philadelphia. The fare for all passengers going through to be *Eight Dollars*, and way passengers paying 10 cents per mile. This line, under the present arrangement, is considered equal at least, to any other *"on this road."* Every attention will be paid to passengers and their baggage; but it will be understood that the proprietors of these stages are *not*, *nor will not*, be answerable for any accidents or miscarriages of any sort, either in loss of baggage or any article that may be put under their charge. The allowance of baggage as usual, and fare as above, *Eight Dollars.*

JOHN H. BARNEY & CO.

jan 13 3   d10t

A period advertisement for a stage from Washington to Philadelphia. The Fountain Inn mentioned in the text was more popularly known as Suter's Tavern.

98.

An 1821 stagecoach advertisement offers a trip from Providence to Worcester that leaves in the morning and arrives that same evening.

Sketch by Captain Basil Hall of an American stagecoach that was obviously the forerunner of the Troy and Concord types. Hall, an officer in the Royal Navy, made this sketch following his American travels in the 1820s. English travelers left many enlightening memoirs about their travels on the old American roads in the nineteenth century.

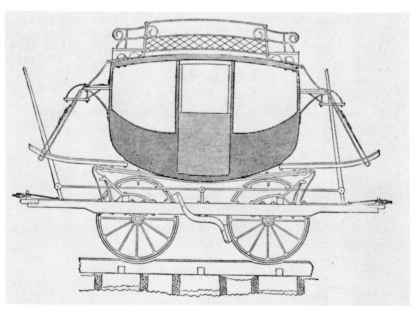

A contemporary drawing by an engineer in 1831 shows the basic design elements of the Albany-Troy coaches.

This 1825 stagecoach of the Philadelphia and Pittsburgh line illustrates the full development of the typical American stagecoach. It had doors, small windows, and, most important, a flat roof with a baggage rack around it. The third feature allowed passengers to ride on the roof.

An 1827 scene of the Fairview Inn on the National Pike near Baltimore. The old road was often crowded, forcing each stage to weave its way through a crowd of covered farm wagons and a herd of cattle.

A stagecoach on the road during the golden years of the early 1830s. This stage was part of the old Phoenix line between Baltimore and Washington, and it made the forty-mile trip in five hours.

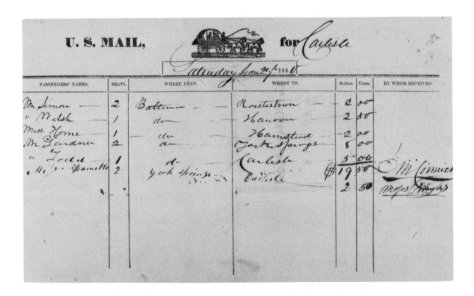

An 1840 waybill. The drivers of mail stages carried waybills that recorded passengers' names, destinations, and fares. The stage in the drawing at the top of the waybill was obsolete in 1840, but the picture may indicate the sense of history and continuity felt by stagecoach proprietors.

An individual waybill of 1850 that served as a stagecoach passenger's ticket.

An extant Abbot, Downing hack passenger wagon, presently in the collection of Jean duPont at Liseter Hall Farm in Pennsylvania. This wagon was originally run on the Boston to New York route. Later, it served the Philadelphia to Pittsburgh route, and, finally, from 1850 to 1858 it covered the Philadelphia to Wilkes Barre route. (Photo courtesy of Jean duPont.)

The Concord coach, the pre-eminent American stagecoach. In 1827,
J. Stephens Abbot, then in the employ of Lewis Downing of Concord,
New Hampshire, built the first model of this stagecoach that was soon
to be world-famous. Not until the Model T did any vehicle of American
manufacture acquire the reputation of the Concord coach.

This Concord coach, built in 1847, is on display in the Smithsonian Institution's National
Museum of American History and is one of the earliest-known surviving models. A six-
passenger "hotel coach," it was used to ferry passengers from railroad terminals to hotels
in the era when railroads were beginning to take over the main routes. The body and gear
are straw-colored, with stripes of black, and are ornately decorated with scroll work, oil
paintings, and gold leaf.

A front view of the 1847 Concord coach shows the thorough
braces, the leather straps slung under the coach's body to
support it. The thorough braces, which were made of thick
oxhide or steerhide, served as shock absorbers. Steel springs
were seldom used on American stages, since they snapped
too easily under the sudden strains of the country's
frequently rough roads.

Interior of the 1847 Concord coach.

Original period pencil drawings from the Abbot, Downing files for what it advertised as a "hack passenger wagon." This vehicle first appeared in the 1820s, but Abbot, Downing continued to produce it even after the firm introduced the Concord coach. The wagon was less expensive than the Concord coach and was used on lines where the service would be particularly hard on vehicles.

POST OFFICE DEPARTMENT,

CONTRACT OFFICE,

April 28th 1841.

SIR:

Your Bid of $ *1,375* ———————— upon Route No. *440*
from *Worcester* ——————— to *Keene*
has been accepted by the Postmaster General. Contracts will be forwarded in due
time. Service is to commence on the first of *July 1841.*

You will request Postmasters to transmit, without delay, a certificate of the
date of commencement of service.

Respectfully,
Your obedient servant,

J. M. Hobbie

First Assistant Postmaster General.

Mr. *Ginery Twichell,*
Barre,
Mass.

This communication from the Post Office Department in 1841 awarded a stage mail
contract for the Worcester to Keene route to a Massachusetts stagecoach proprieter named
Ginery Twichell. In this period, the railroads were beginning to take over the mail, and the
stages were being relegated to smaller routes, such as this one, where the railroads had
not yet penetrated. (Note the courtesies of the day, where the Post Office official signed
himself "Your obedient servant.")

Highway robberies, one of the perils of the road in the nineteenth century. This famous stagecoach cover is a relic from the 1843 Evans, New York, mail robbery. On May 21 of that year, the northbound stage from Erie, Pennsylvania, was headed toward Buffalo when it was held up near the township of Evans, New York. Some six weeks later, a mail pouch from the coach was discovered in the woods, rifled of its contents, except for a few letters such as the above. The remaining letters were taken to Buffalo, where they were stamped at the post office, including with the special hand stamp indicating that they had been involved in the robbery. This is one of three known surviving covers of the episode. (Collection of David L. Jarrett.)

A large Concord mail coach for the open road. This coach, one of the largest Concords built, probably carried twelve inside passengers (a few models that accommodated sixteen were also built) on two regular seats and two rows of jump seats. Additional passengers rode on the roof and beside the driver.

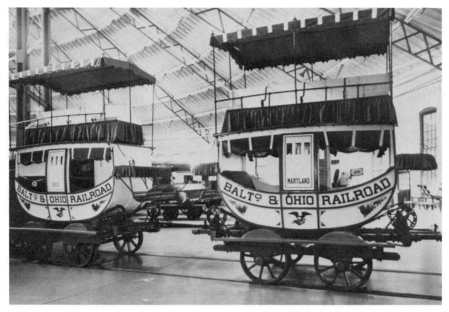

The early railroad cars owed much to the stagecoach for their design, because they appeared to be merely stagecoaches fitted for the tracks. These 1832 railroad cars from the Baltimore and Ohio Railroad are today on display in Baltimore's B&O Railroad Museum collection. (Photo courtesy of the B&O Railroad Museum.)

The stagecoach reaches the Mississippi and then proceeds westward. This 1842 letter was sent on the Boon Stage (sic), which ran from St. Louis to Boone's Lick in central Missouri. (The town had been named for a salt lick discovered by Daniel Boone.) The letter is addressed to Hampton L. Boone, who was Daniel Boone's nephew and in his position as clerk of the Missouri Supreme Court, a post that he held for many years. (Courtesy of Thomas Alexander.)

The Concord goes west. This Concord coach is depicted in California in 1867. After its era of dominance in the East, the stagecoach was to have another golden period west of the Mississippi after the Civil War (as has been romanticized in fiction and drama). The Concord coach was to play a major role in that later era, particularly as the vehicle of the Wells Fargo Company.

The Concord coach, once king of the road, has been relegated to a museum exhibit today. Here is the Smithsonian's Concord coach in its original condition before it was refurbished and restored for display.

IX

The Post Office and the Stages

DURING the first half of the nineteenth century, the stagecoach rolled supreme as the carrier of the United States mail on the nation's leading post roads. In 1835, the first railroad mail contracts were made, but for twenty additional years the stagecoach, in territory east of the Mississippi River, surpassed its rival in mileage of annual mail transportation.[1] And though the railroads gained, through increased frequency of service on their main trunk lines, the stagecoach continued to lead in total mileage of mail transport lines until the Civil War.

Until that war, the major concern of the Post Office Department was the supervision of this vast and complicated network of stagecoach lines carrying the mail. The making of contracts, the arranging of satisfactory connecting schedules, and the checking of performanes involved almost infinite detail. The work eventually absorbed the time of a great number of clerks, but for the first quarter-century, when the growth of the service was comparatively slow, the postmaster general himself conducted much of the correspondence with contractors. From his letterbooks can be traced the beginnings of problems and administrative policies that were to become of major importance when the stagecoach reigned supreme on the post roads.

JOSEPH HABERSHAM, the Georgian who became postmaster general in 1795 during George Washington's second term and served until 1801, was an outspoken supporter of the stagecoach mail service. "While contracts can be made with the proprietors of Stages and Packets on moderate terms they will certainly be preferred to others as it is an object to encourage establishments of such public utility," Habersham wrote shortly after taking office.[2] To Fisher Amers, who had interested himself in securing a contract for the newly established stages on the "Middle Post Road" to Boston, he wrote in 1796: "It gave me pleasure to employ Mr. Miller as it is an object to have the mail carried in Stages, this mode of transporting them is certainly more safe and expeditious than any other and it is proper to give every encouragement to establishments of such general utility."[3]

The rapidly increasing friendliness to stages, evidenced by the letter-books of the postmasters general, from Hazard to Habersham, resulted in part from increasing efficiency in stagecoach operations themselves in the decade 1785 to 1795. The Post Office was also learning to adapt itself to the new institution, as was illustrated by the compromise arrangements worked out on major roads to get the mail through during the spring breakup period. In any case, the clock could not be turned back. The mail was not too heavy and the danger from solitary carriage too great to think of any other policy but encouraging and strengthening the mail stage network.

Habersham's transparent good will toward the stages also may have been motivated in part by the fact that he was from Georgia, a frontier area that felt the need to be bound more closely to the rest of the Union. In that respect, he seems to have been the first postmaster general who believed in using powers within his control to promote transportation and thus facilitate interstate communication. Not yet, however, was the Post Office ready to subsidize stage lines, as it did in later days.

On occasion, Habersham found it necessary to discourage entrepreneurs who looked to his office for aid. In 1797, when business was depressed, he wrote to a proprietor who wished to increase the frequency of his trips and to receive increased pay:

I cannot think it advisable to increase the number of mails on any of the Routes until Trade revives, and things become more settled. The Proprietors of the Stage between New York and Boston already talk of dropping one Line on that route, and the Proprietors in general with whom I have talked on the subject between this city and Baltimore and New York are very much discouraged from present appearances. I do not wish to check any attempts to extend the advantages of Public Stages. You who are on the spot can best determine how far travelling will best defray the expenses of such establishments; but it is necessary that I should not hold out any hopes of encouragement or assistance when I am confident they cannot be realized on the part of the Department.[4]

The Post Office law of 1794 permitted the postmaster general "to provide by contract for the carriage of a mail on any road on which a stage-wagon or other stagecarriage, shall be established, on condition that the expense thereof shall not exceed the revenue thence arising."[5]

A still more liberal spirit was beginning to show itself in Congress. As early as 1797, the statement was made in debate on the Post Office bill that it was "a settled principal that the profits arising from one part of the Union should go to the establishment of post roads in other part."[6] Also, "it was not proper that any money on such a laudable establishment should be put into the Treasury."[7] The first authorization to a postmater general to pay more for stage service than the income from a route was that embodied in the Act of 1802, which permitted Postmaster General Gideon Granger to give a figure that "shall not exceed a sum equal to one-third more than the whole of the present expense" to establish a line through Southern states.[8] Since the "present expense" amounted to more than the income from the route, this represented a liberal allowance.

Granger hailed from Connecticut and was postmaster general from 1801 to 1814. During his long administration, he also developed the practice of advancing pay to contractors to help them set up new lines or gain relief from temporary embarrassments that might endanger their lines. Usually, these advances were limited to one quarter's pay.[9] In his eagerness to establish a line from Wheeling across Ohio to Kentucky, however, Granger granted a year's advance and repented later when he discovered that, instead of its being used to purchase the necessary property and equipment, "the money has been dissipated in gambling, etc."[10] Granger had been given no legal authority for this practice, but he apparently considered himself free to use the income from the Post Office in whatever manner he thought wise, except as Congress imposed restrictions. Any control by the executive branch over Post Office Department funds was loose. At the end of the fiscal year, the postmaster general turned into the Treasury his surplus, or rather, only that part of his surplus that he considered he might spare.[11] The Post Office continued granting advances for several years after Granger left office. A select committee appointed to investigate the Post Office in 1822 found that money advanced to contractors and others in anticipation of their services, and still unliquidated on January 1, 1822, was $54,354. The committee's report added that probably something short of $10,000 of that amount would be lost to the department.[12]

THE AWARDING of mail contracts to the stagecoach lines was one of the Post Office's most bothersome problems during its early years. According to section six of the Act of 1782, public notice of all contracts to be let had to be printed in "one or more of the newspapers published at the Seat of the Government of the United States, and in one or more of the newspapers published in the state or states in which the contract is to be performed" for at least six weeks prior to the time of contracting.[13] This notice was to name the places from and to which the mail was to be conveyed, the time at which it was to be made up, the day and hour at which it was to be delivered, the conditions of the contract, and the penalties for failures. For the first few years, the contracts were made for a year at a time, but a clause in the law of 1794 allowed them to be made for a four-year period if desirable.[14] In the Post Office Act of 1825, the period for which notice had to be published before the time of contracting was lengthened to twelve weeks.[15] These notices eventually became very long, and their publication week after week was the profitable privilege of newspapers in good standing with the administration.

In making the contracts for 1790, the first under the Constitution, Postmaster General Samuel Osgood encountered one of the persistent problems of contracting: that of the lowest bidder. Every year from 1785 on, the contract between Boston and New York had been given to the company headed by Levi Pease, For 1790, however, Pease was underbid by one Daniel Salmon. But neither Salmon nor his two sureties were known at the Post Office, and Osgood eventually awarded the contract to Pease, the old and tried contractor.[16] The postmaster general preferred, naturally, the man who had performed faithfully and whose stock and stages were on the road to a bidder whose line existed only in the imagination. Actually, many bidders completely underestimated the magnitude of their undertaking. "Many Poor People," Osgood reported to Alexander Hamilton, "make Proposals at so low a Rate that it is obvious that the business cannot be done as it ought to be; and consequently there cannot be a strict adherence to the lowest Proposals. Discretion must be used—and the Contract must be given to those who will probably perform the Duty most punctually."[17]

In contracting for the year 1791, Osgood awarded the contracts in accordance with his judgment of the bidder's ability. "I have thot that the public Interest required that I should not confine myself in disposing of the Contracts to the Lowest Proposals," he wrote to President Washington. "It has however occasioned some uneasiness, and the Propriety of my Conduct may be called in Question."[18] His decisions did, in fact, win him enemies among the proprietors, which would have mattered more had he remained in office until the next period of contracting.

Decisions of this sort were among the most difficult ones facing the Post Office in the years before the railroads eliminated competition for contracts. When new contracts failed, the old contractor, the new contractor, the Post Office, and the public all suffered material losses before matters were again adjusted. Such decisions increased in difficulty as the system of connections became more complex and as the routes increased in number. Personal knowledge of the conditions governing each contract became impossible. Decisions of this kind opened the way to charges of bribery and favoritism, usually made by disappointed bidders or opponents of the administration in power.

THE CONDITIONS of a mail contract included a statement of how long the stage must wait at post offices for postmasters to open and close the mail. Until about 1800, such a halt was to be merely a convenient time, "which in some cases may be ten minutes and never exceed half an hour."[19] After 1800, the time was fifteen minutes at offices where a longer time was not specified.[20] By 1824, the time allowed was ten minutes,[21] and by 1830, seven minutes. Of course, passengers were impatient at these delays. One British traveler wrote:

Unfortunately we carried the mail and were detained a tedious time at each village post-office; for instead of having a small bag for each, which might be left without trouble, all the letters are thrown indiscriminately into one large sack, and the passengers are detained while the whole are looked over again and again. The law, I was told, only allowed each postmaster five minutes to sort his letters; but it might just as well be silent on the subject, as from a quarter to half an hour is always employed.[22]

There existed in these delays cause for petty friction between postmasters and stage drivers. Apparently, on occasion, drivers excused their own negligence by blaming the postmasters for delays. At other times, doubtless, certain postmasters were provokingly slow. The following letter from Postmaster General Timothy Pickering to Levi Pease presents one such situation:

Mr. Hobby, Postmaster at Middletown has represented to me that one Rice, a driver for your partner Johnson of Durham, had insulted him outrageously because the mail was not always ready in fifteen minutes; and says he must resign if not exempt from such abuse in the future. It will be proper for you to write to Johnson to correct this evil. Tis not the business of a mail driver to abuse a postmaster, but only to complain to his employer. And if the Postmasters are in fault by detaining the mail let the contractor send his complaints to the General Postmaster.[23]

In the face of additional delays, the establishment of the new post offices, as demanded by a growing country, was difficult. Early offices were a long distance apart. In 1790, for instance, the only offices on the Main Post Road between Boston and Hartford were at Worcester and Springfield. Similarly, between Baltimore and Georgetown, the only post office was at Bladensburg.[24] The smaller villages between were only gradually made post offices. Places where the stage halted for meals had an advantage. An office was established at New Kent Courthouse in 1794, the postmaster general remarking that "as the stage usually stops there, the Contractors can have no objection, on the score of delay."[25]

To minimize delays, it was necessary that a post office be near a tavern, if not at one. The postmaster general, for instance, wrote to the Alexandria postmaster: "Your office is so distant from the stage house that a double delay arises, first at your office in changing the mail and then at his [the contractor's tavern] in changing stages. . . . As the coffee house is kept at the stage house and the stage house and the market is adjoining, it appears that your office ought to be kept near it."[26]

There was another reason, besides the delay at post offices, for the possession of a mail contract being a mixed blessing to stage proprietors. Henceforth, they were subject to the postmaster general's dictation of their schedules. On side roads where a stage ran but once or twice a week, the postmaster general could allow proprietors to set their own times of arrivals and departure.[27] But on the main post roads, where connections were involved, it was important that the hours be fixed in the contract and unexcused failures penalized. The conditions of the contract usually provided also that the postmaster general "may alter the times of arrival and departure at any time during the continuance of the contract, he previously stipulating an adequate compensation for any extra expense that may be occasioned thereby."[28] Naturally, once the changes, eating places, and lodging places were arranged at certain taverns along the road in accordance with the interests of the proprietors, there was strong resistance to any alteration in schedule. Sometimes, there were unreasonable delays in order to accommodate tavern keepers, as when Habersham wrote to Pease:

During the last winter your stages took a whole day in going from New Haven to Hartford only 40 miles merely to accommodate the innkeeper at Hartford with the passengers during the night. Such tardiness is shameful both as it regards an important mail and the mail line of stages. I am confident there cannot be any reason assigned for rejecting the arrangement I proposed than the Interest of tavern keepers who are partners in the line.[29]

"The interest of tavern keepers who are partners" probably seemed sufficient reason to the proprietors themselves for rejecting any contract not to their liking, particularly since only when making their contract did they have any bargaining power. As staging increased on the busier roads, competition often gave the postmaster general the whip hand at the time of contracting.

When the postmaster general attempted to increase the speed of the mails, the proprietors especially objected, on the grounds that their passengers would thereby be disturbed. John Hoomes, for example, expressed a concern for his passengers' rest in 1802, but Gideon Granger answered:

I am sensible that the travellers will not have the same number of hours for refreshment that many of them might wish but Sir, you must reflect that no time is allowed for rest from here thro' the Eastern States. The evil of having one night's rest infringed upon cannot be great to such persons as travel in the stage.[30]

As business grew, stagecoach proprietors met complaints of their passengers on the score of speed by putting on accommodation lines that went more slowly and allowed more time for rest and refreshment.

At the same time, the mails grew in bulk and more of the inside of the mail coaches had to be reserved for them so that the number of passengers they could carry was limited first to six and, later, frequently to four. Those wishing to travel as rapidly as the mails paid usually one-fourth to one-third more for their seats in the "limited" stage. A man might well prefer to pay more for his stage fare and ride most of the night to reach his destination, when he saved on tavern charges by doing so. (The terms *accommodation* and *limited* were later carried over into railroad parlance.)

With each mail, there was sent a waybill on which was entered the number and destination of the letters in the bag. As the mails passed along the route, each local postmaster endorsed on the waybill the stage's arrival and departure times for his office. The waybill was then sent to the General Post Office in Washington, so that the contractor's performance could be checked.[31] The earlier conditions of contract specified that "for every hour's delay (unavoidable accidents excepted) . . . the contractor shall forfeit one dollar and if the delay continue until the departure of any depending mail . . . an additional forfeiture of five dollars shall be incurred."[32] By 1801, a one-dollar penalty was to be paid for every half-hour's delay after the contracted time of arrival.[33] The penalty for delays increased until by 1824 it amounted to a five-dollar forfeiture for every 30 minutes delay at a post office and a fine of twice the normal pay for the trip for missed connections, unless the failure was proved to the department's satisfaction to be unavoidable. In that case, the fine was reduced the amount of the pay for only one trip.[34] At last, the postmaster general had placed in his hands a substantial whip to crack over the mail coach system that he directed.

THE STAGECOACH MAIL SYSTEM had evolved into an operation where the postmaster general in Washington was the overseer of the whole enterprise, while the actual mail routes were contracted out to individual stage line owners. It was thus largely a series of private enterprises monitored by the federal government. The only exception to that practice was the single government-owned line, which ran along the eastern seaboard from 1799 to 1818. It was a unique experiment.

The establishment of a government stage line stemmed not from any particular social philosophy but rather from Postmaster General Joseph Habersham's frustration with the poor service on the Philadelphia-Baltimore section of the Main Post Road during the 1790s. The difficulty of the Susquehanna crossing was one cause of its frequent delays and failures, but the entire road was in notoriously bad condition, especially in winter. Settlement along the way was sparce, and the ordinary taxes were insufficient to keep it in repair. Private companies had no incentive to turnpike it, since it was parallel to the shore and little was carried over it.[35] Part of the trouble may have been in the management of Gabriel Van Horne as long as he held a monopoly from the state of Maryland for the sector between the Susquehanna and the Potomac, but, actually, his successors did not perform much better. Whatever the cause, this section was a weak link in the middle of the chain, affecting and weakening the service both northward and southward. Putting the mail during the spring breakup in sulkies, which carried no passengers, gave only partial relief. In the end, Habersham lost patience and, in February 1799, wrote to the respected Levi Pease, asking his help in getting a government line started:

The persons which have carried the mail between this [i.e. Philadelphia] and Baltimore have performed so unsatisfactorily and are so exorbitant in their demands for a new contract that I determined to set up a line of stages and carry the mail on public account. If you are not much engaged at present I should be glad to have you come and purchase the horses, fix the stands, employ the drivers and in fact set the business in motion.[36]

Habersham also wrote to William Evans, Baltimore tavern keeper and proprietor of the line from Baltimore to Alexandria:

The very abrupt departure of the proprietors of the Line of Stages from Baltimore to this City [Philadelphia] after giving in their second proposals left me no alternative than that of taking immediate steps for the establishment of a line of stages from this place to Alexandria on Public account.

This arrangement is already in considerable forwardness, the stage waggons being engaged, some of the Horses purchased and a person obtained to superintend the Business. . . . If, however, you are willing to contract for the conveyance of the mail between Baltimore and Alexandria at $1,500 a year and will have it properly secured Letters as well as newspapers I will place the contract in your hands for that part of the route. . . . In case you accede to my proposition it will be necessary for your stages to connect with ours as well for the exchange of passengers as of mail.[37]

Faced with this ultimatum, Evans had either to desert his connection with the old Philadelphia-Baltimore line or face competition on his own Baltimore-Alexandria sector of the post road. He accepted the conditions of the postmaster general's letter, so that government line was finally established only on the Baltimore-Philadelphia section of the Main Post Road. Pease arrived to superintend the establishment of the line. The stages were ordered, arrangements were made with taverns along the way for keeping the relay teams, the horses were purchased and distributed on the road, and the drivers and hostlers were engaged.

The old mail contracts expired on March 31, 1799, and during April the mail was carried in government sulkies along the Philadelphia-Baltimore route. The first government stages began to run in May of that year, and the government line was in business. By March 1802, the new postmaster general, Gideon Granger, could report to Congress that the line was a complete success financially. For a year and a half, travelers' fares alone had paid all expenses, so that "the actual profit has been for that time equal to the whole expense of transporting the mail." The "sum repeatedly offered for the public property on the road, exclusive of forage, by persons possessing the means of knowing the profits of the institution, and which it is believed is not the value of it," was $16,000.[38] Furthermore, the postmaster general wrote, "It is proper to remark that the mail has been carried with unexampled regularity and dispatch, within the body of a carriage, in a box prepared for that purpose, less liable to be chafed and injured, and secured from robbery and inclement weather."[39]

In 1810, Granger directed Chester Bailey, a Post Office agent, to extend the government line to Trenton.[40] On December 1, 1813, under the direction of Bailey again, the line was continued to Jersey City. In this direction from Philadelphia, however, the "receipts from passengers was not equal to the expense and support of the line of mail stages"; nor were expenditures equaled even when the equivalent of the cost of carrying the mail by contract was added to the passenger receipts. Nevertheless, "the mail was carried with so much greater regularity than it had been by individuals," and the arrangement was continued by Return J. Meigs after he became postmaster general in 1814. However, according to Meigs, "on closing the accounts for the year 1814, the expenses of the line were greater than we anticipated."[41] In order "to continue the control of that line, without the immediate agency of this Department," Meigs contracted privately with Bailey to carry the mail for 1815. Bailey was to use the government property on the road but to supplement it whenever necessary and to pay all operating expenses. This arrangement continued until 1818 when Bailey purchased the remaining government property on the road and, in partnership with Thomas Ward, carried the mail henceforth under a regular private contract.[42]

The government line was thus terminated, and for the rest of their history, the stagecoaches carried the mails under private contract with the federal government. The government line was abandoned for several reasons: the operation, despite its early success, was not able to run extended lines at a profit; a tremendous amount of the postmaster general's time was spent in supervising stagecoach line management; and individual stage line owners continually complained that the government was competing with private enterprise. In the final analysis, the experiment had not worked.

STAGECOACHES that carried the mail were usually not charged a tariff when they traveled along the toll roads, but one interesting case brought this practice to a head. It involved another of the major stagecoach entrepreneurs of the nineteenth century, Lucius W. Stockton, who had been born in Flemington, New Jersey, in 1799. He later moved to Uniontown, Pennsylvania, and became involved in the staging business, finally becoming owner of the National Road Stage Company—known more popularly at the time as "The Old Line"—which traveled the routes from Cumberland to Wheeling.

In the 1840s, Stockton conceived the idea of putting a mail pouch in each of his passenger coaches so that they could be considered mail coaches as they passed along the National Road and thus exempt from the tolls. The commissioner of the National Road protested, claiming it was a subterfuge, and threatened to ban Stockton's stages from the National Road unless he paid. It was an impasse, and finally the Commissioner decided to enforce his threat by closing the gate five miles west of Uniontown to the Old Line coaches. The commissioner himself supervised the enforcement of his decision at the Uniontown gate as the first Old Line coach pulled up. (The commissioner at that time, incidentally, was William Searight, father of Thomas Searight, author of *The Old Pike*, and the young Thomas was at the scene that day.) The stage drivers, under orders from Stockton, refused to pay, and the gate remained firmly closed. The passengers in the coach became impatient, then angry, and finally they took up a collection among themselves to pay the toll and allow the coach to proceed.[43]

Thus, the impasse remained, and Stockton took the case to court, claiming that the National Road was obstructing the United States mail. The case went all the way to the Supreme Court, but before the final decision was handed down Stockton died on April 25, 1844. Even at that, the decision was against him. The majority decision, written by Chief Justice Roger B. Taney, stated that the exemption for the mails could only be applied to the mails themselves and not to the persons traveling with them; also, the exemption could not be claimed for more carriages than were necessary to carry the mail. As an aftermath to the case, the legislature of Pennsylvania passed a law in 1845 authorizing the collection of tolls from passengers in coaches that carried the mails.[44]

THE POSTAL RATES for mail on the stages were established in 1816, and although the rates varied from time to time, there were no large changes until the major postal reform act of 1845. During that period, the people considered the postage rates quite exorbitant. The charges were based on mileage and the number of sheets per letter, rather than upon weight as was later done. The charge for a single sheet ranged from six cents for thirty miles or less, to twenty-five cents for over 400 miles. Additional sheets or enclosures doubled or trebled the postage. Generally, patrons went to the post office to both mail their letters and call for incoming correspondence, and postmasters often charged regular patrons on a monthly basis, rather than collecting a fee when each letter was delivered. Because of the high fees, many people tried to circumvent the system by having friends or acquaintances carry their mail by hand on the stages for them.[45]

There were no regular issue postage stamps until 1847, and mail was usually sent unpaid, the charges being paid by the addressee. Occasionally, particularly in the case of a suitor writing to his lady, the sender would pre-pay the charges, but this was not the usual custom. Furthermore, the recipient had the right to refuse the letter, and this led to a variety of abuses to avoid postal fees. For instance, a stage traveler might tell his family that he would send a letter on arrival, and the family would then refuse the subsequent letter, knowing that the intended message had been received. Also, a code on the envelope might give the information the sender intended to impart. Or other codes might mean the letter was important and should be opened. A misspelled word, for example, might be used as a code.[46]

In 1840, this arrangement remained unchanged, and there was growing support for postal reform to eradicate the major abuses, particularly the exorbitant rates and the large amount of mail that went unclaimed to avoid postal fees. In that year, Postmaster General Amos Kendall sent George Plitt to England to study the postal reforms that had just been enacted there. Plitt discovered that the British postal reform act of 1840 had been based on an 1837 study by Rowland Hill titled "Post Office Reform: Its Importance and Practicability." The study called for a uniform rate of one pence for mail anywhere in Great Britain, rather than the existing sliding scales. Hill also made a revolutionary proposal that the sender pre-pay the postage and that the government sell "a bit of paper just large enough to bear the stamp which could be affixed to the cover by moistening the gum on the reverse side."[47] Thus, the adhesive postage stamp.

On May 6, 1840, Great Britain issued the first adhesive postage stamp in history, a one-pence black stamp called a "penny black," bearing a portrait of the twenty-one-year-old Queen Victoria. The stamp's color, however, was later changed to a reddish brown because the black cancellation mark was not very distinct on the black stamp, and people sometimes re-used them. Prestamped stationary was also offered for sale. (There had been prestamped stationary briefly in both Paris and Sardina in the eighteenth century.) One pence of postage would carry up to one-half ounce of weight, and two pence up to one ounce. The stamps were an enormous popular success, and letter mail in England doubled in the first year of their use.[48]

Plitt wrote a glowing report on the British system and encouraged the American government to create a postage stamp and adopt the English system. Charles Wickliffe, the new postmaster general (1841–45), opposed the report, particularly the reduction of postal rates. But his successor, Cave Johnson, a Tennesseean appointed by President James

Polk, approved of the report and lobbied for a postal reform bill, which was passed by Congress on March 3, 1845. However, the act only partially reflected the British system. In one variation, it called for a postage price scale based on both weight and distance zones. A "single" letter was considered anything up to one-half ounce, and this single letter could be carried on the stages for up to 300 miles for five cents and for over 300 miles for ten cents. Still, prepayment remained optional, and hand-stampers were provided to post offices bearing the numerals five to ten. There were still no general issue adhesive postage stamps in the United States.[49]

The first regular issue U.S. adhesive postal stamp was born by an act of Congress on March 3, 1847. In July of that year, there were issued a five-cent stamp bearing the portrait of Benjamin Franklin in brown and a ten-cent stamp bearing George Washington's portrait in black. However, their use was still not compulsory. When the rate structure was favorably changed in 1851, a new issue of stamps was released with Franklin on a one-cent stamp and Washington on a five-cent issue. Finally, the use of postage stamps was made compulsory in 1855. Up until 1857, these stamps were issued in flat sheets and had to be cut from the sheets, but after that date they were issued in sheets with perforations.[50]

Therefore, beginning in 1847 some of the mail carried by the stages began to bear postage stamps, and by 1855 all of the mail had stamps affixed. It was then the Indian summer of staging in the East, but the postage stamp was in its healthy infancy. By 1870, just thirty years after that first penny black, more than thirty nations around the world had issued either stamps or franked envelopes.[51]

DURING EACH of the first decades of the nineteenth century, the stages carried more and more mail, until by 1850 there were over 36,000 miles of stagecoach lines carrying mail in the eastern United States. That figure increased to over 45,000 miles by 1853. But it was to be the high watermark for stagecoach mail in the East, and the following years saw a steady decline in the total number of miles. At the same time, in those years before the Civil War, the railroads were significantly increasing the mileage of railroad lines carrying the mail.[52]

The railroad, and later the telegraph and telephone, was to revolutionize our communications systems, but for the first six decades of the nineteenth century, the stagecoach was the principal communications mode for the American public.

X

Newspapers and the Stages

 A PRINCIPAL REASON for the increasing dependence of the Post Office on the country's staging facilities was the growing burden of the newspapers. Until 1792, newspapers had not been carried as part of the mail: They were carried either by private riders or by public riders or stage proprietors who, with the permission of the Post Office, made their own private arrangement with the printers. In either case, by 1788 the Post Office, in the words of Postmaster General Ebenezer Hazard, had "nothing to do with newspapers."[1] The mail stages on the main routes carried newspapers independently of the mail, often apparently without charging the printers. Perhaps, the stage proprietors had some return in advertising: At least, they gained valuable good will. To William Goddard, Baltimore printer, the acting postmaster general complained, in 1791:

Since the Mail has been carried in Stage Waggons the printers have been indulged with the privilege of sending newspapers to their Subscribers free of expense and they now *claim it as a matter of right* not only where the mail goes in the Stages but also where it goes on Horseback . . . Contractors for carrying the mail do not object to their being sent in the Stages without pay; but when the mail goes on Horseback . . . it is impossible to carry them without an extra set of Horses for that purpose. . . .

   The Proprietors of the Stages considered this as a favor, for they were under no obligations to carry Newspapers unless they were paid for it. The printers are notwithstanding very ready to abuse both them and the Postmasters, if there is not the same attention paid to their papers as to the letters.[2]

The Post Office Act of 1792 was the first to establish per copy rates of postage for the carriage of newspapers within the mail. The charge was to be one cent for up to 100 miles and one and one-half cents for any greater distance. The law of 1794 provided that, irrespective of distance, the postage "from any one place to another in the same State shall not exceed one cent."[3] By Senate amendment, there was included in the 1792 Act authorization for mail carriers under contract with the Post Office to continue, if they wished, to carry newspapers outside the mail by private arrangement with printers who cared to employ them.[4] Carriers who wished to take advantage of this provision were required to state in their bids the sums for which they would carry the mail with the newspaper privilege and without it so that the Post Office could compare with other bids and decide intelligently.[5] A provision of this kind was necessary, Representative John Page stated in the debate, lest there be infringement of the liberty of the press. "We have subjected the printers of the papers to a certain tax for sending their papers by the mail, and now it is proposed to cut off from them all opportunity of making their own contracts," he argued.[6] In addition to the safeguard of private distribution, the law granted to every printer of a newspaper permission to "send one paper to each and every other printer of newspapers within the United States, free of postage, under such regulations, as the Postmaster General shall provide."[7] This was a substantial favor. An editor's original contributions were often confined to a note on the weather and the description of an occasional "disastrous conflagration," while he filled his columns with news from other cities and from abroad, all copied from papers which reached his desk free of charge.

Ideal as the law might seem for the printers, a great clamor arose in the press against it. Even James Madison became much excited over what he called the "newspaper tax."[8] Others prophesied that a large class of citizens would be forced to suspend their papers so that only a few newspapers could survive. Timothy Pickering, then postmaster general, wrote to the head of the Committee on the Post Office and discounted the protests of the printers as propaganda and noises made in the hope of the repeal of the law.[9] But the law was not repealed, and enough newspapers were soon sent by mail to cause a severe strain on Post Office facilities. This strain bore disproportionately on the lines that passed through sparsely settled regions and to the frontiers, where there was little private employment of riders.

At the time when the newspapers used horses first and then stagecoaches, they made an infinitesimal contribution to the part of the income of the Post Office that could be used for transportation. This was not only because the rates were low but also because the local postmasters were allowed 50 percent of the postage on newspapers as their commission. Pickering calculated in 1794 that while the newspapers comprised seven-tenths of the mail, the postage received from them was but one-twenty-ninth that received from letters.[10] To Pittsburgh, the most important of the routes to the frontier, newspapers comprised eighty-two percent of the mail.[11] Actually, there was an invisible subsidy of the press by the Post Office, and that subsidy was paid by a tax, in the form of high postage, on all senders of letters, that allowed newspapers to be distributed cheaply to all parts of the country. The result was that instead of the suspension of newspapers, as had been prophesied, they prospered and multiplied until the people of the United States were readers of newspapers to an extent far greater than were the citizens of any other land. The comments of foreign travelers on this point are pertinent. "Our stage . . . carried the mail," wrote John Palmer in 1818, "and it was pleasing to observe the boys and girls running out of the farm-houses at the sound of the post-horn, to catch the numerous newspapers, which our driver distributed en passant. There are but few people but take a newspaper."[12] Another English traveler, John Lambert, wrote in 1814:

The long stages throughout the United States always carry the mail, and it was entertaining to see the eagerness of the people on our arrival, to get a sight of the last newspaper from Boston. They flocked to the postoffice and the inn, and formed a variety of groups round those who were fortunate enough to possess themselves of a paper.

. . . there is scarcely a poor owner of a miserable log hut, who lives on the border of the stage road, but has a newspaper left at his door. . . . The knowledge acquired by newspapers may be superficial, but it gives men a general acquaintance with the world.[13]

Drivers who delivered newspapers at farmhouses along their routes carried those papers by private arrangement with the printers—or "outside the mail," to use Post Office parlance—because newspapers within the mail were in locked bags that were opened only at the post offices by postmasters or their authorized assistants possessing keys. There was provision in the law, after 1794, for collecting or delivering "way letters," as they were called, between offices. The driver had a duty to accept way letters if they were presented more than two miles from a post office. He then delivered them to the postmaster at the next office, who entered them on the waybill and placed them within the bag. The driver was to be paid one cent by the postmaster for each way letter, and this was added to the rate of the letter to be paid by the recipient.[14]

It was also the duty of the driver "to take charge of, and deliver," all way letters committed to his care by a postmaster, and "for every letter so delivered, the mail carrier delivering the same shall be allowed to demand and receive two cents, to his own use, besides the ordinary postage." The driver, however, was not to go off the post road to make such deliveries, and on routes where in the opinion of the postmaster general the speed demanded was inconsistent with the collection and delivery of way letters, the service was not allowed.[15]

Drivers who carried newspapers outside the mail usually acted as collectors for the printers. In effect, they were also agents of the printers in soliciting subscriptions. An advertisement of the Albany–New York Stage proprietors clearly revealed the business arrangements connected with this practice:

The Proprietors of the Stages, having contracted with the Post-Master-General for the Transportation of the Public Mails . . . will cheerfully engage to forward regularly by the same conveyance, the New York, Boston, Portsmouth, Albany, and all the intermediate Newspapers to the different Towns on the Roads, to those who choose to become Subscribers to any of the different Papers.[16]

The stagecoach taverns were the unofficial post offices of the day. Frequently, the official post offices were also located there. In either case, it was important for the newspaper subscriber to be on hand if he wished to be certain of receiving his paper. One Englishman, James Silk Buckingham, widely traveled in the United States, wrote in 1842: "So lightly indeed, are newspapers thought of, as matters of personal property, that it is very common for the idlers of a village to go to the post office on the arrival of the mail, and appropriate to themselves newspapers addressed to others; and this is no more thought of, than the act of stopping a stage near an orchard, to supply all the passengers with fruit."[17] There was certainly greater temptation to such "appropriation" when the post office was in the tavern. Postmaster General Joseph Habersham, in a letter to Noah Webster, explained why this was so often the case.

In a small office the Profits are trifling and persons will not hold them who are well qualified as they find that the duties of the office will interfere with their more profitable occupations . . . but a Postoffice at a Tavern if it produces little or no Commission will in other respects promote the interest of the tavern-keeper; hence it happens that so many of them are Postmasters. The abuses you mention are certainly more easily committed at a tavern than at a private house as people are too generally disposed to use greater freedom at the former under an idea that they must be submitted to . . . for this reason as well as others which could be given I do not think Tavern-keepers are proper persons to be postmasters and where others can be found to act they should unquestionably be preferred.[18]

Habersham secured in the supplementary post office legislation of 1797 a provision subjecting to a twenty-dollar fine any postmaster who delayed any newspaper or permitted any mail of newspapers not directed to his office to be opened.[19] It was found necessary to strengthen this provision in 1810 by including any employee of the Post Office who shall "permit any other person to do the like, or shall open, or permit any other to open any mail or packet of newspapers not directed to the office where he is employed."[20] The fine for employees was increased to fifty dollars, and a fine of twenty dollars might be imposed upon nonemployees who did any of these things. The provisions, apparently, were not strongly enforced.

The Post Office was sometimes accused, especially by papers opposing the administration, of discrimination in the delivery of newspapers. In respect to this, an observation by the English traveler John Lambert in 1814 is interesting:

Each man takes a newspaper that agrees with his politics, or rather directs them; but those who are remotely situated from a town where they are published, must depend upon the *politics of the coachman*, for such papers as he chooses to bring them. One of the drivers during my journey happened to be a *federalist*— No sooner did he blow his horn than up scampered men, women, and children to the Coach, eagerly begging for their favorite paper. If they wanted a democratic one, they must either take a federalist or go without. He had a few of the others with him, but he never would deliver them if he could avoid it.[21]

Since such distribution, as described by Lambert, was outside the mail system, and in accordance with the driver's private arrangements with the printers, the Post Office could not be held responsible for discrimination. And, in Lambert's case, since his visit was from 1806 to 1808, it was a Democratic administration that was permitting its own agents to thus distribute Federalist papers on the side. The practice undoubtedly irked Postmaster General Gidean Granger, and he wrote one forceful letter on the subject to the postmaster at Utica, New York:

I have adopted it as a principle that no person that attempts to give a bias to the public mind unfavorable to the government of the Country and while in the Discharge of the duties of this office, shall be employed as a contractor.[22]

In another letter accepting a contractor's bid for service from Windsor to Burlington in New England, Granger warned that he reserved the right to annul the contract "provided you do not distribute the different political newspapers with strict impartiality."[23]

It may be questioned whether Granger had the right to demand that drivers carrying newspapers privately should carry them impartially, since to do so was to defeat the intention of the provision allowing private contracts with the public riders or drivers. If the drivers refused to distribute Democratic papers privately, the printers could have them sent within the mails and delivered by postmasters. The question was obviously full of potential political and constitutional questions.

There were reasons for the nondelivery of newspapers other than partisanship and their "appropriation" by nonsubscribers. Many printers anxious to get their newspapers into the first mails after printing did not take the time to dry them sufficiently. According to the report of a special committee of the House,

they are thrown into the portmanteaus in a state of moisture that more than doubles the natural weight of the papers when dry. This wet situation of the papers makes them liable also to be easily torn and destroyed by the motion, among the bundles and packages, arising from the carriage or horse that transports them. And sometimes, in travelling from one office to another, whole bundles, as well as single papers, are so worn and defaced, that is is impossble to ascertain to whom, or to what office they are directed, or to read their contents.[24]

After much debate, a clause was included in the supplementary legislation of 1797 providing that newspapers were not to be received "unless they are sufficiently dried and enclosed in paper wrappers."[25] Undoubtedly, the printers considered this a very oppressive regulation, since more than twelve hours would be required to dry their newspapers properly. It was not wholly obeyed.

Stage drivers were known to leave newspapers portmanteaus behind in seasons of the year when the roads were heavy. Their most frequent offense, however, was carrying the newspapers on the board under their feet where they were exposed to all the elements and subjected to the sharp jolting of the carriage, instead of being carried safely within the body.

Habersham carried on a crusade against this practice. He consulted with the contractors urging them to construct a box fixed to insure that the mail was invariably carried within the stage, and in 1796 some of the contractors followed his request. This box had, by 1800, taken the form of a locked trunk built into the fore part of the stage, so that three passengers could be seated upon it with their faces to the rear. The front of the stage, which formerly had been open, was now closed, and the vehicle was entered through a side door. Soon, these stages were running on the leading post routes. On the lesser roads, of course, the old style stage bodies lingered, and from time to time complaints were still received of mail, especially newspapers, being exposed to the rain and mud.

The newspapers' bulk and great weight were responsible for most of these difficulties. Letter writers not only paid to subsidize the transportation of newspapers, but, as a result, received poorer service on their letters. Failures to deliver newspapers properly were a source of much embarrassment to the Post Office because the ungrateful editors always aired such slips. This, in turn, hurt the administration politically, so that the postmaster general soon was explaining to the president or to members of Congress whose constituents needed to be soothed. The cost of newspaper transportation undoubtedly contributed to the high postage required on letters before 1845. But the real problem—the bulk of the stacks of newspapers—could not be solved by inexpensive postage. Instead, no solution was found until the 1830s and 1840s, when the railroads with their significantly larger freight capabilities began to carry the newspapers on the routes previously traveled along the main post roads.

For the first part of the nineteenth century, the stages played a vital and indispensable role in the development and expansion of American newspapers. Newspaper circulation grew to a degree previouely unknown in the world, and it allowed the common man, in the words of John Lambert, to gain "a general acquaintence with the world." The stage's contribution to literacy, education, and the democratic process itself in the nineteenth century was almost incalculable.

XI

Stagecoach Makers

 STAGECOACH MAKING had evolved considerably by 1820, and it would develop even more in the next few decades with the famous eastern stagecoaches of the nineteenth century—the Albany and Troy coaches, and particularly the pinnacle of American stagecoach making, the Concord coach.

Nevertheless, by 1820 stagecoach making and road construction had so improved that drivers and their passengers were experiencing a remarkable acceleration of speed in stage travel. The scheduled time between Boston and New York, for example, had been reduced from six days to thirty-six hours, while the journey from Philadelphia to Petersburg, Virginia, had been cut from seven days to two days and nine hours. And though humans probably could not endure traveling the entire distance without rest, the connecting mail could now pass from Boston to Richmond in five days. The *National Intelligencer*, in the nation's capital, editorialized in 1820: "For three or four of the first years that Congress sat in this city, it was a day's journey for the stages from Baltimore to Washington, and in the winter frequently took twenty hours to complete it. It is now travelled on a turnpike road, not the best in the world, by stages and private carriages, in five or six hours in the summer, and six or seven in the winter."[1] Cutting the time of travel by roughly two-thirds was a notable achievement.

The increased speed of the later model stagecoaches meant that the individual traveler's costs were reduced, since fewer meals and fewer nights of lodging were required on the road. Even at that, competition among the many stage lines served to keep fares at very modest rates.

Thomas Searight recalled that in the 1830s the entire stage fare for a trip from Baltimore to Cumberland, which then continued along the National Road to Wheeling, was only $17.50.[2] Stage travel was therefore not only becoming more rapid; it was also remaining well within the pocketbook of the common man.

THE ALBANY COACH, manufactured by James Goold and Company of Albany, New York, was introduced in the 1820s, and it soon became widely known. Goold, a native of Connecticut, established his factory in 1813 and took in later, as partners, his nephew Walter R. Bush and his son-in-law J. N. Cutler. He specialized in heavy work, and stagecoaches became a featured product of his factory. By 1830, Albany coaches were found south of New Jersey, an indication that some proprietors thought they were superior to coaches obtainable in New Jersey. The newly established Despatch line between Baltimore and Washington advertised in 1829 that it had "provided coaches built in Albany, of the most modern and approved kind. They are hung low and combine ease and safety."[3] The "Splendid Red Coaches" of the Union line between the same cities were also built in Albany.[4]

James Goold and Company made the stagecoach bodies that, placed on flange-wheeled running gears, served as the first cars of the Mohawk and Hudson Railroad in 1831 and 1832. Subsequently, the Goolds did a considerable amount of railroad-car manufacturing. They also were famous as makers of sleighs, including stage sleighs. They had just added a large new factory building to their establishment and were advertising their "increased facilities for the manufacture of all kinds of *pleasure carriages, sleighs,* and *stagecoaches,* from timber selected and seasoned with great care, and of superior workmanship and finish,"[5] when on May 25, 1838, a "Great and Destructive Fire" burned their buildings. According to the *Albany Evening Journal,* "The extensive and valuable coach-making establishment of Messrs. James Goold & Co., yesterday the pride of our city, furnishing employment for many of our citizens and support to numerous families, is now a smoking ruin."[6] At a meeting of citizens the day after the fire, a committee was appointed that raised a $20,000 loan to enable Goold to rebuild his plant. No interest was charged him for five years. Goold rebuilt with such foresight that his factory was still operating in 1879, the year of his death.

ALBANY COACHES were soon eclipsed in fame by those made in the neighboring city of Troy, where manufacturers adopted whatever improvements the Albany coaches could boast and added others of their own. In pattern, the two coaches were basically the same, so that in distant parts of the country no distinction between them was made. In 1827, the Troy *Sentinel* contrasted "our light, elegant and convenient stage-coaches, with the spring seats and easy motion" with "the lumbering vehicle which were in use for the purpose some twelve or fifteen years ago," and remarked editorially, "We are happy to know that the people are indebted to the ingenuity and enterprise of the citizens of Troy for some of these additional conveniences."[7]

There was a competition in Troy between two companies. Charles Veazie set up a factory there within two years of Goold's establishing himself in Albany, and it was continued until 1836. Orsamus Eaton also opened a plant, in 1820. In 1830, the Troy factories together employed about sixty men and turned out about fifty post-coaches and a hundred other carriages worth a total of $50,000. These figures, based on the *Troy Directory for the Year 1830*,[8] if accurate, seemingly indicate that, under the working conditions of the time, no more than two and one-half vehicles per man per year could be produced and that each laborer contributed to the total value of the manufactured goods only $833 minus the cost of raw materials and overhead expenses. Possible additional income was realized from smith, carpenter, and paint repair jobs and other work not included in the totals given above.

This was the beginning of a period of rapid expansion for the Troy firms, however. The spread southward and westward of the fame of Troy coaches was due in part to James Reeside, the "Land Admiral," who used them for his "Splendid Red Coaches" in Pennsylvania and Maryland. "Mr. Reeside exhibited a splendid coach made in Troy, N.Y. by Messrs Eaton and Gilbert, & Charles Veazie," read an item in the *United States Gazette* in 1831:

The coach was painted red, and beautifully lined with red morocco. The whole appliances of the carriage were suited to the elegance of the body, and bespoke the liberality of the enterprising owner. Mr. Reeside ordered a number of these carriages to be built for the new line that is to commence running between Baltimore and Pittsburgh, by the way of Chambersburg, on the 1st of October.[9]

The previous year, Reeside had put Troy coaches on the line between Philadelphia and Easton, Pennsylvania, and the Philadelphia–New York line had been stocked with them a short time before. By 1831, the *Troy Budget* could remark, "Eaton and Veazie have rendered Trojan carriages almost as noted as the wooden horse of old Troy. Their coaches are sent to all parts of the Union and are everywhere noted for their superior beauty and utility."[10]

Troy coaches reached the South some five or six years after their merits were recognized north of the Potomac. In 1825, the line from Wythe Court House, Virginia, to Greensboro, North Carolina, boasted, "The Coaches are made at Troy, N.Y., good and comfortable."[11] The proprietors of the line between Georgetown and Charleston, South Carolina, gave notice in 1837 that they "have placed upon their route an entire new set of Troy built coaches,"[12] and in the following year, the Mail and Telegraph lines, which each run daily over the great southern route from Augusta, Georgia, via Macon and Columbus to Montgomery and Mobile, Alabama, were "furnished with the best Troy built Coaches."[13] West of the mountains, the Maysville-Louisville line, in Kentucky, was in 1838 "supplied with substantial Troy & Lancaster coaches";[14] the line from Nashville to the Mississippi River at Mills' Point had "selected superior Troy coaches";[15] and in Mississippi, the daily lines between Vicksburg and Jackson and between Jackson and Bridgeport, and the triweekly line from Jackson to Grand Gulf and Port Gibson, were all stocked with coaches "of the best Troy manufacture."[16]

Advertisements in the newspapers of the old Northwest similarly indicated the fame and wide distribution of Troy coaches. Proprietors were introducing them on the leading routes in the late 1830s. By 1840, they were found on the lines of the Ohio Stage Company, on Darius Talmadge's routes from Zanesville to Maysville and Cincinnati, on J. P. Voorhees and Company's line in Indiana, on the line run by Frink and Walker from Chicago west to Galena, Illinois, and probably on others.[17] By 1842, for most of their routes throughout Illinois, Frink and Walker were advertising "first rate Troy built coaches."[18] Davis and Moore of Milwaukee, who were associated with Frink and Walker in the line from Milwaukee through Madison, Wisconsin, to Galena, declared in 1843 "their intention to run Troy coaches on the whole of the road,"[19]

James Silk Buckingham wrote in 1842 of the nine-passenger coach "in general use throughout the country" as follows:

These coaches are built with great strength, without which, indeed, they could not endure the shockings and the joltings they receive. They are almost all constructed at Troy, next to Albany in the state of New York, whence they are sent in pieces, to various part of the Union, and put together by coach-builders when they arrive. This, at least, is the practice in the distant states, to which it would be difficult and expensive to convey them when built; but to places near the seat of their manufacture they are conveyed whole. They cost at first hand about $600 . . . when new; though I think in England such coaches could not be made for that sum.[20]

Orsamus Eaton had in 1831 taken Uri Gilbert into partnership, and, as Eaton and Gilbert, the two continued to manufacture stagecoaches until their factory was destroyed by fire in 1852. In 1841, following in the steps of the Goolds, they began manufacturing passenger cars for railroads. They built the first eight-wheel cars run on the Schenectady and Troy Railroad, and, in 1846, cars for the Housatonic Railroad, which won much attention.[21] In 1850, the firm was reported to have built about 100 stagecoaches, 50 omnibuses, 30 passenger cars, and 150 freight cars. When re-established after the fire, the company built only railroad cars.

All of these stagecoaches were constructed in various sizes. The two major size categories were the hotel coach and the mail coach. The hotel coach was smaller, usually seating six, and derived its name from its use chiefly to transport people to and from hotels. The mail coach was larger, carrying from nine to twelve passengers, and was on the open road for longer journeys.

As the coach roof became flatter, with a baggage rack running around its edge, people began to ride outside on the roof of the stage. Earlier, with the rough roads this would have been unthinkable, because the passengers might well have bounced off. But the improved roads and the later flat design of the roof allowed more passengers to be carried on each trip. One and sometimes two passengers could be squeezed in the driver's seat, but other passengers, sometimes as many as six or seven, could sit on the roof itself holding onto the baggage rack.

ONE OF THE leading stagecoach firms in the East did not purchase Troy coaches. Stockton and Stokes had their own coach factory on Belvedere Street, Baltimore, under the direction of Richard Imlay. According to the editor of Niles Weekly Register, who wrote of a visit to the factory in 1831,

Fifty men and thirty lads are employed in this factory—and they are aided by scientific power in a remarkable manner, in every department of this extensive concern. It is ingeniously applied in all possible cases—to the fashioning of iron, the sawing of timber, the smoothing of boards, the turning of iron and wood or metal, &., propelled by the surplus water of the canal leading to the "city mill."[22]

Stockton and Stokes's coaches "have long since obtained the public approbation," concluded the editor. In addition to coaches, his eye was caught by a "splendid rail-road car, called the Virginia, which soon hoped to reach the state after which it was named" on the Baltimore and

Ohio road. Later the same year, the *Register* carried a note that Imlay had thirty railroad cars under construction for different roads, including two for the West Branch Schuykill railroad.[23] In 1832, he built the coaches for the newly opened railroad between Frenchtown and Newcastle.[24] Thus, a third stagecoach factory also was building the earliest cars for pioneer railroads in its territory. Seemingly, Stockton and Stokes in their establishment built coaches under contract for other lines besides their own.

Other large stagecoach interests controlled repair shops at which complete stages at times might be built. Lucius W. Stockton located the repair yards for his lines between Cumberland and Wheeling at Uniontown on the National Road, and coaches were built there. An extensive blacksmith shop was connected with the coach shop. Many mechanics, woodworkers, trimmers, painters, and harness workers were employed. There was even a company store connected with the yard.[25] The "Eastern Stage Yard" in Newburyport, Massachusetts, was a similar headquarters for the Eastern Stage Company of New England, and coaches were built for the company there by Joseph Hale and Nathaniel M. Gurney.[26] In Columbus, Ohio, the repair shops of Neil, Moore and Company developed by 1845 into a factory occupying two buildings, each 180 feet in length, with about forty workmen employed. The construction of railroad cars was also about to be added to the building of coaches in this establishment.[27]

Most large staging centers had resident stagecoach builders, though few of them gained more than a local reputation unless some important stage proprietor was their patron. Coaches made in Ithaca, New York, and in Lancaster, Pennsylvania, were of more than local repute, but their makers are no longer known. Stagecoaches were made in Salem, Massachusetts, by Frothingham and Loring; in Harrisburg, Pennsylvania, by Jacob Fedder and by Henry Grangle; in Pittsburgh by Reddick and Owen and by Hise, Cole and Grear; in Indianapolis by Lashley and Foltz; and in Knoxville, Tennessee, by Barnes Crawford.[28]

The Salem and Boston Stage Company sent an agent to England in 1827 to secure plans for the latest and most valuable improvements to stagecoaches in that country. From his drawings and models, John McGlue and Benjamin Bray of Salem constructed a model, which won much attention when it was exhibited in Boston in 1828. According to the *American Traveller*:

The great improvement is the adaptation of springs to the support of the carriage. The leather thorough braces of our common stages are altogether dispensed with, and in their stead we have sets of firm, steel springs at each end of the coach body, which not only give the vehicle a pleasant, easy, vertical motion, but prevent that violent rocking, which in a common stage, when going at a rapid rate, often throws a passenger from his seat, or causes him to cry out. There is also some improvement in the wheels and boxes. The whole is said to be considerably lighter than the ordinary stages; and the proprietors are so well pleased . . . that orders have been given to finish others immediately.[29]

These coaches were run regularly for some time between Boston and Salem, over what was then one of the best roads in the country. Ordinarily, however, steel-spring coaches were not found practicable on the ordinary roads of the country. Under sudden strains, they snapped too easily. A bow-spring, patented by Thomas Shriver, of Maryland, was used on some stages on the National Road in the early 1840s.[30] Earlier use of the term "steel springs" in advertisements usually referred to the uprights from which the leather thorough braces were suspended. These, if made heavy enough, could be shaped in the form of C springs and contribute to the easy-riding qualities of the carriage. However, the leather thorough braces were indispensable.

The more discerning of foreign travelers were quick to notice that the American stagecoach, though clumsy looking, was well adapted to the roads it traveled. These roads, Buckingham wrote in 1842, "would break to pieces any description of carriage except the ponderous stage-coaches of this country, which are made as heavy and as strong as the union of iron and wood can make them."[31] Captain Robert Barclay found the stage body "resting on strong leather slings instead of steel springs, which indeed would not stand a mile on their roads. It, the body, consequently dances in the air like a balloon, giving a certain kind of variety to the monotony of a journey."[32] According to Alexander Mackey, "Ordinary metal springs would have been useless for the support of a machine destined for such service." It was "heaving and plunging like a vessel in a troubled sea as soon as we got into the open country road."[33] The Concord coach, the supreme achievement of American stagecoach building, still hung on the old leather thorough braces, and when Australia and South Africa, toward the closing years of the nineteenth century, were in the market for stagecoaches, they sent not to the mother country but to Concord, New Hampshire, for them.

LEWIS DOWNING, founder of Downing and Abbot, the firm that created the Concord coach, was the son of a wheelwright at Lexington, Massachusetts, and in growing up he served a four-year's apprenticeship to an older brother in the same business. He arrived at Concord in 1813, as a young man of twenty-one. For thirteen years, Downing made only common wagons and did a general wheelwright's business, working most of that time in a small shop at the rear of his house. He commenced erecting more extensive shops in 1825, planning to branch into chaise and stage manufacturing, and engaged J. Stephens Abbot, a journeyman coachmaker who had learned his trade with Frothingham and Loring of Salem, Massachusetts, to come to Concord to build three stagecoach bodies. Their first coach was completed in July 1827 and was sold immediately to John Shepherd, a proprietor out of Concord on the line running to Burlington, Vermont. The other two were soon sold in Vermont. On January 1, 1828, Abbot was taken in as a partner by Downing, and the firm made coach building a leading feature of their business.

The design of the first Concord coaches was so satisfactory that no major change was ever made in the basic model. The driver's seat was unprotected and only about eight to sixteen inches lower than the roof. The average width of a coach body was four feet, four inches, and its average height was four and one-half feet. The back and front seats inside the coach faced each other, and in addition there was a low, partially adjustable middle seat that had no back except a leather strap that was fastened to one side of the coach and could be hooked across to the other.[34]

Concord was a major staging center of the region; so it was not long before Concord stages made their way into all parts of New England. At the same time, New England lines absorbed the entire stagecoach production of the city's hand-operated shops for some years. The first note of the use of these stages outside of New England was in 1846 when a National Road company announced it had placed "on the road between Brownsville and Cumberland fifty splendid new Troy, Albany, Concord, and Newark made Coaches, of the most improved models," thus all at once calling the roll of the great stagecoach-making centers.[35] The partnership of Downing and Abbot continued until September 1847, when it was dissolved by mutual consent. Abbot continued in business at the old shops built by Downing, while Downing took in his sons as partners and moved up Main Street to a spot near the State House.

Competition between the two establishments seems to have increased the business of both. The Downings commenced with about thirty hands, which increased in a few years to eighty. The old shops that Abbot had taken were entirely destroyed by fire in 1849, whereupon he built a large plant covering about five acres. Extensive shops for their day, Abbot's new facilities were equipped with the latest power machinery. He took his son, Edward A. Abbot, into partnership in 1852, renaming the firm J. S. and E. A. Abbot. Their employees increased from about 75 in 1847 to over 200 just before the Civil War, when much southern trade was coming to them. They had twenty-four forges in operation in their shops, and additional smith work was done outside their yard. L. Downing and Sons, meanwhile, had prospered from a share it held in the Overland and California trade.[36]

Both firms suffered greatly during the Civil War, Abbot's perhaps the most because of the disappearance of its southern market. This situation, doubtless, was a factor in the reunion of the two companies on January 1, 1865, under the name Abbot, Downing and Company. At this time, Lewis Downing, Sr. retired from the business in which he had actively participated for fifty-two years. It had been his practice never to do more business than he could attend to personally. When he died on March 10, 1873, the minister who preached his funeral sermon chose as his text the words from the second chapter of Timothy, "A workman that needeth not to be ashamed."[37] (Lewis Downing, Jr., who later became president of Abbot, Downing and Company, had completed sixty-four years of service in the business when he died in 1901.)

The discovery of gold in the Transvaal, South Africa, in the mid-1880s proved to be the last great boost to the stagecoach business of Abbot, Downing.[38] It never recovered from the depression of the 1890s, though enough work was found to continue running with a reduced force until the twentieth century, when it could turn to manufacturing not railroad cars but Abbot, Downing motor trucks.

The Concord coach was dominant in the Old Southwest just before the Civil War, it was at home along the upper Mississippi, it was found in the hilly areas of central New York and Pennsylvania, and it lingered longest in the Adirondack and White Mountain resort regions not far from where it had its birth.[39] Even the area north of La Crosse, Wisconsin, witnessed a transition in the winter of 1858 from the frontier "mudwagon," as the frontier stage wagons had been dubbed, to "the best 'Concord Coaches,' lined, covered, and with plenty of robes."[40] Here at last, the Concord Coach had passed beyond the empire of the stages from Troy.

The stagecoach order book of J.S. and E.A. Abbot for the last years of its existence as a separate company, 1858–64, and two such order books for the united Abbot, Downing and Company, covering the years 1865–73 and 1873–1902, recorded names and addresses of persons or firms placing orders, dates of receipt and delivery, and the necessary specifications. In 1859, J.S. and E.A. Abbot sent more stagecoaches to Texas than to any other state. Alabama was second, Arkansas and Virginia were tied for third place, and North Carolina and Georgia were tied for fifth. Over 90 percent of the firm's business in this year was with the South. In addition, two sixteen-passenger stages were sent to Melbourne, Australia, and one stage was sent to Chile. Only one small shipment of four coaches was sent to California in the two years 1859 and 1860 combined. In 1864, Ben Holladay sent in a single order for twenty-nine coaches, and the Abbots were forced to turn another order for six coaches for the Overland Mail over to the Downings. In 1865, fifteen stages were sent to Mexico and five to Bolivia for an American stagecoach company operating there. However, nine new stages were ordered from New York State the same year, and Darius Talmadge was ordering Concord coaches for his Lancaster-Columbus line in Ohio. The first order from Alabama after the war came in 1866.[41]

The favorite color for the road stagecoaches, indicated in these books, was red for the body and straw-color for the carriage. Once in a while, the body was straw-colored and the carriage red, and in some instances the entire coach was straw-colored. Other colors were used for the hotel coaches. Coaches could be lined with russet leather, enamel leather, or plush. In the later coaches, glass was used in the doors so that when the leather curtains at the side were lowered, there was still light in the interior of the coach. Orders specified whether oil or candle lamps were wanted. Axle, tire, and track sizes were noted. Almost half the coaches made by the Abbots in 1859 called for one deck seat. Two deck seats were rarely ordered.[42]

The lettering to go on the coach had to be specified with care when an order was made. In addition to the proprietor's name, or the name of the company, the route often appeared. A coach to go to Maine was to be lettered "Gardiner Hallowell & Augusta." Two to go to James R. Powell at Montgomery, Alabama, were to be lettered "Pensacola and Mobile Mail Line." The one for Chile was lettered *Concepcion y Corsonel.*

Few proprietors were particular about the ornamental painting on the panels. "Ornament Neat but not Gaudy," was the request of one. "Put on some nice and neat landscape," another directed. "Ornament up nice and Rich—No *Female* on *doors*", ordered a third. But, the notation for those to go to Bolivia was, "Ornament up Fancy. Put Women in door panel." There were regular stencil designs that could be used when no particular design was specified. "Won't You Come Along," "Under the Vine," "Lady on Horseback" were separate titles. Some proprietors had pictures or portraits "transferred." Proprietors of hotel stages and omnibuses in resort districts frequently wanted pictures of their hotels on their vehicles.[43]

Giving each stagecoach a name became fashionable about 1830. Ordered of the Abbots in 1859 were a Mary Bradford, Malinda Smith, Nelly Long, Julia Horton, Ruth Joe, Lady of the Lake, Gentle Annie, General John L. Bunch, Jeff Davis, J. L. Price and A. V. Brown. When William Henry Harrison, James Polk, and Zachary Taylor passed over the National Road to Washington as presidents-elect, a new stage for each occasion was provided and named The President. Names of favorite politicians were used frequently by mail contractors for their coaches. Searight told the story of Lucius W. Stockton, who, having named one of his coaches for Vice-President John Tyler, ordered the name erased after Tyler as president vetoed the bank bill, saying "I won't have one of my Coaches named for a traitor."[44]

THE CONCORD COACH was a product of eastern staging, but after its important role during the golden years of eastern staging before the Civil War, it was to have another glorious and famous role in the Far West after the war during the years of expansion and development, particularly as the coach of the Wells Fargo Overland Stage of the Gold Rush era. And it would become world-famous, too, with sales to nations all around the globe for the rest of the century. Not until the Model T did any vehicle of American manufacture acquire so great a reputation as did the Concord coach. But, of course, the Concord coach was a period piece, and the twentieth-century motor car doomed it. In 1915, the Abbot, Downing Company announced it would expand into the production of motor trucks, and in 1919 it stated it had just built its last horse-drawn vehicle—a horse-drawn cart for a Boston produce merchant. Finally, in 1925 the Abbot, Downing Co. was dissolved after its abortive motor vehicle venture, and its last remaining asset, the Abbot, Downing name, was sold to the Wells Fargo Company.[45]

Today, a number of those old Concord coaches are exhibited in museums and collections around the country, and many of them are handsomely restored—cleaned, painted, and refurbished. These proud coaches, once the kings of the stagecoach routes, are magnificent exhibits, but one would really have to see the Concord coach alive and functioning to feel its strength, impressiveness, and beauty. One should see it as it was with its power attached, those teams of four or six horses, and the driver mounting the box, gathering his reins and cracking his long whip. Then, one should see the passengers, riding high in the coach, and shouting and waving as the stage rumbles off.

XII

The Stagecoach Tavern

 Thomas Twining, that English traveler in America during the late eighteenth and early nineteenth centuries who chronicled his journeys with such detail and often acerbic criticism, wrote of a trip he took from Baltimore south to Georgetown in April 1796. The stage left Baltimore at 4:00 A.M., filled with ten other passengers, and the twelve-hour trip was apparently quite arduous for Twining. In his account, he complained of the dismal countryside, the roads made soft by spring rains, and the dark and "oppressively hot" interior of the coach. Finally, he wrote with relief about the

welcome report of our driver about 3 in the afternoon that we were approaching Georgetown. We entered this town in half an hour or more, and descended from our prison at the Fountain Tavern.[1]

The Fountain Tavern, which Twining reached so gratefully, was more commonly known in Georgetown as the famous Suter's Tavern. It had been established by John Suter in 1783, and among its regular patrons was George Washington, who conducted some of his most important business there — for example, meeting the proprietors of the lands east of Rock Creek in 1791 and purchasing the site of the Federal City. It was also at Suter's that Pierre l'Enfant, the city planner, and Andrew Ellicott, the city surveyor, made their headquarters and did their significant work, and that the first lots in the new city were auctioned off in Washington's presence.[2] But, for the purposes of this narrative, Suter's Tavern had one other important dimension: It was part of the growing

142.

number of stagecoach taverns that were springing up all up and down the eastern United States.

During the late eighteenth and early nineteenth centuries, the stagecoach tavern was to become one of the most important institutions in the life of the young nation.[3] The busier roads in the earlier decades of the nineteenth century supported an almost unbelievable number of taverns. At one time, there were, for instance, sixty-two taverns functioning simultaneously on the sixty-three miles of the Philadelphia and Lancaster turnpike.[4] Between the thirteenth and eighteenth milestones, a convenient first stage from Philadelphia, there were eleven. Thomas Searight, in *The Old Pike*, named over 400 taverns along the 271 miles of the National Road between Baltimore and Wheeling, including those in the villages through which the great thoroughfare passed.[5] Even in the mountain division, nearly every mile had its tavern. They were not only in the valleys between the ridges but halfway up the long slopes and at the tops of the passes.

On the Mohawk route west from Albany, taverns averaged one per-mile as far as the Palatine church, fifty-one miles away. On one five-mile stretch below Little Falls, twelve of the thirteen dwellings along the road were taverns, And there were fifty along the first fifty-two miles of the Great Western Turnpike, the alternate route from Albany to the west.[6]

These roads were all trunk routes that served an extensive agricultural hinterland, Heavy loads of farm produce moved slowly over them toward market cities on navigable waters. Returning wagons were loaded with merchandise destined for distribution in the interior. Only a small proportion of the taverns on such roads were likely to be stage houses. The majority were "wagon stands" serving the army of teamsters, or to use a term more common to the times, "waggoners." Some would be "drover's stands," patronized chiefly by those who brought heads of cattle, sheep, and hogs from the back country to fattening grounds near the cities. Drovers preferred the lesser roads where little traffic blocked their driving and where softer surfaces saved the animals' feet, but since satisfactory alternate routes were not at hand in many regions beyond the Atlantic coastal plain, all types of taverns flourished along the same highway. On roads parallel to waterways where freight was shipped by boat (for instance, the Hudson River), there were fewer taverns, and a higher percentage, perhaps, were stage houses.

A tavern keeper along a major roadway found it necessary to specialize, for not only did the stagecoach crowds, the wagoners, and the drovers not mix well, but each demanded a special type of accommodation. Wagoners needed a dry wagon yard large enough for their teams to be tied out all night around the wagons. Their horses were rarely stabled. Drovers required large separate plots into which their herds could be turned for the night, or for a longer period if they needed rest. The stagecoach relay teams, on the other hand, demanded good stabling and close care. Wagoners and drovers brought their own bedding and were content to unroll it on the barroom floor around the huge fireplace, but stagecoach passengers stopping overnight demanded better sleeping accommodations. The stagecoach inn was admittedly the aristocratic hostelry of the highway.

As the nation matured, a similar specialization took place among tavern keepers in cities and the larger villages. The stage house in a city, though its accommodations might be elaborate and attractive in many ways, was usually noisy and expensive. In its public rooms, the stranger could not often meet townspeople who might facilitate his introduction to important people and interesting aspects of a city's life. He lost no time, therefore, if he expected to remain a few days, in transferring his baggage to some other quarters that specialized in quiet lodgings or good board and was patronized as much by city residents as by visitors. Some city taverns sought to attract local patronage by providing facilities for meetings of trade groups and fraternal orders and for balls and celebrations. Other taverns in the town made their appeal chiefly to the farmers of the tributary agricultural neighborhoods. In ports or river towns, there were taverns frequented chiefly by sailors or rivermen. Lowest in the scale, in city or country, were those shops that used their tavern license merely as an excuse for selling liquor. The traveler inadvertently happening upon one of these would soon be given to understand, if he did not at once perceive it, that he would find better accommodations farther on.

But other factors also tended to mold the character of the individual tavern. The New England tavern was different from the tavern of the German regions of Pennsylvania or the Shenandoah Valley, and different again from the taverns of the deeper South. Also, there was the chronological factor. The New England tavern of 1830 was as different from the New England tavern of 1790 as the latter was from the Puritan ordinary. The log cabin inn of the Illinois frontier of 1818 appeared two decades later transformed into a brick or frame mansion several stories in height. The older cities in the same period saw such frame structures giving way to more pretentious brick and stone structures with some features, though they were still in the embryo stage, suggesting the modern hotel.

A stagecoach tavern was, by definition, one where relay teams were kept and where, while the horses were being changed, the travelers could leave their cramped quarters for a few minutes to stretch and refresh themselves. Such halting places were at average intervals of twelve miles along all well-regulated stage lines. The 271 miles of the National Road between Baltimore and Wheeling, for example, was divided into twenty-two sections. Consequently, there were twenty-two relay inns along the route. If two rival companies were on the road, as was usually the case upon the National Pike, the number of stagecoach inns doubled. Opposition lines chose different stopping places, and the landlord was expected to offer a commission to the line that used his house.

In older sections of the country, stagecoach taverns were usually located in cities or villages, but as one went westward or southward over the main trails, more and more of them were in the country. Some were located on prosperous farms. Others in wilder, uncultivated districts, as Count Francesco Arese discovered in 1837 in western Virginia, were "nothing more than a posting-station alone in the middle of the forest."[7] Adam Hodgson, traveling through the weary stretches in the South in 1824, also found many of the taverns to be single houses "standing alone in the woods."[8] Between Charleston and Savannah, they were designated as Four Mile House, Eight Mile House, Twenty-Three Mile House, and so on,[9] a type of nomenclature destined later to become familiar in the Far West. Some of the intermediate relay stations scarcely deserved to be called taverns, for seldom was food available for the chance traveler. Along such unfrequented stretches, it was difficult for a stage line to persuade an enterprising man to erect a tavern. Frequently, the stagecoach company found it necessary to construct them and lease them, or hire men to attend them.

The prize tavern locations were those at which the stages stopped for meals or lodgings. Not surprisingly, these key positions were often in the hands of the stagecoach proprietors themselves. At times on routes where there was little competition, this led to abuses. Distances between meals were set to accommodate the proprietors' pocketbooks rather than the travelers' stomachs. One passenger wrote in 1818 about reaching Loudoun, Pennsylvania, at 8:00 A.M. after five hours on the road and complained: "We were not allowed to breakfast at the tavern in this town, as one of the proprietors of the coach had a house at M'Connel's

Ville."[10] Nor was the first eating place in this instance reached until noon. In case of delays and irregularities, there was, in those days, no recourse for hungry passengers, and the stage could not be stopped before the place was reached where proper arrangements had been made.

A landlord whose tavern, in city or country, was desirably located was in a position to be courted by a stagecoach company, and he could impose his conditions. He might, if it seemed desirable to the company, be invited to partnership in order to bind his interests more closely to the common concern. By contrast, a lesser tavern keeper had to be quick to obey the company's will lest he lose his contracts with them. A threat on the company's part to withdraw its stages usually secured ready compliance with its standards. Often, disgruntled tavern keepers, alienated from an existing line, began opposition lines and drew into their alliance others of their fraternity along the road who aspired to be landlords of stage inns.

Sometimes, landlords who had lost their stage connections felt it necessary to save their faces by explanatory notices in the newspapers. In 1814, for example, the host of the Eagle Tavern in Richmond, Virginia, informed the public that

the complaints which have been made against this house have been preceeded (if not entirely) in very great degree from the entry of the stages into the backyard which now being cleared of all the bustle and confusion attending a State House Yard he only asks a trial from those who have hitherto objected to the establishment on account of the stages.[11]

A notice by Jacob Bergen of the Indian Queen tavern in Philadelphia carried more conviction. He announced in 1782 that

the Elizabeth-Town and Baltimore stages, which so greatly incommoded his house, by the noise and trouble occasioned by their coming in late at nights, and setting out early in the mornings, are now removed from hence; he therefore flatters himself that he now has it in his power to accommodate gentlemen, travellers, and others with genteel and peaceable lodgings.[12]

In addition to his income from stage passengers, the landlord of a stage tavern received a substantial amount from the stage company for keeping and caring for its teams and for boarding its drivers. On important lines, a relay tavern might keep two or four teams of four or six horses each, while taverns located in stagecoach centers would have forty to eighty horses in their stables. In summer, when travel was heavy and extra coaches were frequently sent over the roads, there might be additional teams. Often the tavern keepers owned teams that they hired to the company either regularly or in busy seasons and emergencies. Tavern keepers who did not have the privilege of feeding passengers might be paid at a higher rate for keeping stage teams. E. S. Abdy, traveling in the Great Valley of Virginia in 1834, learned that innkeepers kept the horses for a coach and a driver for $350 a year in addition to the profit from passengers' meals, and that "where the contractor has not the benefit of providing for the passengers, he is paid $500.00 a year."[13]

Horsekeeping was the heaviest item in the bills of any stage line. One tavern keeper on the Philadelphia-Pittsburgh road in 1830 received $681.35 for keeping five teams and drivers and extra horses for three months.[14] According to vouchers from the records of the lines from Zanesville, Ohio, to Maysville, Kentucky, or to Cincinnati in 1838, tavern keepers were receiving $400 a year for boarding a four-horse stage team and its driver.[15] One bill for a team without the driver for three months amounted to $85, or the rate of $340 a year.[16] A package of vouchers for 1852 listed substantially the same charges.[17] How much profit remained for the innholder after his heavy feed bills and other expenses were paid is impossible to ascertain. Most tavern keepers not actually located in a large city had a farm in connection with their tavern upon which they raised not only their horse feed but a substantial part of the table fare for their guests, as well.

LIKE MANY another American institution, the stagecoach inn was defined most sharply in the writings of foreign observers, who were quick to sense its variations from the hostelries of their own lands. To Americans, who wrote of their travels, its features were too familiar to call for comment. Foreign travelers necessarily spent much of their time in public vehicles and public houses, however; so critics sometimes charged that their interpretations of American life were too much influenced by their experiences there.

One discovery that foreigners soon made was that only minimal personal service was available at taverns and in connection with stagecoach journeys. Necessary items for guests (according to American standards of the time) were provided. Anyone who asked for more was considered presumptuous. If a request was made politely, and was not too difficult to fulfill, it was granted. But the foreigner who presumed to give orders to the landlord or tavern help, as if he were in his own country, was ignored. The landlord was a free, equal, and busy man. Help was expensive and independent, and any innkeeper who required his employees to be ever at the beck and call of his guests was likely to find himself without help.

This attitude was a natural in a young country where so many opportunities were offered that no one of initiative would spend time merely serving someone else. In the more mature economy of European countries, an entirely different psychology prevailed. There, only a portion of the population could win its living directly from nature, and an ever larger portion had to get theirs second-hand in the service trades. Most Europeans of wealth supported a small bevy of servants and when they traveled were accompanied by one or more of them. Such wealthy individuals were used to having things done for them. Americans, on the contrary, were expected to take care of their own wants. They helped themselves into stagecoaches and looked after their own baggage; they carried their own candles to their tavern bedchambers at night and frequently took up their own water if they were so fastidious as to wish to wash in their rooms.

South of Mason and Dixon's line, where slaves performed most of the routine tasks of a tavern, the psychology was different. There, guests might give their orders in whatever tone they pleased. Whatever their manner, they were not likely to receive attention any quicker than in the North. The slaves did no more than their master expected them to do, unless a guest took it upon himself to make them some special present.

With respect to the introduction of the custom of tipping, foreign travelers made some very interesting comments. Richard Parkinson, here from 1798 to 1800, wrote, "It is not usual to give servants any thing at taverns, but there are some Englishmen who do it and it is a growing evil, and of disagreeable consequences to travellers."[18] James Stuart, traveling in the country exactly thirty years later, observed that "if they are American, and not of colour," waiters "will seldom receive any money from a passenger, and so generally consider the offer as an insult, that it is not advisable to make it. On the other hand, whenever the waiters are people of colour, or Irish, or generally speaking, European, they will not object to receive a douceur; but let the traveller if he intend to give one do it in private; and let him take an opportunity to let the waiter know his intention in time, for otherwise he will not expect anything, and may perhaps in that case turn out less attentive to your requests than the American, who will seldom refuse if your application be made as a matter of favour in civil terms."[19] Captain Frederick Marryat, the novelist, whose American travels were in 1837 and 1838, wrote: "The Americans are apt to boast that they do not have to pay for civility, as we do in England, by feeing waiters, coachmen, etc. In some respects this is true, but in the cities the custom has become very prevalent... In some of the hotels at New York, and in the principal cities, you not only must fee, but you must fee much higher than you do in England, if you want to be comfortable."[20] Thus, a maturing society found itself, despite its earlier ideals, gradually accepting the attitudes of older societies across the Atlantic.

ONE OF the most difficult mental readjustments that foreign travelers found themselves obliged to make in this country related to the social standing of their host. In European countries, innkeeping was a humble and somewhat menial occupation, but it was quite the contrary in America. "Innkeepers here are men of the first rank," wrote the duc de La Rochefoucauld Liancourt in 1799.[21] "The hotelkeepers of the country are the noblesse of the district," echoed Patrick Shirreff as late as 1835.[22] Francis Hall, writing about his 1816 journey, said: "The innkeepers of America are, in most villages, what we vulgarly call 'topping men,' field officers of militia, with good farms attached to their taverns... they are apt to think... that the travellers rather receive, than confer a favour by being accommodated at their homes."[23] Adam Hodgson wrote in 1824 that the landlord was, "in general, well informed and well behaved, and the independence of manner... appears to rise naturally from easy circumstances, and a consciousness that, both with respect to situation and intelligence, he is at least on a level with the generality of his visitors."[24]

There were several reasons for the high position that, in this period, landlords held in the esteem of their townsmen. Timothy Dwight, writing in 1821, explained the situation in New England:

Our ancestors considered an Inn as a place, where travellers must trust themselves, their horses, baggage, and money; where women as well as men, must at times lodge, might need humane and delicate offices, and might be subjected to disagreeable exposures. To provide for safety and comfort, and against danger and mischief, in all these cases, they took particular pains in the laws, and administrations, to prevent Inns from being kept by vicious, unprincipled, worthless men. Every innkeeper in Connecticut must be recommended by the Selectmen, and Civil Authority, Constables and Grand Jurors of the town, in which he resides; and then licensed at the discretion of the Court of Common Pleas. Substantially in the same manner is the business regulated in Massachusetts and New Hampshire. In consequence of this system men of no small personal respectability have ever kept Inns in this country.[25]

In sections of the country where such strict regulation was not traditional, other circumstances operated to elevate the innkeeper's position. Frequently, a pioneer taverner's location at a strategic crossroads, river crossing, or desirable valley site became the nucleus around which eventually clustered a little store, a blacksmith shop, a post office, and other institutions of a village settlement. Often the tavern keeper was honored with the postmastership, and not infrequently did the new post office bear his name.

As long as tavern keeping remained one of the more profitable businesses of the day, it was respectable and attracted able and energetic men. Their contact with all types of people gave them experience and self-confidence. They were often good politicians, and the best of them held the trust of the common people and served frequently in public offices, local and state. In the isolated communities of their day, they were often among the best informed about current events because their position gave them special channels of communication with the outside world. Stages brought the news of notable occurrences along their routes. In stage taverns, the leading newspapers were at hand.

Another source of the tavern keeper's popularity lay in his office as host to the militia on training day. If, as a result, he could not be elected at least a major, he had missed his calling. Having once held the rank, the title was his for life. Foreigners who took their military titles seriously and considered even a captain to be a kind of superior fellow expressed their surprise at this. "At first," wrote Hodgson, "I was a little surprised, on enquiring where the stage stopped to breakfast to be told, at Major Todd's; to dine? At Colonel Brown's."[26] Another traveler commented, "The titles which the landlords of Globe Inn, where I now am, bear, sound unusual in such a connection to an Englishman, and I find it difficult sometimes to address them without a smile: one of them is a general of brigade, and a member of the legislature; his partner is a colonel and sheriff of the district: their bar-keeper is distinguished as a major: and the superintendent of the negroes, or head waiter, is a captain."[27]

Placing so much emphasis upon the landlord probably gave him more than his due. The real responsibility for the excellence of an inn rested with its hostess. Its culinary attractions, its cleanliness, and its general air of comfort, if they existed, were of her contriving. If she failed, it was almost impossible for a man to redeem the reputation of a house. "Shepherd would keep a good tavern," wrote Timothy Bigelow of the inn in Canojoharie, New York, "if his wife was as attentive, neat and active as he is."[28] Apparently, hostesses generally measured up to their tasks. One proof lay in the number of widows who continued to keep taverns successfully after their husbands' deaths. Searight mentioned a dozen or more inns along the National Road kept by widows and said that they usually kept the best houses along the way.[29]

Tavern keepers always had plenty of daughters, or so it seems, for travelers rarely failed to mention them. They must have been a considerable attraction to an inn. Thurlow Weed remembered the great popularity of Mrs. Cary's inn at Westmoreland, New York, where six or seven attractive and accomplished daughters known to all travelers as "Mother Cary's chickens" made the house pleasant for its guests.[30] The daughters, of course, came in for their full share of the cleaning, cooking, and waiting on tables. But Europeans who looked for coquetry were usually doomed to disappointment. One traveler noted their "grave deportment and air of cool indifference." Francis Hall observed penetratingly in 1818, "Their behavior is reserved in the extreme, but it enables them to serve as domestics, without losing their rank of equality with those on whom they attend."[31]

But, of course, there was always the exception, and John Melish, who traveled in the eastern part of the United States from 1806 to 1811, reported on one interesting experience. During a stage journey, he and his fellow passengers had stopped to water their horses at a small tavern near what is today McConnelsburg, Pennsylvania. Melish described the tavern as "a miserable log cabin" that was kept by an old Irishwoman who had a son and two daughters, "one of them rather handsome." He wrote, "And from inquirey we learned that the old hag picked up a miserable pittance at this place by selling whiskey and—the chastity of her daughters!"[32]

RARELY in stage taverns was a landlord his own bartender. If he stepped behind the bar to mix a drink, it was only as a special honor to some guest. The bartender was an establishment's chief employee and was usually the most important personage except the host and hostess. His duties included those which today fall to the hotel clerk, a functionary who appeared only after the introduction of hotel lobbies in the 1840s and 1850s. All requests in tavern days were made known at the bar, and all payments were made there. The kitchen, dining room, and stable were outside the bartender's province, but otherwise, in the absence of the landlord, he gave the orders to the tavern help.

"The furniture of the bar-room is invariably the same,"wrote Captain Marryat, "a wooden clock, map of the United States, map of the State, the Declaration of Independence, a looking-glass, with a hair-brush and comb hanging to it by strings, *pro bono publica* — sometimes with the extra embellishment of one or two miserable pictures, such as General Jackson scrambling upon a horse, with fire or steam coming out of his nostrils, going to the battle of New Orleans, & C. & C."[33] Traveling across New York in 1830, John Fowler found the walls of the barrooms "covered with advertisements of elections — fares of stages and steamboats, when and where running — auctions — sales of land — sales of stock — sales of merchandise — sales of everything that can be sold — quack medicines without end — the most prominent being specifics for dyspepsia."[34]

Just before meal hours when all were waiting for the gong to ring, the barroom crowds became loud and noisy. Also, just before stage time, there was much activity as travelers came in to set down their baggage and fortify themselves at the bar for their long journey. The stage office and stage books were in the barroom, unless the house was a sufficiently important central point to have a stage office in a separate room with a special stage clerk.

A foreign traveler described the scene. Although only five or six persons were seated, not one of the fifteen or sixteen chairs was available to the stranger who entered the room. "Each of these individuals occupied three or four chairs. He sat upon one, laid his legs upon another, whirled around a third and perhaps chewed the paint from the back of the fourth.... none of them offered to resign me a chair; but I suppose the clouds of tobacco vapor which filled the room prevented them from observing that I wanted one."[35] James Stuart noted that "backgammon-boards, and checquer-boards are in the bar-rooms generally all over the country" and that the bartender frequently played with the loungers. Cards, he reported, were seldom seen.[36] A livelier, more intimate atmosphere usually prevailed in the evening, when the locals dropped in to learn the news. Crops, trade, local gossip, public questions and politics, and theology were leading themes of conversation. Notices that might have been roughly equivalent to newspaper advertisements were stuck on the barroom walls. Tobacco chewers managed to get near the fireplace, or, after stoves came into use, they calculated their distances from the large sandbox that served as a spittoon.

Somewhat gloomy in contrast to the barroom was the public parlor, usually on the opposite side of the entrance hallway. Here the ladies rested before or after meals if the stagecoach allowed enough time, and here family parties might congregate or a man enter to talk with some lady. But rarely did males venture there of their own accord. Apparently, most of these parlors were poorly and tastelessly furnished, but some were made attractive and comfortable by the better hostesses. Harriet Martineau painted a pleasant picture about 1835 when she wrote that "the hotel parlours, in various parts of the country, were papered with the old-fashioned papers, I believe French, which represented a sort of panorama of a hunting party, the ladies in scarlet riding-habits, as I remember the landlord of the inn at Bray, near Dublin, to have been proud of in his best parlour. At Schenectady, the Bay of Naples, with its fishing boats on the water, and groups of lazzaroni on the shore, adorned our parlour walls."[37]

Though every chamber had, or was supposed to have, its bowl and pitcher, most men preferred to make their toilet in the barroom, where there were public towels and, as has been noted, a mirror and comb. In summer, the wash basin might be moved outside to a wooden bench on the porch or beside the well. It was especially difficult to procure hot water in one's room, and, said Stuart in 1828, "it is very general practice for travellers to shave in public in the bar-room, where there is always a looking glass."[38] John Howison recorded an exemplary incident: "I entered a tavern, and desired that water might be sent into a room. 'Water,' exclaimed the landlord, 'Why, here's water, and towels enough in the bar—I guess all the gentlemen washes there.'" Howison added, "I surveyed the bar room curiously, and found things in such a state, that I would rather have worn the coat of dust I had received while in the stage, than attempted ablution in it."[39]

It must be said in favor of the Englishmen that they, at least, desired not to stop with washing face and hands. Stuart observed in 1833 that "the practice of travellers washing at the doors, or in the porticos or stoops, or at the wells of taverns and hotels once a day, is most prejudicial to health; the ablution of the body, which ought never to be neglected, at least twice a day in a hot climate, being altogether inconsistent with it." He added, "I have found it more difficult in travelling in the United States to procure a liberal supply of water at all times of the day and night in my bedchamber, than to obtain any other necessary."[40] The average American of the day, it must be admitted, was notably careless in his toilet. The story was told by Captain Marryat in 1839 of a traveler in Indiana who had not yet finished his morning toilet when the stage was ready at the door. The driver sent the bartender to get the passenger, and word came back that he would be there directly. 'What is he about?' asked the driver impatiently. 'Cleaning his teeth,' was the answer. 'Cleaning his teeth!' roared the driver; 'By the ——,' and away went the horses at a gallop leaving the passenger behind.[41]

MEALS were served at fixed hours, and a guest had to be present at the appointed time. Otherwise, he would very likely go hungry, though under the American plan, which universally prevailed, he was charged for the meal he had missed. In the great cities where patronage was sufficient, the landlord might ease the situation slightly by setting two tables, one half an hour after the other. If a stagecoach was expected but was late, the landlord naturally held food for the passengers after the regular dinner hours.

In the better taverns in large towns and cities, a bell rang twice before meals. Between the sound of the warning bell and the final bell, a guest was expected to make his toilet and plant himself in a strategic position before the dining room door. One traveler described the ensuing scene at a notable stage tavern in Augusta, Georgia: "Negroes are stationed at each door of the dining room, and when the second bell announces that all is ready, they turn the key, and escape as for their lives,—a general rush is made by the hungry company who were eagerly waiting outside, and without ceremony they commence a general attack upon the smoking board."[42] In smaller taverns, the anouncement was merely "Dinner is served."

The diners were all seated at one long table. This was essential in connection with the genuine old-fashioned American *table d'hote*. Only in the largest city dining rooms where perhaps several hundred were fed was there likely to be a second table. Everyone helped himself to a convenient chair and sat down without waiting for his neighbor. In a smaller tavern, the landlord would preside personally over his more intimate group and probably would invite ladies and prominent guests to take seats near him at the head of the table.[43]

The American *table d'hote* was another institution that developed because of the high price of labor. It was time-saving to bring the food to the table in large serving dishes as at a family dinner, instead of bothering with small dishes for individual portions. Diners helped themselves to whatever appealed to them and waited on each other. Waitresses needed only to keep water glasses, coffee cups, and serving dishes filled. There was no clearing away of dishes between courses because all courses from soup to desert were on the table at the beginning. This sped up the meal, especially since a diner passed immediately from one course to another without waiting for his neighbor. To a foreigner's utter astonishment, some Americans were up and gone within ten or twelve minutes. So efficient was the *table d'hote* arrangement that the dining room probably would be cleared in less than half an hour.

The *table d'hote* manner of dining was not conducive to conversation at meals, however. Long tables prevented the group intimacy that the small separate tables of cafes encouraged. Americans on the whole tended strictly to business while in the dining room and postponed their conversation until the meal was over. Then it was the fashion for men to retire to the barroom or piazza and converse while resting and smoking a "segar."[44] To the European mind, this manner of dining was little less than vulgar. The democracy of the common table was bad enough. "You are, however, pretty sure against the conversation of unpolished people, because the Americans are usually mute at table," was the caustic comment of Prince Maxmillian of Weid;[45] while Patrick Shirreff remarked caustically "A meal in the United States and Canada is simply a feeding, and not in any degree a conversational meeting."[46]

But in the quantity and quality of its food, the American tavern was outstanding. A "really superb dinner" was Henry Tudor's comment at Fredericktown, Maryland; "nowhere in the world do people live better than in the United States…and in very few countries do the public live half so well."[47] "In America a traveller's sufferings are rarely connected with the table," said Thomas Hamilton in 1834; "Go where he may, he finds abundance of good and wholesome food."[48] It cost dearly in a new country to build and furnish a tavern in the style to which foreign travelers were accustomed, but to set a good table was an easier matter. The kitchen was supplied directly from the farm of the landlord or one of his neighbors. There were few middlemen involved in the marketing of food, even in the cities. On the frontier, farm products were supplemented by game and wild fruits. Besides, it was partly the style of service that was responsible for the variety of dishes on the American table. Americans, in order to save labor, brought everything to the table at once, and there allowed the traveler to make his own choice.

Breakfast seemed to be the leading meal, and well it might have been to stagecoach passengers, for they generally set out at two, three, four, or five o'clock in the morning and were on the road until seven or eight o'clock before a stop was made for their first meal. Appetites were sharpened by the morning ride. Charles Fenno Hoffman in 1835 drew a picture of the passengers eagerly attacking "the huge piles of buckwheat cakes that smoked along the board flanked each by a cold apple-pie." "The beef-steak was decidedly the favorite dish," he added.[49] "They always gave us plentiful fare," wrote Francis Hall in 1819, "particularly at breakfast, where veal-cutlets, sweetmeats, cheese, eggs, and ham were most liberally set before us."[50]

"Dinner is little more than a repetition of breakfast, with spirits instead of coffee," Hall also noted. He added, "I never heard wine called for; the common drink is a small cyder: rum, whisky, and brandy, are placed on the table, and the use of them left to the discretion of the company, who seem rarely to abuse the privilege. Tea is a meal of the same solid construction with breakfast, answering also for supper."[51]

James Stuart wrote in 1833 that "Virginia dinners were more abundant, if possible, than elsewhere," and described one as consisting among other things of roast turkey, a whole ham, roast beef, canvass-back ducks, a pie of game, potatoes, and hominey.[52] South of Virginia, the meals seemed to be very uneven. They could still be good in the taverns of conscientious landlords in the cities, but food was more expensive and more difficult to secure in variety. According to Charles J. Latrobe in 1825: "Both the mode and style of entertainment for the traveller were vastly inferior to those of the more Northern States; and the same remark applies to the whole South as far as one could judge. The meals were scanty and invariably the same. Fresh meat was rarely seen, and the whole population seemed to exist on salt provisions alone, with now and then the addition of a little poultry and pastry."[53] Tyrone Power recorded an 1836 conversation with his landlady at a lone log tavern on the much traveled road between Columbus, Georgia, and Montgomery, Alabama, when she informed him that "the mere necessities of living were very limited; that butcher's meat was only attainable at Columbus, and that any attempt to rear a stock of poultry was ridiculous, as the Indians of the country invariably stole every feather."[54]

American cooking in the hotels of the larger cities was better even than in London taverns, according to Captain Marryat, but he complained of the grease and corn bread in the back country. "In a new country pork is more easily raised than any other meat, and the Americans eat a great deal of pork, which renders the cooking in the small taverns very greasy, with the exception of the Virginia taverns, where they fry chickens without grease in a way which would be admired by Ude himself, but this is a state receipe, handed down from generation to generation."[55]

The charge for meals was usually higher to stage passengers than to persons traveling in any other style. "Here [Bedford, Pennsylvania] I perceived that they made a difference in the charge between the passengers in the stage and those on horseback." wrote John Melish in 1811: "the former paying 31¼ cents, and the latter only 25 cents [for breakfast]. I inquired into the reason of it, and was informed that it was in consequence of being obliged to prepare victuals for a certain number of passengers by the stage whether they came or not."[56] Fortesque

Cuming had found the same discrimination in prices in 1808, but further west near Pittsburgh, both he and Melish discovered that the charge to all comers for breakfast was but a quarter.[57] If prices decreased in going toward the frontier, they were high along the Atlantic seaboard.

THE SMALLEST ITEM in tavern expenses was the charge for lodging, and judging from many descriptions, it was the side of tavern hospitality that was most neglected. As the stagecoach era progressed, the time allowed on the main routes for night stops so dwindled that one had little opportunity to enjoy one's bed. In the earlier decades, the unimproved state of the roads did not permit much night travel. The stage set out at "sunrise" or at five o'clock, or in summer perhaps at four o'clock, and it reached its destination ordinarily between six and eight in the evening. Even in later years, such hours were customary on frontier lines where the earlier road conditions existed or on local lines where there was no real need for speed. But on the major highways, as the roadbed improved, greater speed, shorter stops, and longer journeys each day were the rule for through coaches. The hour of starting in the morning was pushed back to three or two o'clock, and in some instances, even to one o'clock; and the scheduled hour of halting for the night was nine o'clock. Frequently, the coach was an hour or two late, and sometimes it barely arrived in time to enable the passengers to obtain something to eat before their next day's coach was at the door.

Under such conditions, passengers were not likely to be too critical of their beds. Captain Marryat spent six successive days and nights on the road on a return trip from Louisville, Kentucky, to Baltimore in 1837 and wrote that he "was glad when the coach stopped for a few hours, to throw off my coat and lie down on a bed."[58] Harriet Martineau wrote in 1838 of similar short halts during her southern tour: "While the meal was preparing, it was my wont to lie down and doze, in spite of hunger; if I could find a bed or sofa, it was well . . . under conditions like this a good bed would only increase the torture of being so prematurely awakened."[59]

If the usual charge of 12½ or 25 cents for lodging seems ridiculously small, it must be remembered that this did not mean a room to oneself, as in a modern hotel. It meant a bed, or more accurately, if the bed were double, one's share of a bed. Americans of the period considered such accommodations to be quite sufficient, and probably would not have thought it worthwhile to pay more for anything better. Most of them had grown up under the primitive housing conditions of a pioneering society, and much of the frontier spirit of accommodation to circumstances persisted. The frontier landlord was duty-bound to find room for every guest who applied, even if it meant assigning two or three strangers to the same bed and finding floor space around the fireplace for any who appeared after the beds were filled to capacity.

Individual bedrooms required heating arrangements and additional furniture, and they were more troublesome to keep clean. American standards had not yet been raised to such levels. Unless they were traveling with their families, men had no thought of separate bedrooms. As soon as possible, however, a landlord added a few smaller rooms to his establishment in order to make it possible to accommodate women travelers, families, and noted guests. This was the way of evolution in the older east, where taverns were built with large common bedrooms down to 1820, as well as in the west.

John Davis, who traveled up and down the Atlantic seaboard between 1798 and 1802, left many interesting descriptions of the taverns of the region. At Frenchtown, Maryland, for instance, there were only six beds for sixteen stagecoach passengers, with the large beds expected to hold three each. Davis proposed to sit up by the fireplace all night, "but sleep overcame me and I retired to bed undisturbed by the nasal trump of my bed-fellow who snorted like a horse."[60] Frederick DeRoos in 1826 also cited instances of three in a bed and reported at one place that he secured a single bed only "after a desperate struggle" and not without "undergoing a severe objurgation from the landlady, who could not understand such unaccommodating selfishness."[61] Thurlow Weed wrote of the old days when "a traveller who objected to a stranger as a bed-fellow was regarded as unreasonably fastidious." It was not so bad, of course, when one could select his partner and both could retire at once, but, continued Weed, "nothing was more common, after a passenger had retired, than to be awakened by the landlord, who appeared with a tallow candle, showing a stranger into your bed."[62]

By the second quarter of the nineteenth century, a traveler in the older regions no longer found it difficult in stagecoach inns to get individual beds, for accommodations had caught up with the demand. He might still be shown to a room with several beds, however, unless he insisted on a private room. G. T. Vigne wrote about 1830 that his request for a room with a single bed seldom failed. On one occasion in Kentucky, however, when he persisted in his demand, he remarked, "The landlord . . . thought I must be ill."[63] Patrick Shirreff, returning east from Illinois a few years later, recorded that he found "the hotels gradually improve on leaving Springfield, Illinois, and many of those in the State of Ohio appeared to be everything a reasonable person could wish, with the exception of the want of single-bedded rooms."[64] By this time in the larger cities, not only were single rooms available, but bedrooms with adjacent private parlors were provided for those who could afford them.

Frequently, because of fatigue, or the shortness of the stops, and also, sometimes, discouraged by the appearance of the bed, travelers lay down without undressing. In the South, wrote Martineau, "If there are no sheets, or yellow ones, the ladies spread their dressing-gowns over the bed, and use their cloaks for a covering. They wrap up their heads to baffle the draft from a broken window behind the bed, and as soon as they are fairly dreaming they hear the stage horn, see a light under the door, and the black woman looks in to admonish them to dress in haste, which they do sick and dizzy."[65] The freshness of the morning air when once on the road and the beauty of the sunrise stealing through the forests eventually dissipated the feeling of fatigue, and a hearty American breakfast atoned for all.

LIKE THE STAGE DRIVERS, many tavern keepers also became celebrities of a sort along the well-traveled routes. Thomas Endsley, for instance, was the owner of the popular Endsley House near Somerfield, Maryland. He had been born near Richmond, Virginia, in 1787, the only child of Swiss immigrant parents, and he migrated to Maryland in 1819 where he became involved in the tavern profession. He first rented the old Frost House at Frostburg, and then in 1823 he bought an old farm near Somerfield for $8,000. Hard working and industrious, Endsley refurbished the delapidated farm, made it productive again, and constructed a large stone tavern on the property. Endsley House soon acquired a reputation as one of the most pleasant taverns on the National Road: The rooms were neat and clean, and the table was marvelous, supplied mostly with fresh produce from Endsley's farm. He signed a contract with Lucius Stockton for coaches on the Old Line, and as long as the line was in existence all the Stockton coaches stopped at Endsley House. Endsley, who soon became quite wealthy, himself joined the local militia, and became, like so many other tavern keepers, "Captain" Endsley. He had eight children, and one of his daughters, Mary Ann, married the legendary stagecoach driver, Redding Bunting (who was discussed in chapter 7).[66]

William Sheets was another prominent tavern owner of the period, although he had a much more checkered career than Endsley. Born in

Virginia in 1798, he first became a wagoner and then a stagecoach driver on the National Road. He next tried his hand at tavern keeping, but he went through a series of failures, caused mostly by his excessive drinking. At age forty, he finally decided to straighten himself out: he quit drinking and took a lease on the Negro Mountain House on the National Road. From that point on, his fortunes soared. His business prospered, he purchased the tavern, and he became a wealthy man. In 1855, at the age of fifty-seven, he realized that the glory days of eastern staging were over, and he moved to Jefferson County, Iowa, where he involved himself in profitable land speculation until he died at the age of ninety-four.[67]

THE AMERICAN SUCCESS STORY of tavern keeper Thomas Endsley was unfortunately marred by one tragic flaw—he was a noted slave hunter, capturing runaway slaves and returning them to their owners. On one occasion, he cornered three fleeing slaves who were resting in his barn, and he managed to subdue two of them by himself. Fortunately, the third escaped and was able to make his way to safety in Canada.[68]

The golden days of eastern staging were also the last, sad days of slavery in America, and accounts of that inhuman practice are part of the records of life on the stagecoach routes. For instance, a tract of property that was being sold in Washington County, Pennsylvania, in 1784 for later use as a tavern was sold for forty shillings an acre, payable "in installments of money, iron, and one negro."[69]

And there are many accounts of skirmishes with runaway slaves. Thomas Searight told of one Richard Shadburn, who had been a wagoner for many years on the National Road. Shadburn was actually a runaway slave: He had been born a slave in Virginia and had escaped as a young man. He was apparently of fair complexion, and he had been able to pass as a white man for many years. One day in 1842, Shadburn had stopped at McGruder's tavern in Pratt's Hallow, Maryland, to rest and water his horses, when his subterfuge was discovered. In one of the arriving stagecoaches was Shadburn's original owner from Virginia, who recognized his runaway slave. The owner shouted for help from the other passengers, and they tried to catch Shadburn. One man grabbed the runaway slave, but he managed to wrestle himself free. Then the owner fired a pistol at the fleeing Shadburn, but he missed. Richard Shadburn fled, leaving his wagon behind, and he continued his journey until he arrived in Canada, where he spent the remainder of his life.[70]

But there were also, happily, opponents of slavery during that period. Endsley himself had five sons, and they all grew up to be staunch abolitionists. Then there was William Willey, a shoemaker in Endsley's own town of Somerfield. An abolitionist, he assisted fugitive slaves, harboring as many as eight or ten in a single night, as they made their way along the underground railroad to freedom. Willey is said to have hidden, fed, and assisted more fugitive slaves than any other person on the old National Road.[71]

Fortunately, as eastern staging entered its Indian summer period in those years before the Civil War, the days of American slavery were numbered, and the time of Lincoln's Emancipation Proclamation in 1863 was not far away.

THE WORD *hotel* was imported from France into eastern cities at the end of the eighteenth century. The first known use of it in the United States was in 1790 by Joseph Corre who called his newly opened Broadway tavern in New York "Corre's Hotel." The City Hotel, opened in 1794 on Broadway just below Trinity Church, was the first well-known institution to adopt the word. One of the largest inns in the country, the headquarters for several important stage lines, and a conspicuous center of metropolitan life in the first two decades of the nineteeth century, the City Hotel undoubtedly helped to popularize the new style in names. The Tammany Hotel was opened in 1810, and by the end of the War of 1812 there were the Planter's Hotel in Charleston, the Columbia Hotel in Richmond, the Pittsburgh and Western hotels in Pittsburgh, Butler's Hotel in New Haven, and others. By 1830, every town of consequence west to the Mississippi had its "hotel." Also, there existed widespread use of the simple word *house*, usually preceded by the landlord's name, a fashion that came in as the use of the old-fashioned tavern signs and names declined. In competition with these two movements, the word *tavern* began to lose its place, and by the end of the Civil War, it was infrequently heard.

All houses bearing the name *hotel* before 1829 were merely "over-size inns," according to Jefferson Williamson, the hotel's historian.[72] They retained the atmosphere of inns. The first to mark a distinct change, the "true grandparent of all the swagger hostelries that dot the land today,"[73] was the Tremont Hotel in Boston, which opened in 1829. Its impressive list of innovations entitled it to the honor. It was the world's largest at the time, filling an entire city block and containing 170 rooms. It was designed by Isaiah Rogers, who subsequently designed the Astor Hotel in New York, the Burnet House in Cincinnati, the Galt House in Louisville, and the Charleston Hotel in Charleston, all of which represented the best in hotel architecture at the time and set the example for lesser hostelries. The Tremont also possessed the first "lobby," though until after 1850, this room was usually known as the "office."

The modern hotel belongs to the railroad age as completely as the wayside inn is associated with stagecoach days. The institution that it became was made possible only by the concentration of travelers at rail centers. By the time that the Astor Hotel, the first to outclass the Tremont, was built in New York in 1836, the stages were on the retreat in eastern metropolitan districts. The few local lines that remained made their headquarters at lesser hotels where some of the old-time atmosphere lingered.

THE VAST NETWORK of stagecoach taverns during the golden days of eastern staging illustrated another important contribution of the American stagecoach—it supported, directly or indirectly, a considerable population.

There were, of course, the proprietors and the drivers. But there were also stage office agents in the leading cities and managing agents who traveled the roads, inspected the horses, vehicles, and facilities, received the money, and paid the bills in periodic settlements with tavern keepers and blacksmith shops. There were the stable hands. There was the landlord and his help in the stagecoach taverns. There were the coachsmith, blacksmith, and farrier (or horseshoer) in a service industry so technical that it called for specialization and so busy that it supported such a division of labor. Finally, there were the farmers, who found in the stage lines a market for the horses they raised and for oats, corn, and hay this working stock consumed.

In the nineteenth century, there was therefore a genuine stagecoach industry in the eastern United States—indeed, a stagecoach culture.

XIII

Steamboats and Stages —
Rivals and Partners

 ALMOST FROM THE BEGINNING of the story of the American stagecoach, there seemed to be a seesaw struggle between land travel and water carriers. At first, the sailing packets were without doubt more efficient than the clumsy early wagons that traveled over primitive roads, and they were preferred wherever there was a waterway. But with the improvement of stagecoach design and road construction and the finite number of waterways, stages began to gain ascendancy. Often, though, there was a partnership between land and water, part of a journey would be taken by stagecoach, and part of it by ship.

A new chapter in this struggle began in 1807 when Robert Fulton demonstrated in the Hudson River that the steamboat was commercially practical. Interest in reviving the old land-water combination routes increased, although the steamboat did not really come into its own in eastern waters until the 1820s.

After his successful demonstration, Fulton and his partner, Chancellor Robert R. Livingston, won an exclusive privilege from the State of New York to run steamboats on its waters. Thus, the Hudson was their domain, and before the outbreak of the War of 1812 they had five boats operating on the river and on Jersey waters connected with New York harbor. Popular interest in the innovation was tremendous, and stage lines running parallel to the Hudson must have felt the competition at once. The steamboat line along the east side of the river probably ceased operation for the winter season of 1810. That winter, under the banner *Steamboats Defeated and Stages Revived!*, a notice appeared in the New York *Evening Post* that "The New York and Albany Mail Stage will commence running on Sunday, 10th December, on the east side of Hudson river, everyday—and arrive in Albany in 57 hours."[1] The following winter much the same winter stagecoach arrangements were explained under a notice headed:

> Since Steam Boats are no more the rage
> We'll introduce our New-Mail Stage
> As going by steam is out of date,
> Pray take your seats ere 'tis too late.[2]

The only other route upon which the competition of the steamboat was felt seriously before the War of 1812 was the one across New Jersey between New York and Philadelphia, still the most important travel route in the country. The Fulton-Livingston interests, because of their exclusive privilege in New York waters, including those of New York harbor, found themselves able also to control the approaches to the various east Jersey ports, much to the disgust and discomfiture of their chief rival, Colonel John Stevens of Hoboken, who in 1808 had launched his *Phoenix*, the fruit of much experimental labor and a better boat than his opponents' *Clermont*.[3] For a time, Stevens ran the *Phoenix* between New York and New Brunswick, New Jersey, where his passengers changed to stagecoaches if they were enroute to Philadelphia. Faced with the threats of competition and legal action, however, he was persuaded to send his boat around New Jersey—the first steamboat to navigate ocean waters—into the Delaware, where in July 1809 it was placed in regular operation between Philadelphia and Trenton.[4]

Stevens swallowed his pride sufficiently to cooperate with the Livingstons in working out by 1810 the first through steamboat-stage service across New Jersey, with a Livingston boat, the *Rariton*, taking passengers from New York to New Brunswick and the *Phoenix* accepting them at Bordentown. Rival stage lines, traveling somewhat different routes, competed bitterly for the traffic between the landings until the season on 1812. That year, Stevens and Livingston worked out an agreement with three stage operators and established a system for selling through passages: The captains of the steamboats collected the passage money and issued the tickets, while the stage operators charged twenty-five cents less than usual for their portion of the route and allowed the steamboat proprietors to keep the difference as a commission for each passenger procured. The stage operators were each to provide the same number of coaches and were to share the passengers equally.[5]

Only the mail stages that traveled via Trenton and the Swiftsure line still further to the north continued to operate without steamboat connections at either end. Perhaps significantly it was in these years that the mail line deteriorated to the point where the postmaster general was forced to extend the public line first to Trenton, then to New Brunswick, and finally, in 1813, to Jersey City.[6] The Swiftsure line was also fortified with a mail contract and obviously profited considerably from local travel. To its regular newspaper notice, the Swiftsure line in 1810 added a defiant postscript:

N.B. The Steamboat (or rather Smoak Boat) advertises to travel more expeditiously than any Line except the Mail. We therefore beg leave to inform the public, that they leave New York three hours before we do, and do not arrive in Philadelphia until our passengers have had a comfortable refreshment, if then! and the fare and expenses on the road are nearly double to ours.[7]

At the same time, the advertisements for the *Rariton* boasted:

Such as wish to avoid a dangerous ferry, mud, dust and mosquitoes, will undoubtedly give the preference to this elegant and easy mode of travelling, where breakfast, dinner and tea is served up during their progress, in a style more agreeable than many of the Road Taverns.[8]

The earliest steamboats may not have been much faster than the stagecoaches. They were from the first, however, a fascinating novelty and a welcome relief after hours of highway jolting. What traveler would prefer to sit cramped between his fellow passengers in a stage for hours when he could move about freely on the cool, clean-aired deck of a river steamer? The newer steamboats built during and after the War of 1812 were more comfortable and more efficient and averaged double the speed of the earlier ones, so that any stagecoaches attempting competition on parallel routes were left far behind. The stage lines, since they could not compete, were soon forced to act as feeders to the steamboats and to take the passengers from steamboat terminals. They profited from the steamboats in the long run; the steamboats, by making passage easier, cheaper, faster, and more enjoyable, seemed to stimulate far more travel than there had ever been before.

Two FACTORS slowed the extension of steamboat service into New England and southern waters: the Fulton-Livingston monopoly and the War of 1812. The monopoly granted by New York aroused opposition throughout New England but especially in Connecticut. Connecticut was interested in encouraging its own steamboats and felt they should be permitted to enter New York harbor at will if it was expected to reciprocate. The monopoly in 1815 placed the *Fulton* in service between New York and New Haven, and there was a later attempt in 1817 to run to New London and Norwich in connection with the stage line to Boston. So intense did the feeling become that Connecticut was induced to pass a retaliatory act in 1822 forbidding New York steamboats to enter Connecticut waters.[9]

Also, in 1817 the Fulton-Livingston interests had sent their *Firefly,* a slow and awkward little vessel, to Rhode Island to run between Newport and Providence. But these ports were dominated by long-existing packet lines and by strong packet interests, all determined to give battle. Here, the swift, efficient, and relatively comfortable sailing boats had reached their highest development, and the clumsy steamboat found itself outclassed. The packets agreed to take passengers between the two cities for twenty-five cents and to refund the money if they did not arrive before the steamboat. The *Firefly* was soon withdrawn, and the packets reigned unchallenged in Rhode Island waters for another four years.[10] Ill luck also dogged the first steamboat in Boston harbor, the *Massachusetts,* which likewise arrived in 1817. On her first run—an excursion—to Salem, her machinery broke down, and the passengers had to be returned to their homes in stagecoaches. The event was a blow to the boat's prestige; it was little patronized and soon withdrawn, a commercial failure.[11] Wrote the Reverend William Bently of Salem in his diary: "The certainty of reaching Boston in two hours at two thirds of the distance by water, gives every advantage to the Stage. We have 21 miles to the Town and then all the inconveniences of entering and leaving the boat when thirteen miles may carry us to the bridge from the entrance of the Turnpike and we can be taken up and put down at the places we may chuse."[12]

SOUTHERN WATERS proved more hospitable to steamboats once the British fleet lifted its blockade. A small steamboat had been sent to Baltimore before Chesapeake Bay was closed and was, in March 1814, placed in motion on the upper bay, running to Frenchtown three times a week, but its operations were soon interrupted by the appearance of the British naval forces.[13] Additional steamboats could not enter the bay until 1815. Captain Moses Rogers then brought the *Eagle* around and in July paced her on the run between Baltimore and Elkton at the head of the bay. Stages carried passengers across the narrow peninsula to Wilmington, then the steamboat *Vesta* conveyed them up the Delaware to Philadelphia. This "New Steamboat Line" thus offered the same kind of connected land-water service between Philadelphia and Baltimore as had been inaugurated across New Jersey five years earlier.[14]

A few months earlier—in May 1815—the steamboat made its debut in Potomac waters when the *Washington*, a boat constructed by Fulton in response to an order placed in 1813 by the Potomac Steam Boat Company, was finally delivered. It was put in service to run from Washington down the Potomac river to the mouth of Acquia Creek, from which landing passengers were carried by stages the remaining eight miles to Fredericksburg. After a few experimental runs, a schedule was fixed that provided for the steamboat to leave Washington at 2:30 P.M., after the early stages had arrived from Baltimore. The boat reached the mouth of Acquia Creek the same night so that passengers going south could lodge in Fredericksburg, and returned to Washington the next morning in time for passengers to take the afternoon stages to Baltimore. By this arrangement, almost a day was cut in the previous time it took to travel between Baltimore and Fredericksburg, since passengers were now transported in either direction in nineteen hours.[15] The successful operation of the *Washington* on the Potomac meant the end of the stage line from Alexandria south to Fredericksburg, except in winter. The steamboats of that day with their flimsy paddlewheels could not operate with even small quantities of ice in the water. So they would be laid up for a few months, and the stage line from Alexandria to Fredericksburg would be revived.[16] Similarly, in winter the stages would be put into service between Baltimore and Elkton.[17] But in summer, when travel was heaviest, two of the worst stretches of the old Main Post Road were avoided by using the steamboat lines.

Stagecoach interests were from the very first tied in closely with the Potomac steamboat venture, more so than in the case of any similar enterprise farther north. William Crawford, landlord of the Union Tavern in Georgetown, and John Davis, host of the Indian Queen in Washington, who were both proprietors of the Baltimore-Georgetown stage lines, invested heavily in stock of the steamboat company. Meanwhile, Hazelwood Farish of Fredericksburg, proprietor of several of the newly established stage lines fanning out from that city, became Secretary-Treasurer, and later President, of the Potomac Steam Boat Company.[18] The steamboat depended on the stagecoach interests for its connections at either end. On the other hand, the staging interests that controlled the steamboat were relatively secure against competition. The situation was the reverse of that across New Jersey, where the steamboat entrepreneurs controlled both ends of the route and bought interests in the stages in order to bind all elements into a more unified enterprise.

The expansion of steamboating on the waters of Chesapeake Bay was rapid once the War of 1812 was over. In 1816, a second steamboat, the *Chesapeake,* arrived to take over the Baltimore end of a second line to Philadelphia, the stages this time crossing between Frenchtown and Newcastle.[19] By 1819, three such steamboat-stage combinations were in service, one leaving Baltimore in the morning and reaching Philadelphia the same evening and the two others leaving in the evening and reaching Philadelphia the following morning.[20] A new steamboat, the *Virginia,* commenced in 1817 to run regularly once each week between Baltimore and Norfolk, leaving the former place each Thursday morning and the latter each Monday morning. By 1819, a second boat, the *Roanoke,* was also on this run, the two providing service twice a week each way. This short-cut route between North and South would become more popular after 1820. That year, a line of stages was established to run southwest from Norfolk and intersect the Main Post Road at Fayetteville, North Carolina, thus providing a speedy and more comfortable alternative to the conventional North-South route. The *Maryland* was then providing service twice a week from Baltimore to Annapolis and across the bay to Easton on the Eastern Shore.[21]

THE ADJUSTMENTS required among the stage lines following the introduction of steamboats might have proceeded more smoothly had it not been for the seasonal complications. Each autumn when the steamboats were laid up by ice, stages had to be ready to handle the passengers. Usually, staging arrangements had to be organized anew each winter. Many of the same proprietors might be involved year after year, but there naturally was less stability than when staging operations were uninterrupted. Stable arrangements had to be made, and horses and drivers found and placed on the road—all for only a few months of service. Coaches, and usually sleighs to combat the weather of the season, had to be available for the same brief period and stored in idleness for the rest of the year. The early form of organization, where stage lines were run by the proprietors living along a road, could not handle seasonal operations like these as economically and efficiently as could the new large stagecoach companies that were beginning to control many different lines within a region. As travel thinned in winter, these businesses could draw off horses and equipment from their inland routes and use them to stock the roads parallel to bays and rivers.

Travel along interconnecting routes of stagecoaches and steamboats was therefore a seasonal venture in the nineteenth century. John Quincy Adams recounted in his diary one such trip he made from New England to New York in December 1829, the same year he had completed his one term as president:

Soon after the Clock struck four I was roused by the Stageman, and took my seat in the Carriage. The driver went to two other houses and took in two passengers, entire Strangers to me. We rode about two hours in the dark, and reached Dedham about Sunrise. We were immediately followed by three other Stages of the same line entirely full. We breakfasted at Dedham...Precisely at Noon we came to the lower wharf at Providence called India Wharf, where the new Steam boat, President, and Captain Bunker was waiting, and in ten minutes we had left the wharf.[22]

On board the steamboat that afternoon, Adams met Daniel Webster and his daughter, plus several members of the U.S. House of Representatives, and the trip then continued down Long Island Sound. But it was not a pleasant one for Adams: He complained of being "thoroughly chilled," and spent a sleepless night before landing in New York at 6:00 A.M.

Adam's discomfiture during the journey is evident in his diary—the early rising to catch the stage, the ride in the dark morning with "entire Strangers," the cold and sleepless boat ride, the journey of twenty-six hours—and he obviously was yearning for a faster, more pleasant way to travel. Such relief was now beginning to appear; the previous year, in 1828, the Baltimore and Ohio, the first U.S. passenger railroad, commenced operation.

The sound of the railroad whistle would be heard more insistently in the East during the next few decades, and the railroads would run in direct competition with the stagecoach along the major stage lines. This time there would be no land-water partnership; this time the railroads would win outright, gradually driving the stage off its traditional routes.

XIV

West to the Mississippi

WHEN THE three states forming the first tier west of the Appalachian barrier—Kentucky, Tennessee, and Ohio—were each admitted to the Union, there were as yet no stagecoach lines within their borders. No line had crossed the mountain ranges, and only a few had reached their eastern foothills. The mail stage establishment of the Post Office Department was only seven years old when Kentucky was admitted in 1792, only eleven years old when Tennessee was admitted in 1796, and only eighteen years old when Ohio was admitted in 1803. In those years, the stagecoach was still basically an institution of the eastern seaboard, and it would require the first third of the nineteenth century for it to penetrate on a regular basis to the frontier territories to the west. Actually, satisfactory stagecoach service there would only be achieved during the Jackson regime of the 1830s, when the frontier was able to make its influence sufficiently felt in Washington to gain Post Office subsidies for frontier undertakings.

The first stagecoach service across the Appalachian ridges to western waters was established in July 1804 by John Tomlinson and Company and went to Pittsburgh on the Ohio. For several years previously, stages had been running from Philadelphia west as far as Chambersburg. Now, one of these stages each week crossed the main ridges via Bedford, Somerset and Greensburg to the forks of the Ohio, and by autumn it provided the service twice a week.[1] The stages left John Tomlinson's Spread Eagle Tavern in Market Street, Philadelphia, every Tuesday and Friday at 4:00 A.M. and arrived at Thomas Feree's Fountain Inn, Water Street, Pittsburgh, seven days later. Since Chambersburg was reached in two and one-half days, more than four days were consumed struggling across the mountain ridges to its west.

John Tomlinson had been a stage proprietor operating westward from Philadelphia for a number of years, and in 1804 he held the mail contract between Philadelphia and Lancaster. A letter to him from Postmaster General Gideon Granger showed that the impetus for the establishment of the Pittsburgh service came from the Post Office Department. Granger was then endeavoring to complete a line of stages via Pittsburgh, Wheeling, and Zane's Trace, Ohio, to Lexington, Kentucky, and Nashville, Tennessee. Thence, the mail would be carried horseback over the Natchez Trace to New Orleans, which had become part of the United States territory the previous year. All this was on his mind when he wrote Tomlinson on March 4, 1804:

I wish to give every reasonable aid to the establishment of a line of Stages from Lancaster to Pittsburgh; and will give you $6000 per annum for the conveyance of the mail on that Line, and make the contract for four years; the mail to be carried twice a week, once in a stage (and once in a Sulkey or on horseback if you prefer it.)[2]

By the end of 1804, Granger had taken the next step in pushing stage service westward by contracting with Henry Westbay of Cannonsburg and John Scott of Washington, Pennsylvania, to take the mail from Pittsburgh southwest through their respective towns to Wheeling, where the starting point of Zane's Trace lay across the Ohio River. And by July 1805, Granger had likewise contracted with Andrew Marshall of St. Clairsville, Ohio, to establish a line of stages over the Trace from Wheeling to Frankfort, Kentucky.[3] On July 19, he wrote enthusiastically to President Thomas Jefferson: "I have closed contracts for the establishment of a line of mail coaches from Wheeling, Virginia through the state of Ohio, to Frankfort, Kentucky; when these lines go into operation all the States will be knit together by lines of public carriages. The terms are $7000 per annum and one years pay in advance."[4] Granger's hopes, unfortunately, were premature. The Trace was not ready for stages, and despite much money expended by the Post Office, it was 1809 before a line ran from Wheeling with any regularity.

The contract with Marshall represented an instance in which the practice of paying in advance backfired. Marshall was still employing only riders in March 1806, and apparently had sublet the western end of his undertaking to Nathan Willis of Chillicothe. Granger wrote Willis in April that Marshall had failed to carry according to contract and probably was "not competent to the undertaking."[5] To another man, he wrote: "The amount of 1 year's pay was made to Marshall in advance with which he proposed to furnish himself with horses and carriages. It appears that instead of furnishing himself with the property necessary to carry his contract into effect, the money has been dissipated in gambling, etc., and that he has not now the means of performing it."[6] To Willis, Granger added: "I do not wish you to set your stages in motion between Chillicothe and Frankfort until they are in operation between Wheeling and Chillicothe, but as soon as that is the case you must be in operation."[7]

There was a report in July that Marshall had started his stages,[8] but in August, Granger directed his department's special agent, Phineas Bradley, "to repair to the State of Ohio and negotiate with Andrew Marshall for the relinquishment of his...contracts...and to make such further additional arrangements for the transportation of a mail twice a week on said route in mail coaches if practicable."[9] For unknown reasons, this was not done. Perhaps it was already too late in the year for a new venture. In the spring of 1807, Granger wrote to George Beymer, Willis's partner, "If Marshall's line of Stages is not in operation by the 1st of next month, I authorize you to extend your line over his part of the route."[10] Stage service of some sort was provided that summer, presumably, because on October 17 Granger wrote Willis and Beymer, "In consequence of the badness of the roads, on which you are conveying the mail in Stages, I consent to have you resort immediately to the winter arrangement and to have you carry the mail on horseback until the 1st of May next."[11]

The next season, the situation apparently was worse. Surprisingly, Granger gave up in the middle of the summer. On July 16, 1808, he wrote Willis: "The numerous embarrassments that we have experienced in the transmission of the mail under the direction of yourself, Beymer, and Marshall by Stage and the numberless complaints that have resulted from the failures, delays, and tardiness of the mail have induced me to propose a different mode of conveying it." He then released the contractors from all obligations to convey the mail in stages and directed them to use a horse at all times.[12] The following summer, the entire route was put into the hands of new stagecoach contractors, Jacob Ayers of Zanesville, at $3,200 per annum for the road between Chillicothe and Wheeling, and James Johnson of Great Crossing, Kentucky, at $5,177 per annum for the road from Chillicothe to Frankfort. There were still complaints of delays and trip failures, but they seem to have been little different from those on other routes.[13] In the summer of 1809, stage service over Zane's Trace and the Maysville Road was, at last, firmly established.

THE ONLY ROAD in the "Old Northwest" over which stagecoaches operated before the War of 1812 was Zane's Trace. Until about 1832, this
was the busiest and most important thoroughfare in Ohio. It served the
more thickly populated areas of the state, and passed through three of
the older inland trading centers—Zanesville, Lancaster, and Chillicothe,
each of which had been founded on the Trace (at the crossings of the
Muskingum, Hocking, and Scioto rivers, respectively). Chillicothe was
then the state capital. Stages plowed through the natural mud of this
pioneer track for nine years before Columbus was founded and for
twenty-two years before the eastern stretch between Wheeling and
Zanesville was incorporated into the National Road.[14]

This pioneer road from Wheeling to Maysville was important, however, not only to Ohio. Its national importance lay in its being the
shortest and most practical route from Washington, Baltimore, Philadelphia, and all the northern and northeastern states to Kentucky and
central Tennessee. From Maysville, it continued in an almost direct line
to Lexington and Nashville, and thence via the Natchez Trace to
Natchez and New Orleans.

Postmaster General Granger had been sending the mail toward New
Orleans along three routes: east of the Alleghenies through Georgia;
down the Great Valley through Knoxville; and through Ohio and Ken-
tucky. On each of them, he had met similar delays and frustrations.
Down to 1827, the "great mails" through and beyond Ohio into the
Southwest were carried over the Ohio route. Even after 1827, the mail
from north of Washington went west and southwest via the National
Road and Zane's Trace.

The route across Ohio via Zane's Trace was of national importance
for another reason, as well. It was then the main land route to the West.
From Lexington, Kentucky, a branch reached westward through Frankfort to Louisville, the growing city at the falls of the Ohio. Crossing the
Ohio at this point, it traversed southern Indiana to Vincennes, and then
crossed southern Illinois to St. Louis. Before the days of the steamboats,
most of the communication with the early settlements of Indiana, Illinois, and Missouri and with the trading and military posts of the upper
Mississippi and Missouri river frontiers passed over this road. And it was
also over this road that the first stagecoach was to reach the Mississippi.

In these early years, the Ohio River and Zane's Trace were comple-
mentary to each other, since both were necessary to complete a transportation circuit. Zane's Trace was to the upper Ohio what the Natchez
Trace was to the lower Ohio and Mississippi, namely the return trail.
Before the conquest of these rivers by the steamboat, travel on them

was almost wholly downstream. It was 1817 before many steamboats able to ascend the Ohio were constructed, and it was well into the 1820s before enough of them plied the river to maintain schedules. By that time, travel was increasing so rapidly that both steamboats and coach lines had plenty of patronage. Many who descended the Ohio returned by land for variety and to see something of the interior of Ohio, which at this time was a much-talked-of region. Not until the 1830s were steamboats considered safe and proper carriers of the mail, and by this time, the speed of the stages over the National and Maysville roads had so increased that the "great mails" continued to be sent by stage. After the 1830s, mail for Indiana, Illinois, and Missouri continued west from Zanesville over the newly constructed National Road, but glory enough remained for the Maysville Road in carrying Kentucky mails and Kentucky statesmen. Its most profitable years were those between 1835 and 1845.

The first stagecoach service to Columbus was inaugurated in 1816, the year it replaced Chillicothe as the state capital. The stage came not from Zanesville to the east, as might perhaps be expected, but up the Scioto Valley from Chillicothe to the south. Phillip Zinn had taken the contract to carry the mail weekly, and one of his sons usually drove the light, round-topped, two-horse wagon that he placed on the road. In the spring of 1818, he began service twice a week, and in 1819 he announced that one of the trips would "be performed with a large and elegant new stage and four horses." Usually an overnight stop was made at Circleville, although for a time he promised, on the northward trip, "if the moon shines, and the roads are favorable, [it] will go through to Columbus."[15]

Possibly in 1819, when he secured the mail contract for that route, Zinn also established the first stage line between Lancaster and Columbus.[16] It was sometime in 1820 or 1821 before G. C. Harrington started the first stage line between Zanesville and Columbus, using the road leading through Newark and Granville. It ran irregularly, however, and no permanent line served Columbus from the east until May 1823. These three lines were a forecast of how Columbus was eventually to become the hub of stagecoach activity in the state. William Nail, who bought the Bell Tavern in Columbus and renamed it the Red Lion, bought into both Zinn's and Harrington's enterprises, and with them eventually created a great network of lines running out of Columbus. This system ultimately developed into the Ohio Stage Company, probably the greatest grouping of staging interests east of the Mississippi to be brought together into one organization.[17]

In 1818, Cincinnati, which was already the largest city in Ohio by a large margin, was connected with Dayton by a stage line that crossed over the ridge to Hamilton on the Miami River and then ascended the Miami Valley.[18] There was also a demand for stage service from some point on Zane's Trace across the hills of southwest Ohio to Cincinnati, but its establishment was probably delayed by the hard times that commenced in 1819.

It was probably John Metcalf, the pioneer mail carrier between Erie, Pennsylvania, and Cleveland, Ohio, who started the second stage line in Ohio, because in 1815 he provided himself with a light carriage that had two seats for passengers besides the driver's box. Aaron and Edwin Harmon, when they secured the postal route in 1818, put the mail back in wagons, but when their control of the road was threatened that year by others establishing a stage line from Cleveland east to Painesville, the Harmons took Metcalf into partnership, purchased large coaches, and began the first four-horse service in northern Ohio.[19]

These were the pioneer lines in Ohio. For several years after 1820, there was almost no extension of staging activity. There was also a suspension of much needed road work and bridge building. As a marginal business activity of the nineteenth century, frontier expansion was among the first enterprises to feel the era's economic depression. By 1823, the tide was turning in Ohio. In the next seven years, the pattern of stagecoach communication was shaped, and by 1830 Ohio was ready for its busiest decade of staging, having arrived at that threshold but a few years behind New England and the mid-Atlantic states.

THE EARLIEST stage lines in the entire trans-Appalachian West were not in Ohio but in Kentucky. Started in 1803, they preceded even the crossing of the Alleghenies to Pittsburgh. These were two lines that ran out of Lexington, the "Athens of the West." The first, advertised in August by John Kennedy, left Lexington every Thursday morning by Winchester and Mt. Sterling for the Olympian Springs in Bath County, some forty-seven miles eastward, where the stage arrived the same evening. This apparently was a seasonal line, established to carry the inhabitants of the Bluegrass to the "Bath of Kentucky" developed and owned by Colonel Thomas Hart, father-in-law of Henry Clay.[20]

The second line was the Lexington and Frankfort Stage inaugurated a few months later by John Kennedy and William Dailey. It ran twice a week from the start, leaving Lexington on Mondays and Fridays at daybreak. The road chosen was that through the now-extinct town of

Leesburg, where the partners purchased a tavern and stables that were operated as a halfway station.[21] Both these stage lines had their headquarters on the public square in Lexington in a fine tavern known as Travellers Hall. Henry Clay purchased the tavern in 1808, renamed it the Kentucky Hotel, and leased it to Cuthbert Banks, who made it Lexington's chief social center of the day.[22]

The next advance in Kentucky staging was a line from Lexington to Louisville at the Falls of the Ohio, initiated by James Johnson in June 1817. The "great western mail," which came over Zane's Trace into Kentucky, was divided at Lexington into that which continued southwest to Tennessee and New Orleans and that which went westward through Louisville and Vincennes to St. Louis. Johnson's venture thus marked a new westward thrust on the route stretching toward Missouri. The move also hinted that Johnson was interested in the entire line to Wheeling, and in 1817, he received the contract between Wheeling and Pittsburgh. Soon, however, he turned his interests to steamboating and left the actual direction of his staging business to his son, Edward P. Johnson, who took over the mail contracts and, in time, vastly extended them, becoming the unquestioned stagecoach king of the Bluegrass region in the 1830s.[23]

BEGINNING IN 1820, several attempts were made to extend stage service from Louisville across southern Indiana to Vincennes and then into southern Illinois to St. Louis. Much attention was given to this route, which played a role in the development of southern Indiana and Illinois: Until about 1835, it was the chief thoroughfare across these states.

Late in 1819, James Foyles of Vincennes entered into a contract to carry the mail weekly in stages between Louisville and Vincennes, a distance of about 126 miles. The road over which he traveled, known variously as the Buffalo Trace, the Vincennes Trail, and (to Indiana settlers) the Kentucky Road, was the oldest highway in the state, having been used by early traders and by approximately two-thirds of the settlers who moved into the southern part of Indiana. Foyles's stage was in operation by April 1820 and consumed practically three days traveling each way.[24]

In 1821, a notice appeared that "The Union Line of Stages in connection with the Louisville line will commence on the 5th day of September inst." to run regularly from Vincennes to St. Louis, thus completing a through line to Missouri in the year that the territory graduated into statehood. Passengers leaving Louisville early Saturday morning reached Vincennes Monday evening, left there again early Tuesday, and arrived finally at St. Louis sometime Friday afternoon if there were no delays, thus consuming an entire week on the road.[25] The 165-mile stretch across Illinois was straight and level compared to that across the Indiana hills, but it was a much newer road. There were but three or four infant settlements along the way, and houses of entertainment were few and poor.[26] The stagecoach in this instance was almost in advance of settlement.

Like Lexington, Kentucky, St. Louis had several local stage lines radiating from it before it was connected with the outer world by stage service. The Kaskaskia and Edwardsville stages, both started in 1819 were the earliest in Illinois. The stage from St. Louis across to St. Charles on the Missouri River, a distance of about 20 miles, was started by Nathaniel Simonds in December 1818 and, from its beginning, ran three times each week each way.[27] It was the first stage line west of the Mississippi River and represented the spearhead of stage service into the West in 1820. A line to Franklin, opposite Boone's Lick, was started in March 1821.[28] It, in its turn, extended stagecoach service west of the Mississippi more than halfway across Missouri.

The stagecoach was no longer restricted to the eastern seaboard states of the young Republic; it had now rolled westward to the frontiers of the expanding nation, reaching and crossing the Mississippi. It was the second major epoch in the history of the American stagecoach. The third epoch, a romantic and dramatic one, was yet to take place in the Far West after the Civil War.

XV

The Indian Summer of Eastern Staging

 THE TWO DECADES from 1820 to 1840 can probably be called the golden years of staging in the East. It was a period just before the railroads began their major development, a time when stagecoach routes continued to multiply, and when increased numbers of passengers were riding the stages with great enthusiasm.

Late in 1823, for instance, a new line of stages was inaugurated to run from Jersey City through northeast Pennsylvania to Oswego on the Susquehanna and then into western New York, roughly along the route the Erie Railroad was later to take. What this new route meant to the citizens of Montrose, Pennsylvania, was illustrated by the diary entry of Jerre Lyon of that town on New Year's Day, 1824:

Huzza! Huzza! for the new stage; this evening about 7 o'clock the new stage direct from New York. What a shouting! It was saluted by the drum and fife, and by the cheers of the populace. A number of buildings were brilliantly illuminated.[1]

An idea of just how vigorous the stage coach activity was during that period can be obtained from some records of staging in and out of Boston. As was discussed in chapter 8, the number of stage lines running out of the city increased from forty in 1820 to sixty-one in 1825.[2] And in June 1826, the *American Traveller* reported: "We have more than seventy different lines of four and six horse stages, which regularly depart from the city in every direction, and send out, many of them, daily and hourly coaches...It is no uncommon sight to behold twenty-five and even thirty stages pass down in a single day on the turnpike to Salem, conveying from nine to seventeen passengers each."[3]

That growth was to continue for another decade, as the March 1835 issue of *Badger and Porter's Stage Register* indicated. In 1835, some 110 separate lines out of Boston were listed, not quite double the sixty-two listed ten years earlier, but the number of coaches arriving and departing weekly, up to 526 from 256 in 1825, had more than doubled. Since more coaches, especially those to nearby towns, were by then carrying more passengers on outside seats, over 250,000 persons were leaving Boston each year and as many arriving. This was probably the high point, however, because in 1835 New England's first three railroads were being completed—the Boston and Providence, the Boston and Lowell, and the Boston and Worcester.[4]

THE RAILROAD's first victories over the stagecoach occurred on the major and most heavily traveled routes. A stark example of that confrontation was the popular Baltimore to Washington route, where as late as 1829 there were ten stage lines operating between the two cities. But as the intercity railroad was being built during the early 1830s people began taking the train as far as the roadbed had been completed and then transferring to a stagecoach to complete the journey. The stagecoach on that once proud main line was thus quickly turned into a trunk line. Finally, on August 24, 1835, the railroad was completed into Washington, and the postal contract was given to it.

But the story of staging on the Baltimore road was not quite over; it was to breathe one final gasp. The railroad, feeling it now had a monopoly, thought it could make its own demands for carrying the mail and passengers. Its fares for passengers were, according to a complaint in the *Washington Globe*, "unprecedently and provokingly exorbitant."[5] Passengers also missed the old stagecoach courtesy of being picked up at their homes or hotels, whenever possible. They complained that they now had an additional transportation charge of getting themselves and their baggage to and from the railroad depots in both cities.

In October 1837, Postmaster General Amos Kendall decided to put the mail contract back in the hands of stage owners, this time James Williams of Washington, who was then running the Annapolis and Leonardtown lines, and John H. King of Georgetown.[6] These two owners put two lines of stages on the old road to run morning and afternoon. They emphasized that "for the accommodation of families and others, they will be taken up and put down at all the principal hotels, and intermediate places, at any reasonable distance."[7] Their fare was $2.50, later reduced to $2.00. The *National Intelligencer* for December 1837, noted that these stages "have been, so far, well encouraged."[8]

But in January 1838, Postmaster General Kendall, after long negotiations, came to terms with the railroad and annulled the contract with Williams and King, allowing them one month's extra commission, as he was permitted to do by law.[9] Deprived of their mail income, the two proprietors promptly dissolved the stage line.

THE RAILROAD'S conquest of the stagecoach usually was not so quick and final. The Great Western mail, for instance, was in 1838 taken off the stage line to Frederick, Maryland, and was transported via the railroad to Relay, at which point it was transferred to the Washington Branch. But, the Frederick stage line did not collapse, though it lost its importance as a through line and reduced its service from daily to three times a week.[10] The line managed to survive on that basis as a local line until the 1860s, finally terminating service shortly after the end of the Civil War.

And, of course, the railroad's confrontation with the stagecoach was neither universal nor immediate. The first railroads were built along the major routes, leaving the secondary routes to the stages, and it did require a great deal of time to construct the railroad network. Unlike a stagecoach, which could roll as soon as it was constructed, the railroad had to wait for the roadbeds to be built and the rails to be laid. As a matter of fact, the stage continued slightly to surpass its rival in annual miles of mail transportation until the Civil War. However, the final outcome became inevitable on July 7, 1838, when Congress designated every railroad as a postal route. As more miles of rail were laid year after year, the stages steadily declined, while the mileage for railroads regularly increased.

The postmaster general's *Annual Report* for 1860 used mileage figures for 1849 to 1860 to illustrate the declining use of the stage and increasing use of the railroad to transport the mail in the years just before the Civil War (see Table). These figures compared only the miles of stage and rail *routes* on which the *mail* was carried, rather than the total number of miles that were traveled. No reliable figures are available today for the *total* stagecoach mileage of the multitudinous major and minor stage lines during those years, but the postmaster general's statistics indicate fairly well what was transpiring for the stage overall. For many lines, the mail contract was the lifeline of financial survival.

Stages carrying the mail reached their apogee in 1853, covering over 45,000 miles, but then the decline set in. By 1860, the eastern stages were carrying less mail than they were eleven years earlier. On the

Miles of Stagecoach and Railway Lines Carrying Mails 1849–60

Year	Stagecoach Mileage East of the Mississippi	Railroad Mileage
1849	33,134	5,497
1850	36,511	6,886
1851	42,388	8,225
1852	43,171	10,146
1853	45,174	12,415
1854	44,647	14,440
1855	39,112	18,333
1856	38,317	20,323
1857	°	22,530
1858	36,151	24,431
1859	39,900	26,010
1860	32,040	27,129

SOURCE: Postmaster General's *Annual Report* (Washington, 1860).

other hand, the railroads had increased their mileage almost fivefold—from a little over a modest 5,000 miles to over 27,000 miles, almost equal to the eastern stages. And that ratio would continue dramatically in the decades following the Civil War.

The postmaster general's report also broke down those figures by states, further indicating what was happening. In states with more rural areas and where the railroad did not penetrate, the stage was better able to sustain itself. In Maine, for instance, the mail mileage dropped during that period from 2,362 miles to 1,999 miles, a decline of only 363 miles. But in populous New York State, the decline was from 5,803 miles to 4,358 miles, a difference of over 1,400 miles in mail stage activities.

Other figures in the report indicated what was happening west of the Mississippi. While eastern staging was experiencing its Indian summer, staging in the West was beginning a whole new epoch. For instance, in Texas in 1850, there were only 727 miles of mail stage, but that had increased to 3,930 miles by 1860. And while there were no mail contacts at all for stages in California in 1850, there were 4,955 miles by 1860.[11]

One epoch of staging was dying, while a new one was being born.

NEVERTHELESS, there was still one area of staging that would remain dominant throughout the East before the Civil War and that, in fact, would increase and develop there for the remainder of the century. Representing a new and final dimension of eastern staging, this aspect would keep the stagecoaches rolling along a number of smaller routes while they were rapidly disappearing along the major routes. Its development began in the 1830s and was illustrated by an 1824 advertisement in the Georgia *Augusta Chronicle:*

On the 1st of July, or sooner or later, as may suit the convenience of passengers, the subscriber will start to Greenville, S.C., from one to four comfortable four horse post coaches for the express accommodation of all persons disposed to visit or pass the summer months in that section of the country. The same coaches will return to Augusta, between the 1st and 15th October next, thereby offering great accommodation and convenience.[12]

The Greenville mentioned in the advertisement was located in the foothills of the Blue Ridge in the northwest corner of South Carolina, and it was just beginning to become fashionable as a vacation spot of summer hotels and boarding houses and second homes. The new line to Greenville was successful, and during the following decades there were a number of similar lines throughout the East. This was to be eastern staging's last dimension: the lines into the vacation areas of the mountains, where the railroads would not penetrate for many years to come.

The hilly and mountainous regions of the East were forbidding territories for the railroads. The costs of initial construction on their steep grades, plus the operation and maintenance expenses, were much more severe in the mountains. At the same time, those sparsely settled areas furnished little traffic or income. Significantly, no railroads were built into mountainous areas before the Civil War, except to cross them to richer regions beyond. Thus, there was at the base of this mountain fringe a figurative shore line against which the railroad tide flowed and ebbed, leaving open territory for the stagecoaches.

For the rest of the century, the eastern stagecoach made those resorts available to thousands who otherwise could not have reached them. Indeed, the growth in popularity of the mountain resorts was one of the remarkable social phenomena of that period of increasing industrialization in the United States. Residents of the growing urban areas seemingly yearned for a temporary flight back to nature. Furthermore, after the Civil War, when the stagecoach had largely disappeared from the major routes of the East, it was a unique experience for young people who had never before ridden in a stagecoach to climb aboard, roll off, and indulge in a chapter of romance from the past.

There were numerous different areas of mountain staging in the nineteenth century—not just the Greenville region of South Carolina, but other places, too, such as Asheville Sulphur Springs in North Carolina and the Virginia Springs region. Farther north was one of the most popular resort areas in the East, the Catskills in New York. Still farther north in New England were the White Mountains.

THE STORY OF staging in the Catskill Mountains was typical of this dimension of the eastern stage when the stagecoach proprietors who previously associated themselves with the tavern and the post office began to be associated with the resort hotel. The Catskills were the most accessible by far of the northern mountain groups, and the first stage of a vacation trip there was usually by steamboat up the Hudson. The steamboats landed their passengers at the little town of Catskill, and from that point there had to be an inland journey to the mountains. It was here that the stagecoaches played their final role.

The pioneer in the development of the Catskill tourist trade was Erastus Beach of Catskill. His career and that of his son, Charles L. Beach, illustrated the close relationship between the mountain resorts and the stagecoach business in mountain areas. Erastus Beach in 1819 became the owner of a livery business in Catskill and soon became interested in stage lines passing through the city. Eventually, he and his son, under the name of E. Beach and Company, became proprietors in the line between New York City and Albany on the west side of the Hudson River and also in the important line from Catskill west to Ithaca. The mail contracts for these lines and for others were taken in the name of the company, which employed some 40 coaches and nearly 200 horses. Partners for other portions of the lines changed, but the Beach interests in Catskill remained the stabilizing influence in the staging operations of this region until the building of the Delaware and Ulster and the West Shore railroads in the 1870s.[13]

In 1822, Beach took his first party of tourists by stagecoach into the Catskill Mountains. Beach was so impressed with the possibilities that the next year he organized a stock company called the Catskill Mountain Association to construct a road up South Mountain and there on a ledge near the top, where the view over the Hudson Valley was unobstructed, to build a hotel that would permit visitors to remain overnight or longer amid mountain scenes and atmosphere. A temporary lodging house was opened on June 28, and the first season was made notable by the arrival of General Lafayette and his retinue. Erastus Beach himself drove the coach that took the celebrated Frenchman to the top of the mountain. The original Catskill Mountain House was opened in 1824, the first and probably the most historic of all American mountain hotels.

In 1839, Charles L. Beach leased the hotel from the association, and in 1845 he became the sole owner. He was the proprietor of this house for sixty years. Eventually, he owned some 3,500 acres of the mountain plateau, in which were constructed some seven miles of carriage road and many miles of trails leading to scenic points.[14]

As early as 1825, guidebooks were mentioning the stagecoach trip to the summit of the Catskill Mountains.[15] The fare for many years was one dollar for the fourteen-mile trip from Catskill. Theodore Dwight's 1826 edition of *The Northern Traveller* referred to the "large and commodious house of entertainment erected at Pine Orchard," as the site was known, "the ascent—performed without fatigue, in a stage coach, which goes and returns regularly twice a day."[16] Four to five hours were required for the ascent from Catskill, and two hours only for the descent. The inevitable halfway taverns were seven miles out from Catskill at the foot of the main mountain. The stage line to the mountains was, of course, operated by the Beaches themselves. The Mountain House coaches met all river boats landing at Catskill. In the height of the season, four or five coaches were often required to accommodate one boatload of passengers destined for the mountain resort.[17]

For fifty years after it was built, the Catskill Mountain House remained the only important place of entertainment in the Catskills. A second period in the history of the Catskills was opened, however, by the building of the Ulster and Delaware railroad from Kingston west through the southern and western sections of the mountains, thereby making more accessible an entirely new region. Mammoth mountain hotels of the style that was so popular in the last three decades of the century were soon being built. The Laurel House near Kaaterskill Falls was one of the first rivals of the Mountain House. In 1878, the Overlook Mountain House, located on a high mountain to the south of Pine Orchard, was opened. It had stage connections from West Hurley, the first station on the Ulster and Delaware line. There was also a twelve-mile stage line from Saugerties Landing. In 1881, the Grand Hotel, on Summit Mountain in the southwestern part of the Catskills, and the Hotel Kaaterskill, on the summit of Kaaterskill Mountain, were opened. The Kaaterskill was described as "the finest mountain hotel in the world." Besides "elegant beds," it boasted of elevators, gas, electric bells, and the "celebrated Germania Orchestra from Philadelphia." By then, there were also many smaller hotels and excellent summer boarding houses in the central Catskill villages of Hunter and Tannersville and in Cairo, Freehold, Windham, and Prattsville, villages in the northern Catskills, along the old Susquehanna turnpike over which at least two daily stage lines passed. In the 1870s, several daily stage lines also ran from Catskill to Palenville, to Cairo and Prattsville, and through Kaaterskill Clove to Tannerville and Hunter.

The Catskill Mountain Railroad, which began in 1882 from Catskill to Palenville, eliminated the stage trip to the foot of the mountains, leaving only the actual ascent to the Mountain House and the lines through the Clove to Hunter. However, local stage lines increased rather than diminished through the remainder of the century. In a guidebook to the Catskill region published in 1905, fifty-one different lines were listed, with the greater number of them being only six to ten miles long.[18]

The stagecoach, during its twilight years in the East, was reduced to the benign task of carrying vacationers in an often seasonal enterprise. This was far different than the golden years, when it was vitally involved in intercity transportation and the mail. The stage, it seemed, had almost come full circle in America. The earliest covered coaches had started simply, carrying small numbers of passengers over primitive and largely undeveloped areas, and here at the end, the stage was again carrying few people and was back in the sparsely populated areas of the mountains.

For the individual passenger who made the transition from stagecoach to railroad in the nineteenth century, there was both gain and loss. The gains came in the form of greater speed and comfort, and, particularly, more convenient hours for travel. Stagecoaches, usually those scheduled for long trips, routinely departed at excessively early hours in the morning to gain the greatest amount of travel hours for the day. Except in winter, stages were regularly scheduled to travel from 80 to 100 miles daily. Since the coach's average speed, including all the stops, probably was only six miles an hour, from fourteen to eighteen of each day's twenty-four hours had to be spent on the road.

From 1815 on, for instance, all Boston-Albany stages expecting to cover 170 miles in two days started at 2:00 A.M. Stages from Boston to Portland started at 3:00 A.M., and stages to Hartford at 4:00 A.M. Local lines could afford to depart somewhat later—between 5:00 and 8:00 A.M. These early starts allowed the maximum amount of travel hours per day and therefore often saved travelers the expense of an extra night's lodgings on the road. The faster railroads, of course, departed at more convenient hours and eventually even offered sleeping accommodations on board.

But there was some loss in the transition, too. For one thing, the stages attempted, as far as possible, to pick up passengers at their homes or hotels and deposit them there at the end of the trip, a convenience that saved them an extra leg of their journey. Moreover, travelers of the old roads recalled the extraordinarily good food, often freshly picked produce from nearby farms, that was served at the stagecoach taverns en route. Finally, travelers remembered, with some nostalgia, the very gentle mood that seemed to pervade a stagecoach ride.

This mood was described by Nathaniel Hawthorne, who himself had a close association with the stagecoach industry. In 1819–20, at age sixteen, Hawthorne kept the ledgers for the Boston and Salem Stage Company, which was run by his uncle, William Manning. After his graduation from Bowdoin College, Hawthorne continued to work on the books of the stage company during the afternoons of his long reclusive period in Salem when he was doing his early creative writing.[19] He later recalled, in his lovely prose, a trip in July 1838, when he departed from Northampton, Massachusetts, in a stagecoach:

Left Northampton the next morning, between one and two o'clock. Three other passengers, whose faces were not visible for some hours; so we went on through unknown space, saying nothing, glancing forth sometimes to see the gleam of the lanterns on wayside objects.

How very desolate looks a forest when seen in this way…Sometimes we passed a house or rumbled through a village, stopping perhaps to arouse some drowsy postmaster, who appeared at the door in shirt and pantaloons, yawning, received the mail, returned it again, and was yawning when last seen. A few words exchanged among the passengers, as they roused themselves from their half-slumbers, or dreamy, slumber-like abstraction. Meanwhile dawn broke, our faces became partly visible, the morning air grew colder, and finally cloudy day came on. We found ourselves driving through quite a romantic country…and rattled on at the rate of ten miles an hour. Breakfast between four and five,—newly caught trout, salmon, ham, boiled eggs, and other niceties,—truly excellent.[20]

Hawthorne captures the unique and friendly flavor of the old stage-coach road in the East for us—the early departure, the excellent breakfast, and the darkened ride through "quite a romantic country." But our historical recollection of the eastern American stagecoach should not be merely a nostalgic one for a quaint old mode of travel. Rather, we should remember the stagecoach as an institution that determined the very pace of the nation's life during the first half of the nineteenth century, and that had critically important tasks to perform: It had to provide the mass transportation system needed by a young nation; it had to maintain communications in the Republic by moving the mail; it had to sponsor literacy and the spread of information by delivering the newspapers. And the old stagecoach did its job well.

Notes

I Colonial Stage Lines

1. The full significance of these observations can be studied in the excellent work by Arthur Pierce Middleton, *Tobacco Coast: A Maritime History of Chesapeake Bay in the Colonial Era* (Newport News, Va., 1953).
2. Joan Parkes, *Travel in England in the Seventeenth Century* (New York, 1925), pp. 53-58.
3. A fine treatment of the colonial post office is contained in William Smith, *The History of the Post Office in British North America* (Cambridge, Mass., 1920).
4. I. N. Phelps Stokes, *Iconography of Manhattan Island*, 6 vols. (New York, 1915-28), 4: 303, 959.
5. Mary Newton Stanard, *Colonial Virginia, Its People and Customs* (Philadelphia, 1917), p. 130.
6. *Collections of the Massachusetts Historical Society*, 5th ser. 5, (1878): 450, 484.
7. William Penn owned both a coach and a calash in Pennsylvania before 1700. See John F. Watson, *Annals of Philadelphia and Pennsylvania in the Olden Time*, 3 vols. (Philadelphia, Pa., 1845), 2:105.
8. *The Bicentennial Book of Malden* (Boston, 1850), p. 219.
9. Joseph Bennett, "History of New England," in *Proceedings of the Massachusetts Historical Society*, 1st ser. 5 (1862): 124.
10. Joseph B. Felt, *Annals of Salem* (Salem, Mass., 1827), p. 316; and Sylvester Judd, *History of Hadley* (Northampton, Mass., 1863), p. 391.
11. *Boston Town Records, 1742 to 1757* (Boston, 1885), pp. 178, 181.
12. For reprints of several notices, see G.W.W. Houghton, *Colonial Coaches of New York* (New York, 1890), pp. 11–13.
13. Ibid., p. 13.
14. Phaetons were four-wheeled vehicles for two horses. Lighter than coaches or chariots, they were introduced into the colonies about 1760.
15. Stanard, *Colonial Virginia*, p. 131.
16. Hugh Jones, *The Present State of Virginia* (London, 1724), p. 32.
17. "Observations in Several Voyages and Travels in America," *London Magazine* 15 (1746): 623.
18. Calvet M. Hahn, "The Swift-Sure Letters," *S.P.A. Journal*, October 1979 and June 1980.
19. S. A. Drake, *Old Boston Taverns* (Boston, 1917), p. 116. See also references to the Wardells in the *Reports of the Record Commissions of the City of Boston*.
20. John Nelson to Henry Lloyd, March 8, 1717; printed in Temple Prime, *Descent of John Nelson* (New York, 1894), p. 37.
21. Advertisement, *Boston News-Letter*, April 4–11, 1720.

22. Travel across New Jersey in colonial times is treated in the *Proceedings of the New Jersey Historical Society*, n.s. 7 (1922): 97–119.

23. William Adee Whitehead, *East Jersey under the Proprietary Governments*, 2d. ed., rev. and enl. (Newark, N.J., 1875), pp. 235–37.

24. *Documents Relating to the Colonial History of the State of New Jersey*, New Jersey Archives, 1st ser. 3 (1881): 187 (cited as N.J. Archives).

25. Ibid., pp. 176, 186–88, 250–51, 327.

26. Ibid., 11 (1894): 162.

27. Ibid., p. 309.

28. Ibid., p. 521.

29. Ibid., 12 (1895): 21.

30. Ibid., pp. 22, 29, 94.

31. Ibid., p. 681.

32. Ibid., p. 209.

33. Advertisement, *Pennsylvania Journal*, June 16, 1757.

34. N.J. Archives 26 (1904): 500, 513, 545.

35. Ibid., 27 (1905): 477, 550.

36. Advertisement of Jacob Rush, *Pennsylvania Gazette*, May 7, 1761.

37. Advertisement of Dowdle and Oakford, Ibid., July 22, 1762.

38. Ibid., June 2, 1763.

39. Advertisement, *Pennsylvania Journal*, July 16, 1764.

40. Advertisement, *Pennsylvania Packet*, October 12, 1772.

41. Advertisement, ibid., May 23, 1774.

42. Advertisement, *Boston News-Letter*, April 9, 1761.

43. Advertisement, ibid., April 15, 1763.

44. Advertisement, *Boston Post-Boy*, March 31, 1766.

45. Advertisement, *Boston Gazette*, November 28, 1770.

46. Advertisement, *Massachusetts Gazette*, August 8, 1771.

47. Advertisement, *Boston Gazette*, August 9, 1773.

48. Advertisement, *Boston Post-Boy*, July 20, 1767.

49. *New England Town and Country Almanack for 1769* (Boston).

50. Advertisement, *New-York Journal*, May 28, 1772.

51. Ibid., March 3, 1772.

52. See also advertisement, *Boston Evening Post*, July 6, 1772.

53. N.J. Archives, 26 (1904): 134, 214, 484, 496.

54. Ibid., p. 289.

55. Ibid., 28 (1906): 235.

56. Advertisement, *Pennsylvania Gazette*, December 3, 1767.

57. *Pennsylvania Journal*, April 11, 1771.

58. Advertisement, ibid., April 11, 1771.

59. Advertisement, *Dunlap's Pennsylvania Packet*, March 20, 1775.

60. Advertisement, *New-York Gazette*, June 20, 1768.

61. Advertisement, *Pennsylvania Chronicle*, February 27–March 6, 1769.

II Revival after the Revolution

1. For a list of the receipts of each post office in 1799, see *American State Papers: Documents, Legislative and Executive, of the Congress of the United States*, 38 vols. (Washington, D.C., 1832–61), vol. 27, *Post Office Department* (1834), pp. 8–12 (cited as *American State Papers: Post Office Department*).

2. Advertisement, *New Jersey Gazette*, November 25, 1778.

3. Advertisement, *Pennsylvania Gazette*, February 17, 1779.

4. Advertisement, *New Jersey Gazette*, October 4, 1780.

5. Johnson was born in 1744 in Littleton, New Jersey (Mary Ball Johnson Pease et al., eds., *Mahlon Johnson Family of Littleton, New Jersey: Ancestors and Descendants,* 1931, p. 708).

6. Advertisement, *New Jersey Gazette,* January 31 and May 9, 1781.

7. Advertisement, ibid., April 17, 1782.

8. Advertisement, *Pennsylvania Journal,* July 4, 1782.

9. Advertisement, *Royal Gazette* (New York), June 14, 1783.

10. Advertisement, *Pennsylvania Journal,* September 10, 1783.

11. Advertisement, ibid., March 1, 1783.

12. Advertisement, *Pennsylvania Gazette,* June 11, 1783.

13. Advertisement, *Pennsylvania Packet,* August 23, 1783.

14. Ibid.

15. *Maryland Journal,* January 2, 1784.

16. Ibid., May 6, 1783. The early history of this route is covered in greater detail in Oliver W. Holmes, "Stagecoach Days in the District of Columbia," *Records of the Columbia Historical Society* 50 (1952): 1–42.

17. *Index to the Journals of the Senate and House of Delegates of the State of Maryland,* 3 vols. (Annapolis, 1856–57), 1:523.

18. William W. Hening, ed., *The Statutes-at-Large, Being a Collection of All the Laws of Virginia, 1619–1792,* 13 vols. (Philadelphia and New York, 1823), 11:395.

19. Ibid, p. 467.

20. *Connecticut Courant* (Hartford), July 29, 1783.

21. For references to Pease and a more detailed account of the establishment of the first successful New York–Boston stage line, see Oliver W. Holmes, "Levi Pease, the Father of New England Stage-Coaching," *Journal of Economic and Business History* 3 (1931): 241–63.

22. Andrew Ward, *History of the Town of Shrewsbury* (1847), p. 407–09.

23. *Massachusetts Spy* (Worcester), October 30, 1783.

24. Advertisement, ibid., June 3, 1784.

25. Advertisement, *New-York Packet,* October 15, 1784.

26. *Massachusetts Spy,* November 4, 1784.

27. Advertisement, *New-York Packet,* May 26, 1785.

28. *Massachusetts Spy,* November 4, 1784.

29. *Salem Gazette,* September 1, 1784.

30. *Pennyslvania Gazette,* March 21, 1781.

31. *Laws of the State of New York,* 8th session, chap. 52, 1886 ed., 2:99.

32. Advertisement, *New York Packet,* April 25, 1785.

33. Petition of John Hoomes; manuscript in Archives Department, Virginia State Library, Richmond.

III   Stagecoaches and the Mail —
A Debate of the Confederation Period

1. Hugh Finlay, *Journal Kept by Hugh Finlay* (Brooklyn, 1867), p. 18.

2. Ibid., p. 32.

3. Worthington C. Ford et al., eds., *Journals of the Continental Congress, 1774–1789,* 34 vols. (Washington, D.C., 1904–37), 23:673 (cited as *Journals of the Continental Congress*).

4. Papers of the Continental Congress, vol. 61, fols. 181–85; in Record Group 11, National Archives, Washington, D.C.

5. Ibid., vol. 41, fols. 199–200, 255–56.

6. Ibid.

7. *Journals of the Continental Congress,* 28:489.

8. Calvet M. Hahn, "Mail on Wheels," *Stamp Collector*, March 14, 1981. Hahn offers an adroit discussion of this whole interesting historical question.

9. *Journals of the Continental Congress*, 29:525–29.

10. Ibid., 24:527.

11. Ibid.

12. Ibid., 29:527–8.

13. Ibid., p. 684.

14. A copy of the contract is in the Papers of the Continental Congress, vol. 61, fol. 265.

15. Hazard to Alexander Hamilton, August 1, 1786.

16. Hazard to Congress, February 22, 1787.

17. Hazard to Hamilton, August 1, 1781.

18. *Journals of the Continental Congress*, 41:271.

19. See the figures and comparisons in the Papers of the Continental Congress, vol. 61, fol. 421.

20. *Journals of the Continental Congress*, 31:690–92.

21. Hazard to Congress, October 11, 1787.

22. Papers of the Continental Congress, vol. 61, fol. 565.

23. *Journals of the Continental Congress*, 23:673.

24. *New-York Journal*, February 21 and April 17, 1788.

25. Papers of the Continental Congress. Petitions in vol. 42, fol. 101, and vol. 41, fol. 254. The resolution is in vol. 41, fol. 250.

26. Ibid., vol. 59, fols. 331–47.

27. Hazard to Jeremy Balknap, March 5 and May 10, 1788.

28. Communication signed "Sentinel," *The Independent Gazateer* (Philadelphia), January 7, 1788.

29. George Washington, *The Writings of Washington*, ed. Worthington C. Ford, 14 vols. (New York, 1889–93), 11: 290–92.

IV   The Stages Roll—1790 to 1800

1. Records of the United States Post Office Department, Postmaster General's Letter-books, A:13, 198–99; in Record Group 28, National Archives, Washington, D.C. (cited as Postmaster General's Letterbooks).

2. Ibid.

3. Ibid., B:242–50, 293.

4. Ibid., B:466, 493.

5. Ibid., F:139; and advertisement of Levi Pease and Company, *Columbian Centinel* (Boston), November 19, 1796.

6. Advertisement, *Columbian Centinel*, May 1, 1793.

7. *New Hampshire State Papers*, 12 (1893): 660.

8. E. P. Walton, ed., *Records of the Governor and Council of the State of Vermont*, 8 vols. (Montpelier, 1876), 4:33.

9. David Willard, *Willard's History of Greenfield* (Greenfield, Mass., 1904), p. 760.

10. Postmaster General's Letterbooks, B:16; and advertisements of Israel Hatch, *Columbian Centinel*, January 10 and February 11, 1795.

11. *Columbian Centinel*, February 7, 1795.

12. Holmes, "Levi Pease," pp. 241–63.

13. J. Munsell, *Annals of Albany*, 1:248, and 3:96, 99.

14. Advertisement, *Albany Gazette*, September 12, 1793.

15. Timothy Pickering to Hugh White, July 8, 1794, and to Hendrick Troy, August 4, 1794.

16. Pickering to Jason Parker, September 6, 1794.

17. Postmaster General's Letterbooks, B:9–20.

18. Samuel Osgood to President Washington, December 16, 1790.

19. Pickering to Alexander Furnival, January 9, 1792.

20. *New York Journal and Weekly Register*, January 7, 1790.

21. *Commercial Advertiser* (New York), May 9, 1799.

22. *Aurora and General Advertiser* (Philadelphia), July 1, 1799. See also Hahn, "The Swift-Sure Letters."

23. *Documents Relating to the Revolutionary History of the State of New Jersey*, N.J. Archives, 2d ser. 1 (1901): 346–47.

24. Watson, *Annals of Philadelphia*. 2:466–67.

25. *American State Papers: Post Office Department*, p. 9.

26. The Treasurer's account of money received for stage licenses each year may be found in successive volumes of the *Votes and Proceedings* of the New Jersey General Assembly.

27. William Patterson, *Laws of the State of New Jersey* (Newark, 1800), p. 451.

28. U.S., Congress, *Annals of Congress*, 2nd Cong., 1st sess., 1792, p. 304 (cited as *Annals of Congress*).

29. Postmaster General's Letterbooks, C:190.

30. Pickering to Furnival, May 30, 1794.

31. Morton L. Montgomery, *History of Reading, Pennsylvania* (Reading, 1898), p. 45.

32. Advertisement, *General Advertiser* (Philadelphia), July 3, 1792.

33. See Charles Landis, "The Beginnings of Artificial Roads in Pennsylvania" and "The First Long Turnpike in the United States" in *Lancaster County Historical Society Papers* 23(1919): 99–107 and 20(1916): 205–26, 235–58, and 265–334, respectively.

34. Advertisement, *Claypoole's Daily American Advertiser*, May 1, 1797.

V   The Early Stagecoaches

1. Thomas Twining, *Travels in America 100 Years Ago* (New York, 1894), p. 59.

2. Charles W. Janson, *The Stranger in America* (London, 1807), p. 202.

3. Ibid., p. 171.

4. Jean Pierre Brissot de Warville, *New Travels in the United States of America Performed in 1788* (London, 1792), p. 172.

5. Francois, duc de La Rochefoucauld-Liancourt, *Travels through the United States of America and Upper Canada in the Years 1795, 1796, and 1797*, 2 vols. (London, 1799), 2:132.

6. John M. Duncan, *Travels through Part of the United States and Canada in 1818 and 1819*, 4 vols. (New Haven, 1821–22), 2:6.

7. John Bernard, *Retrospections of America, 1797–1811* (New York, 1887), pp. 33–34.

8. Twining, *Travels in America*, p. 94.

9. Isaac Weld, *Travels through the States of North America and the Provinces of Upper and Lower Canada during the Years 1795, 1796, and 1797*, 4th ed., 2 vols. (London, 1807), p. 27.

10. Postmaster General's Letterbooks, H:302.

11. Ibid., H:318.

12. Ibid., H:391.

13. Ibid., I:159.

14. Ibid., K:514.

15. Advertisement, *Evening Post* (New York), August 21, 1817.

16. Advertisement, *Albany Argus*, December 29, 1818, and January 12, 1819.

17. Advertisement, ibid., December 29, 1818.

18. Duncan, *Travels through Part of the United States*, 2:316.

19. Karl Bernhard, Duke of Saxe-Weimar-Eisenach, *Travels through North America during the Years 1825 and 1826*, 2 vols. (Philadelphia, 1828), 2:157.
20. Basil Hall, *Travels in America*, 3 vols. (Edinburgh, 1829), 1:93–94.
21. *American Traveller* (Boston), July 26, 1825.

VI Perils of the Road

1. Robert Barclay, *Agricultural Tour in the United States and Upper Canada* (London, 1842), p. 29.
2. John Melish, *Travels in the United States of America in the Years 1806, and 1807, and 1809, 1810, and 1811*, 2 vols. (Philadelphia, 1812), 1:143.
3. Duncan, *Travels through Part of the United States*, 2:8.
4. Tyrone Power, *Impressions of America*, 2 vols. (London, 1836), 1:299–300.
5. Duncan, *Travels through Part of the United States*, 2:12–15.
6. Charles J. Latrobe, *The Rambler in North America*, 2 vols. (Philadelphia, 1835), 2:12.
7. Frederick Marryat, *A Diary in America*, 3 vols. (London, 1839), 2:165.
8. William Dalton, *Travels in the United States and Upper Canada* (Appleby, England, 1821), p. 67.
9. Bernhard, *Travels through North America*, 2:27.
10. Advertisement, *Evening Post*, January 22, 1828.
11. Charles Lyell, *Travels in North America*, 2 vols. (New York, 1845), 2:62.
12. Marryat, *Diary in America*, 2:165.
13. La Rochefoucauld-Liancourt, *Travels through the United States*, 1:17.
14. Weld, *Travels through the States*, 1:37–38.
15. Amelia Murray, *Letters from the United States, Cuba, and Canada*, 2 vols. (London, 1856), p. 290.
16. Adam Hodgson, *Letters from North America* (London, 1824), 2:131.
17. See, for example, *Revised Statutes of the Commonwealth of Massachusetts, 1836*, p. 389; *Revised Statutes of the State of New York, 1852*, 2:105; and *A Digest of the Laws of Pennsylvania, 1856*, p. 761.
18. H. P. Warren et al., *History of Waterford, Oxford County, Maine* (Portland, Maine, 1879), pp. 177–78.
19. *Evening Post*, February 7, 1822.
20. *American Traveller*, February 27, 1826.
21. Advertisement, *Evening Post*, May 5, 1825.
22. Alexander Mackey, *The Western World*, 3 vols. (London, 1849), 2:260–64.
23. Thomas Searight, *The Old Pike* (Uniontown, Pa., 1894), p. 155. This fine work has in some respects the value of an original source, since the author, the son of a well-known tavern keeper on the road, lived through the years of the pike as a boy and a young man.
24. Edward Thomas Coke, *A Subaltern's Furlough*, 2 vols. (New York, 1833), 1:193–94.
25. *New Hampshire Sentinel* (Keene), December 30, 1826.
26. *Niles Weekly Register*, May 12, 1832.
27. *Virginia Herald* (Fredericksburg), May 18, 1802.
28. *Chicago Democrat*, August 6, 1834.
29. Searight, *The Old Pike*, p. 16.
30. *Ohio State Journal*, June 18, 1842.
31. *Sargamo Journal* (Springfield, Ill.), July 1, 1842.
32. *American Advertiser* (Richmond), January 31, 1784.
33. *Columbus Sentinel* (Ohio), March 26, 1831.
34. James S. Buckingham, *America, Historical, Statistic, and Descriptive*, 3 vols. (London, 1843), 3:202.

35. Robert Sutcliff, *Travels in Some Parts of North America in the Years 1804, 1805, and 1806*, 2nd ed. (York, 1815), p. 44.
36. See R. S. Kirby and P. S. Lawson, *The Early Years of Modern Civil Engineering* (New Haven, 1932). The subject of bridge building, like that of road making, has too many ramifications to be given detailed treatment in this book.
37. For examples of baggage robbery see *Virginia North-Western Gazette* (Wheeling), February 3, 1819; *Star and North Carolina Gazette* (Raleigh), February 24, 1831; and *American Traveller*, May 18, 1827.
38. Gerham A. Worth, "Recollections of Cincinnati" (Albany, 1851); reprinted in *Quarterly Publication of the Historical and Philosophical Society of Ohio*, 11 (1916): 8.
39. U.S., *Statutes at Large*, 1:237, 736.
40. *City of Washington Gazette*, March 14, 16, and 20, 1818.
41. The "Confession" was reprinted in *The Life of the Celebrated Mail Robber and Daring Highwayman, Joseph Thompson Hare, Highwayman and Pirate's Own Book* (Philadelphia, 1846).
42. *Niles Weekly Register*, September 19, 1818.
43. *Charleston Courier*, February 10, 12, 18, and 22, 1819.
44. *Niles Weekly Register*, April 17, 1819.
45. Ibid., November 3, 1821.
46. Ibid., July 12, 1825; and *Columbus Gazette* (Ohio), July 24, 1823.
47. *American State Papers: Post Office Department*, pp. 62–63.
48. Ibid.
49. Searight, *The Old Pike*, pp. 157–58.

VII   The Stage Driver

1. Marryat, *Diary in America*, 2:12.
2. *American State Papers: Post Office Department*, pp. 62–63.
3. Bernard, *Retrospections of America*, p. 35.
4. Buckingham, *America*, 2:477.
5. James S. Buckingham, *The Slave States of America*, 2 vols. (London, 1842), 1:234.
6. John R. Gedley, *Letters from America*, 2 vols. (London, 1844), 1:50.
7. John Fowler, *Journal of a Tour in the State of New York in the Year 1830* (London, 1831), p. 69.
8. Searight, *The Old Pike*, pp. 156–57.
9. Brissot de Warville, *New Travels through a Part of the United States and Canada* (New York, 1849), pp. 138–39.
10. James Dixon, *Personal Narrative of a Tour through a Part of the United States and Canada* (New York, 1849), p. 107.
11. Power, *Impressions of America*, 1:177–78.
12. Duncan, *Travels through Part of the United States*, 2:17.
13. Coke, *A Subaltern's Furlough*, p. 78.
14. George Combe, *Notes on the United States of North America during a Phrenological Visit in 1838–9–40*, 3 vols. (Edinburgh, 1841), 1:38.
15. Twining, *Travels in America*, p. 63.
16. Buckingham, *The Slave States*, 1:238.
17. Power, *Impressions of America*, 1:335–36.
18. Latrobe, *Rambler in North America*, 2:53.
19. Charles Dickens, *American Notes* (London, 1842), p. 50.
20. Weld, *Travels through the States*, 1:38.
21. Hall, *Travels in North America*, 1:109.
22. Harriet Martineau, *Retrospect of Western Travel*, 3 vols. (London, 1838), 1:337.

23. John Lambert, *Travels through Canada and the United States in the Years 1806, 1807, and 1808*, 2nd ed., 2 vols. (London, 1814), 2:31.

24. James Stuart, *Three Years in America*, 2 vols. (New York, 1833), 2:64.

25. Buckingham, *America*, 3:217.

26. Henry Tudor, *Narrative of a Tour in North America*, 2 vols. (Philadelphia, 1836), 1:448.

27. Postmaster General's Letterbooks, H:403, 407.

28. John Palmer, *Journals of Travels in the United States of North America and in Lower Canada Performed in the Year 1817* (London, 1818), p. 43.

29. "Western Stage Company—General Account Ledger"; manuscript in the Pennsylvania Historical Society.

30. Records of the Eastern Stage Company; manuscript in the Essex Institute, Salem, Massachusetts.

31. "Book of Records Belonging to the Proprietors of the Boston and New York Mail Stages"; manuscript in the American Antiquarian Society, Worcester, Massachusetts.

32. Searight, *The Old Pike*, p. 142.

33. Postmaster General's Letterbooks; P:227.

34. In a folder of miscellaneous papers among manuscript papers and records of stage-coach proprietor Ginery Twitchell in the American Antiquarian Society, Worcester, Mass.

35. *Boston Recorder and Telegraph*, February 27, 1826.

36. Ibid., March 6, 1826.

37. Searight, *The Old Pike*, pp. 169–70.

38. Ibid., pp. 152–53.

39. O. O. Winther, "Stage Coach Service in Northern California, 1849–53," *Pacific Historical Review*, 3 (1934): 389.

40. Morris Schaff, *Etna and Kirkersville* (Boston and New York, 1905), p. 74.

VIII   The "Step-lively Era" in the East

1. Postmaster General's Letterbooks, M:7.

2. Ibid.

3. The figures for 1811 and 1816 are in *Niles Weekly Register*, 11:341. The figure for 1820 is from *American State Papers; Post Office Department*, 183.

4. Although the turnpike and the stagecoach were closely associated, as the road and the vehicle always are, the full story of that important topic must be left to other writers. See, for example, Joseph A. Durrenberger, *Turnpikes: A Study of the Toll Road Movement in the Middle Atlantic States and Maryland* (Valdosta, Ga., 1931); and Frederic J. Wood, *The Turnpikes of New England and Evolution of the Same through England, Virginia, and Maryland* (Boston, 1919).

5. F. R. Diffenderfer, "The Philadelphia and Lancaster Turnpike," in *Papers Read Before the Lancaster County Historical Society*, 6 (1901): 116–49.

6. Julius P. Sachse, *The Wayside Inns on the Lancaster Roadside*, 2nd ed., (Lancaster, Pa., 1912), p. 132.

7. Wheaton J. Lane, *From Indian Trail to Iron Horse: Travel and Transportation in New Jersey, 1620–1860* (Princeton, 1939), p. 159.

8. Ibid., p. 160.

9. R. S. Rantoul, "Some Notes on Old Modes of Travel," *Essex Institute Historical Collections*, 11 (1872): 43.

10. Searight, *The Old Pike*, pp. 185–87.

11. John Adams Paxton, *The Philadelphia Directory and Register for 1819* (Philadelphia, 1819), p. 77.

12. "List of Stages from Boston," *Isaiah Thomas, Junior's, Massachusetts, Rhode Island, New Hampshire, and Vermont Almanack for 1801* (Worcester, Mass., 1800).

13. "List of Stages," *The Boston Directory* (Boston, 1820), pp. 19–21.

14. *The Boston Directory* (1825), pp. 18–23.

15. Maine was a part of Massachusetts until 1820, but present-day terminology for the area is used in this chapter.

16. James W. North, *History of Augusta* (Augusta, Maine, 1820), p. 333.

17. George A. and Henry W. Wheeler, *History of Brunswick, Topsham and Harpswell, Maine* (Boston, 1878), p. 323.

18. *Private or Special Laws of the State of Maine*, vol. 1, *1820–1828* (Portland, 1828), pp. 295, 360.

19. Advertisement, *Independent Chronicle* (Boston), April 3 and September 25, 1800.

20. Postmaster General's Letterbooks, M:295.

21. *The Albany Register and Albany Directory for the Year 1815* (Albany, 1815), p. 9.

22. Munsell, *Annals of Albany*, 7:133.

23. *American Traveller*, October 12, 1827..

24. Advertisement, *Maryland Gazette*, October 24, 1786.

25. The story of Twining's fortunes may be followed in his several memorials to Congress in the Papers of the Continental Congress, vol. 41, fols. 255–56, 259–62.

26. Hening, *Statutes-at-Large* (Va.), 12:618–19.

27. Ibid., 11:467.

28. Ibid., 13:106–08.

29. *The Statutes at Large of South Carolina* (Columbia, 1839), 5:281–82.

30. Ibid.

31. Postmaster General's Letterbooks, L:164.

32. *American State Papers: Post Office Department*, p. 29.

33. Ibid., pp. 24–25.

34. Advertisement, *Richmond Enquirer*, April 21, 1820.

35. *Amerian State Papers: Post Office Department*, p. 29.

36. Advertisement, *Raleigh Register*, May 19, 1820.

37. *American Beacon* (Norfolk, Va.), April 11, 1818.

38. *Charleston Courier*, May 16, 1820.

39. Ibid.

40. *Alexandria Herald*, January 4, 1819.

41. *Richmond Enquirer*, April 21, 1820.

42. Ibid., January 13, 1814.

43. Ibid., April 21, 1820.

44. *Raleigh Register*, January 15, 1819.

45. Ibid., February 26, 1819.

46. Advertisement, *Carolina Centinel* (New Bern, N.C.), May 9, 1818.

47. Postmaster General's Letterbooks, I:59.

48. Clarence E. Carter, ed., *Territorial Papers of the United States* (Washington, D.C., 1934–), vol. 4, *Southwest Territory*, pp. 343–45, 354, 397, 416–17.

49. Julian P. Bretz, "Early Land Communication with the Lower Mississippi Valley," *Mississippi Valley Historical Review* 13 (June 1926): 4–5.

50. Habersham to secretary of war, March 12, 1801.

51. Postmaster General's Letterbooks, M:231–34.

52. Ibid., N:171.

53. Ibid., D:330.

54. Ibid., O:318.

55. Ibid., P:11.
56. Ibid., Q:95–101.
57. Ibid.
58. Advertisement, *Alabama Republican* (Huntsville), May 6, 1820.
59. Edward C. Betts, *Early History of Huntsville, Alabama, 1804–1870*, rev. ed. (Montgomery, Ala., 1916), pp. 32–34.
60. Advertisement, *Southern Advocate and Huntsville Advertiser*, December 30, 1825.
61. Advertisement, *Augusta Chronicle*, April 25, 1821.
62. *Montgomery Republican*, June 19, 1821.
63. *National Intelligencer*, May 9, 1817.
64. Paxton, *Philadelphia Directory for 1819*, p. 72. This publication cited these two routes as the longest routes of connecting stages in the United States.

IX   The Post Office and the Stages

1. For the beginnings of railway service in 1835, see the extended treatment in "A History of the Railway Mail Service," published as U.S., Congress, *Senate Executive Document No. 40*, 48th Cong., 2d sess., 1885, serial no. 2261 (cited as Senate, "History of Railway Mail Service").
2. Habersham to William Rotch, November 4, 1795.
3. Ibid., January 26, 1796.
4. Habersham to Simeon Lester, April 15, 1795.
5. U.S., *Statutes at Large*, 1:357.
6. *Annals of Congress*, 4th Cong., 2d sess., 1797, pp. 2061–62.
7. Ibid., pp. 2058–59.
8. U.S., *Statutes at Large*, 2:191.
9. Postmaster General's Letterbooks, M:465.
10. Granger to Nathaniel Willis, April 14, 1806.
11. Table, *American State Papers: Post Office Department*, p. 41.
12. Ibid, p. 97.
13. U.S., *Statutes at Large*, 1:234.
14. Ibid., 1:356.
15. Ibid., 4:104–05.
16. Postmaster General's Letterbooks, A:19–21.
17. Ibid., A:38.
18. Ibid., A:198–99.
19. *Columbian Centinel*, July 23, 1794.
20. *Universal Gazette* (Washington), July 16, 1801.
21. *New Hampshire Patriot* (Concord), August 16, 1824.
22. [Mark] Beaufoy, *Tour through Parts of the United States and Canada* (London, 1828), p. 64.
23. Pickering to Pease, April 26, 1793.
24. *American State Papers: Post Office Department*, pp. 9-12.
25. Postmaster General's Letterbooks, C:315.
26. Ibid., D:123.
27. Ibid., F:98.
28. *Federal Gazette* (Baltimore), January 3, 1798.
29. Postmaster General's Letterbooks, I:305.
30. Ibid., L:311.
31. Ibid., A:154–56.
32. "Proposals for Carrying the Public Mails," *Federal Gazette*, January 3, 1798.
33. "Proposals," *Universal Gazette*, July 16, 1801.

34. "Proposals," *New Hampshire Patriot*, August 16, 1824.
35. "Turnpike Road to Baltimore," signed "American Traveller," *Federal Gazette*, February 19, 1806.
36. Postmaster General's Letterbooks, H:192.
37. Ibid., H:371.
38. Granger to James Jackson, March 23, 1802.
39. Ibid.
40. Postmaster General's Letterbooks, Q:72, 209–11.
41. *American State Papers: Post Office Department*, pp. 99–102.
42. Ibid.
43. Searight, *The Old Pike*, pp. 18-19.
44. Ibid.
45. Carl H. Scheele, *A Short History of the Mail Service* (Washington, 1970), p. 66.
46. Ibid., pp. 73–76.
47. Mervyn Savill, *The Romance of the Postage Stamp* (New York, 1962), pass.
48. Ibid.
49. Scheele, *History of the Mail Service*, p. 73.
50. John N. Luff, *The Postage Stamps of the United States* (New York, 1902), pass.
51. Savill, *Romance of the Postage Stamp*, pass.
52. The Postmasters General's *Annual Reports* (Washington) from 1849 to 1860 contain tables showing the lengths of mail coach routes and also the number of routes by states. The figures used in this and later chapters of this book are calculated from the table in the *Report* for 1860. For a comparison with railroad operations see also Senate, "History of Railway Mail Service."

X   Newspapers and the Stages

1. Hazard to Belknap, March 5, 1788.
2. Postmaster General's Letterbooks, A:257–59.
3. U.S., *Statutes at Large*, 1:238, 362.
4. Ibid., 1:238, 362; 2:600–01.
5. Pickering to John Scull, Postmaster General's Letterbooks, B:11.
6. *Annals of Congress*, 2d Cong., 1st sess., 1792, pp. 284–86.
7. In Section 21 of the Acts of 1792 and 1794 and Section 26 of the Act of 1810.
8. Madison to Edmund Pendleton, December 6, 1792.
9. Pickering to Murry, December 31, 1792.
10. Postmaster General's Letterbooks, C:157–58.
11. Ibid.
12. Palmer, *Journal of Travels*, p. 200.
13. Lambert, *Travels through Canada and the United States*, 2:497–98.
14. U.S., *Statutes at Large*, 1:360.
15. Ibid.
16. *New-York Journal*, January 4, 1787.
17. Buckingham, *Slave States*, 2:352.
18. Postmaster General's Letterbooks, D:245.
19. U.S., *Statutes at Large*, 1:512.
20. Ibid., 2:600–01.
21. Lambert, *Travels through Canada and the United States*, 2:498.
22. Granger to Thomas Walker, August 2, 1803.
23. Granger to Parrit Blasdell, June 19, 1804.
24. *American State Papers: Post Office Department*, pp. 16–17.
25. U.S., *Statutes at Large*, 1:512.

XI Stagecoach Makers

1. *National Intelligencer*, September 4, 1820.
2. Searight, *The Old Pike*, p. 181.
3. Advertisement, *United States Telegraph*, December 18, 1829.
4. Advertisemet, ibid., February 9, 1830.
5. Advertisement, *Daily Albany Argus*, May 26, 1838.
6. *Albany Evening Journal*, May 26, 1838.
7. *Troy Sentinel*, May 8, 1827.
8. Quoted in A. J. Weise, *Troy's One Hundred Years*, pp. 168–70.
9. Quoted in the *American Traveller*, August 12, 1831.
10. Quoted in ibid.
11. Advertisement, *North Carolina Standard*, June 26, 1835.
12. *Charleston Courier*, March 7, 1837.
13. Ibid., February 6, 1838.
14. *Maysville Monitor*, January 4, 1838.
15. *Kentucky Gazette* (Lexington), April 26, 1838.
16. *The Mississippian* (Jackson), February 9, 1838.
17. Advertisement, *Daily Pittsburgh Gazette*, January 23, 1840.
18. Advertisement, *Chicago Democrat*, November 30, 1842.
19. *Madison City Express*, July 6, 1843.
20. Buckingham, *Slave States*, 2:41.
21. *Daily Albany Argus*, January 20, 1846.
22. *Niles Weekly Register*, August 20, 1831.
23. Ibid., November 19, 1831.
24. Ibid., March 3, 1832.
25. Searight, *The Old Pike*, pp. 164–66.
26. *American Traveller*, June 12, 1827.
27. Alfred E. Lee, *History of the City of Columbus, Capital of Ohio*, 2 vols. (New York and Chicago, 1892), 2:321–22.
28. Advertisement, *Pittsburgh Gazette*, September 14, 1827, and March 30, 1832.
29. *American Traveller*, May 20, 1828.
30. *Daily Ohio Statesman*, December 10, 1842.
31. Buckingham, *Slave States*, 1:191.
32. Barclay, *Agricultural Tour*, p. 29.
33. Alexander Mackey, *The Western World*, 2:213.
34. For fine account of the early years of Abbot Downing and Company, see "Carriage Manufacturing in Concord," *Concord Daily Mirror*, January 2, 1865.
35. Advertisement, *Daily Commercial Chronicle* (Pittsburgh), February 27, 1846.
36. These and subsequent facts are taken largely from "Carriage Manufacturing in Concord."
37. Joseph F. Lovering, *A Sermon Commemorative of Lewis Downing* (Concord, 1873).
38. *Concord Evening Monitor*, May 3, 1897.
39. The distribution of Concord coaches after 1865 can be studied by noting the orders in the two order books of Abbot, Downing and Company covering the period 1865–1902. They are in the collection of the New Hampshire Historical Society, Concord (cited as Abbot, Downing order books).
40. *La Crosse National Democrat*, October 12, 1858.
41. Abbot, Downing order books.
42. Ibid.
43. Ibid.
44. Searight, *The Old Pike*, p. 164.
45. *Historical New Hampshire*, 20 (November 3, 1965).

XII   The Stagecoach Tavern

1. Twining, *Travels in America*, p. 99.
2. Bessie W. Gahn, *George Washington's Headquarters in Washington* (Silver Spring, 1940).
3. For a view of the tavern on a busy stagecoach route, see the fifteen chapters on the inns of the National Road in Searight, *The Old Pike*. See also Alice Morse Earle, *Stage-Coach and Tavern Days* (1900; reprint ed., New York, 1969). Many of Earle's observations are firsthand recollections from her youth, and thus this work has some of the character of a primary source. In the latter chapters of her book, she has some amusing, if slightly credulous, sections about taverns that were believed to be haunted by the spirits of past travelers of the road. For a modern and popular account of the stagecoach tavern, see the early sections of Horace Sutton, *Travelers: The American Tourist from Stagecoach to Space Shuttle* (New York, 1980).
4. F. R. Diffenderfer, "Philadelphia and Lancaster Turnpike," p. 122.
5. Searight, *The Old Pike*, pp. 192–297.
6. Good summaries of the taverns along these major New York roads are to be found in Jeptha R. Simms, *The Frontiersmen of New York*, 2 vols. (Albany, N.Y., 1882–83), 1:356–63.
7. Count Francesco Arese, *A Trip to the Prairies and in the Interior of North America, 1837–1838*, trans. Andrew Evans (New York, 1934), p. 34.
8. Hodgson, *Letters from North America*, 1:21.
9. Lambert, *Travels through Canada and the United States*, p. 239.
10. Henry B. Fearon, *Sketches of America*, 2nd ed. (London, 1818), p. 185.
11. Advertisement, *Richmond Enquirer*, January 29, 1814.
12. Advertisement, *Pennsylvania Packet*, August 10, 1782.
13. Edward S. Abdy, *Journal of a Residence and Tour in the United States of North America, from April, 1833, to October, 1834* (London, 1835), p. 310.
14. "Ledger Containing General Accounts for the Western Road"; manuscript in the Pennsylvania Historical Society, Philadelphia.
15. Tallmadge Stage records; manuscript in Ohio Historical and Archeological Society at Columbus.
16. Bill of Jacob Brechill, ibid.
17. Package for first and second quarters, ibid.
18. Richard Parkinson, *A Tour in America in 1798, 1799, and 1800*, 2 vols. (London, 1805), 1:254–55.
19. Stuart, *Three Years in North America*, p. 86.
20. Marryat, *Diary in America*, 1:102.
21. La Rochefoucauld-Liancourt, *Travels through the United States*, 1:44.
22. Patrick Shirreff, *A Tour through North America* (Edinburgh, 1835), p. 49.
23. Francis Hall, *Travels in Canada and the United States in 1816 and 1817* (London, 1818), p. 57.
24. Hodgson, *Letters from North America*, 1:21.
25. Timothy Dwight, *Travels in New England and New York*, 4 vols. (New Haven, 1821–22), 1:428.
26. Hodgson, *Letters from North America*, 1:21.
27. William T. Harris, *Remarks Made during a Tour through the United States of America in the Years 1817, 1818, and 1819* (London, 1821), p. 66.
28. Timothy Bigelow, *Journal of a Tour to Niagara Falls in the Year 1805* (Boston, 1876), pp. 17–18.
29. Searight, *The Old Pike*, pp. 195ff.
30. Thurlow Weed, "A Chapter from the Autobiography of Mr. Thurlow Weed"; reprinted in *The Galaxy*, April 1870, p. 18.

31. Hall, *Travels in Canada and the United States*, p. 57.
32. Melish, *Travels in the United States*, 1:33–34.
33. Marryat, *Diary in America*, 1:103.
34. Fowler, *Journal of a Tour*, 72.
35. John Howison, *Sketches of Upper Canada and Some Resolutions of the United States of America* (Edinburgh, 1821), 291.
36. Stuart, *Three Years in North America*, 1:129.
37. Martineau, *Retrospect of Western Travel*, 1:127.
38. Stuart, *Three Years in North America*, 1:86.
39. Howison, *Sketches and Some Resolutions*, p. 291.
40. Stuart, *Three Years in North America*, 2:273.
41. Marryat, *Diary in America*, 2:273.
42. Harris, *Remarks Made during a Tour*, p. 66.
43. Palmer, *Journal of Travels*, p. 150.
44. Ibid.
45. Maximilian of Wied, *Travels in the Interior of North America, 1832–1834*, trans. H. Evans Lloyd, 3 vols. (Cleveland, 1906), 1:52.
46. Shirraff, *Tour through North America*.
47. Tudor, *Narrative of a Tour*, 2:443.
48. Thomas Hamilton, *Men and Mariners in America*, 2 vols. (Edinburgh, 1834), 2:5.
49. Charles Fenno Hoffman, *A Winter in the West*, 2 vols. (New York, 1835), 1:92.
50. Hall, *Travels in Canada and the United States*, p. 57.
51. Ibid.
52. Stuart, *Three Years in North America*, 2:302.
53. Latrobe, *Rambler in North America*, 2:18.
54. Power, *Impressions of America*, 2:143.
55. Marryat, *Diary in America*, 1:108–09.
56. Melish, *Travels in the United States*, 2:40.
57. Ibid., p. 48.
58. Marryat, *Diary in America*, 2:210.
59. Martineau, *Retrospect of Western Travel*, 2:37–38.
60. John Davis, *Travels of Four Years and and a Half in the United States of America during 1798, 1799, 1800, 1801, 1802* (London, 1803), p. 357.
61. Frederick F. DeRoos, *Personal Narrative of Travels in the United States and Canada in 1826* (London, 1827), 85–86, 90.
62. Weed, "Autobiography," p. 9.
63. G. T. Vigne, *Six Months in America*, 1:279–80.
64. Shirreff, *Tour through North America*, p. 287.
65. Martineau, *Retrospect of Western Travel*, 2:44–45.
66. Searight, *The Old Pike*, pp. 324-25.
67. Ibid., pp. 325–27.
68. Ibid., p. 337.
69. Ibid., p. 260.
70. Ibid., p. 202.
71. Ibid., p. 337.
72. Jefferson Williamson, *The American Hotel: An Anecdotal History* (New York, 1930), pp. 10–11.
73. Ibid., p. 13.

XIII   Steamboats and Stages—Rivals and Partners

1. Advertisement, *Evening Post*, January 2, 1810.
2. Advertisement, ibid., December 31, 1810.

3. See Lane, *From Indian Trail*, pp. 173–218.

4. Ibid., pp. 179–82.

5. Ibid., p. 182.

6. See chapter 9.

7. Advertisement, *New York Evening Post*, September 7, 1810.

8. Advertisement, ibid., September 5, 1810.

9. Edward C. Kirkland, *Men, Cities, and Transportation: A Study in New England History, 1820–1900*, 2 vols. (Cambridge, Mass., 1948), 1:20–22.

10. Seymour Dunbar, *A History of Travel in America* (4 vols., 1915; 1-vol. reprint ed., New York, 1937), pp. 404–06.

11. Ibid., p.404.

12. Quoted in Kirkland, *Men, Cities, and Transportation*, p. 25.

13. Advertisement, *National Intelligencer*, March 21, 1814.

14. Advertisement, *Baltimore Patriot*, July 5, 1815.

15. *National Intelligencer*, January 9, February 9, July 10, and December 14, 1813; January 10, May 13, and July 1, 1814.

16. Ibid., December 2, 1817.

17. Advertisement, *Baltimore Patriot*, December 15, 1815.

18. *National Intelligencer*, July 8, 1812.

19. Ibid., April 26, 1817.

20. Samuel Jackson, comp., *The Baltimore Directory Corrected up to June, 1819.*

21. Ibid.

22. Diary of John Quincy Adams; manuscript in the Massachusetts Historical Society, Boston.

XIV West to the Mississippi

1. Advertisements, *Philadelphia Gazette and Daily Advertiser*, July 3 and December 3, 1804.

2. Postmaster General's Letterbooks, M:446.

3. Ibid., N:131, 317, 516.

4. Ibid., N:305.

5. Ibid., N:516.

6. Ibid.

7. Ibid.

8. Ibid., O:51.

9. Ibid., O:90.

10. Ibid., O:364.

11. Ibid., O:469.

12. Ibid., P:263.

13. Ibid., Q:95–101, 304.

14. Philip D. Jordan, in chapter 3: "Ebenezer Hews a Trace," *The National Road* (Indianapolis and New York, 1948), furnishes the best account of the pioneer days of this route. It is often a surprise to realize how late the National Road was opened through the center of Ohio, Indiana, and Illinois, to the Mississippi. Not until 1828 was horseback mail service established directly between Columbus and Indianapolis, and not until 1832 was there stagecoach service over this route. In 1834, the road was extended, via Terre Haute and Springfield, to St. Louis, and stage service over it was complete, fourteen years after the first coach had reached St. Louis over the Vincennes route.

15. Lee, *History of Columbus*, 1:344–45.

16. Postmaster General's Letterbooks, Z:109–17.

17. Lee, *History of Columbus*, 1:345, 346.

18. *History of Dayton, Ohio* (Dayton, 1889), p. 139.
19. *History of Ashtabula County, Ohio* (Philadelphia, 1878), p. 28.
20. Advertisement, *Kentucky Gazette*, August 9, 1803.
21. J. Winston Coleman, *Stagecoach Days in the Bluegrass* (Louisville, 1935), pp. 34–35.
22. Bernard Mayo, *Henry Clay, Spokesman of the New West* (Boston, 1937), p. 197.
23. These ventures can be followed in considerable detail in the *Argus of Western Amer-America* (Frankfort, Ky), 1819–1821.
24. See George R. Wilson and Gayle Thornbrough, *The Buffalo Trace* (Indianapolis, 1946).
25. Advertisement, *Indiana Centinel*, November 18, 1820.
26. *History of Marion and Clinton Counties* (Philadelphia, 1881), p. 191.
27. J. Thomas Scharf, *History of Saint Louis City and County*, 2 vols. (Philadelphia, 1883), 2:1, 432.
28. *Missouri Gazette*, April 4, 1821.

XV   The Indian Summer of Eastern Staging

1. Quoted in Emily C. Blackman, *History of Susquehanna County, Pennsylvania* (Philadelphia, 1873), p. 325.
2. *Boston Directory* (1820, 1825).
3. *American Traveller*, June 30, 1826.
4. *Badger and Porter's Stage Register*, no. 3 (1825), pp. 14–16, and no. 59 (1835), p. 30.
5. *Washington Globe*, October 1, 1835.
6. Route Registers for Maryland, 1836–39, pp. 552–53.
7. Advertisement, *Washington Globe*, October 1 and November 13, 1837.
8. *National Intelligencer*, December 4, 1837.
9. Route Registers for Maryland, 1836–39, pp. 552–53.
10. Ibid., pp. 584–85.
11. Postmaster General's *Annual Report* for 1860. See also footnote 52 in chapter 9.
12. Advertisement, *Augusta Chronicle*, May 19, 1824.
13. R.P.H. Vail, "Along the Hudson in Stagecoach Days," *Outlook* 80 (June 24, 1905): 489–96, contains an extended account of the Beach activities, obviously written from first-hand information secured perhaps from Charles L. Beach himself (who had died in 1903 at the age of 93) or from members of his family.
14. Ibid.; and "One Hundred Years Young," *Catskill Recorder*, June 29, 1923.
15. [Theodore Dwight], *The Northern Traveler and Northern Tour* (New York, 1825), p. 15.
16. Ibid., p. 38.
17. Ibid.; and Robert J. Vandewater, *The Tourist; or Pocket Manual for Travellers on the Hudson River, the Western Canal, and Stagehead* (New York, 1835), p. 31.
18. Richard S. Barrett, *The Eagle Guide to the Catskill Mountains* (Brooklyn, N.Y., 1905), pp. 79–80.
19. Mark Van Doren, *Nathaniel Hawthorne* (New York, 1949), pp. 8–9, 14, 28.
20. Nathaniel Hawthorne, *Passages from the American Note-Books of Nathaniel Hawthorne* (Boston, 1885), pp. 126–27.

Select Bibliography
of Primary Sources

Unpublished Official Records

Files of the Connecticut General Assembly, 1784–97. Connecticut State Library, Hartford.

> This series contains important documents relating to early stage lines through Connecticut, including petitions for and against exclusive privileges for certain proprietors.

Maryland "Red Books." Maryland Hall of Records, Annapolis.

> This miscellaneous assemblage of early official records of the state of Maryland includes some papers of the State Senate and House of Delegates. In volume 31, numbers 53, 54, and 55 relate to Gabriel Van Horne's exclusive privilege to run stages between the Susquehanna and Potomac rivers. Other documents concern Robert Hodgson's exclusive privilege on the Eastern Shore.

Papers of the Continental Congress. Record Group No. 11, National Archives, Washington, D.C.

> Especially valuable for this study is volume 61, which contains most of the papers relating to the postal service during the Confederation period.

Records of the United States Post Office Department. Record Group No. 28, National Archives, Washington, D.C.

> These records, which were originally kept in the Library of the Post Office, contain invaluable information about the mail operations of the stage lines in the nineteenth century. The most useful items are the following:
>
> a) Postmaster General's Letterbooks, volumes A (October 1789)–Z (December 1821), except J and V, which never existed. Each volume of this series has its own index of addresses, making it easy to pick out letters to specific contractors. Many letters to Congressmen, postmasters, and others also contain pertinent information. Starting over with a new alphabet, this series continues after 1821.
>
> b) Letterbooks of the First Assistant Postmaster General, volumes A (October 1793)–C (March 1800). These volumes contain copies of letters relating chiefly to postmasters' accounts and balances and of letters to contractors. They are sometimes helpful in showing that stage service had been started by a particular time, and there are occasional details of interest that supplement the Postmaster General's Letterbooks. This series may have continued past volume C, which is filled to its last page, but no later volumes have been found.
>
> c) "Ledger A, No. 6," May 1782–March 1790. This single volume is an exceedingly valuable financial record of the Confederation period. Included in it are the accounts of the stage proprietors, recording the periods of their service and the

amounts they were paid. The signficance of the figure *6* in the title, which has been carried through several rebindings, is unknown.

d) Route Register, 1814–17. This record lists all postal routes of its period, printing the names of post offices and the established schedules of service for each route. This was the first route register and the only one before 1820.

Unpublished Personal Papers and Contracts

Gideon Granger Papers. Manuscript Division, Library of Congress, Washington, D.C.

This portfolio includes the postmaster general's papers on political subjects and affairs of the Post Office, with the latter being semiofficial or personal in character.

William Gulick Papers. Princeton University Library, Princeton, N.J.

These papers relate to the business interests of the Gulick family in staging enterprises across New Jersey from about 1812 to 1835. They are contained in eighty-eight folders distributed throughout the "General File," chiefly under "Gulick," but some folders are filed under other headings such as the names of partners Thomas Ward, Thomas Lyon, and Gen. J. N. Cumming. Many folders hold little but receipted bills, but others provide information on the complicated and ever-changing arrangements between partners in staging ventures and on the Gulicks' relations with steamboat owners. These papers are also excellent records of the costs of coaches, horses, horse feed, coach repairs, labor, tolls, and other needs of a staging business.

Return J. Meigs's Letterbook as Postmaster General, 1820–21. Manuscript Division, Library of Congress, Washington, D.C.

This volume contains copies of Meigs's letters to committees and members of Congress, relating chiefly to the congressional investigations of the Post Office during those two years. This letterbook could be considered official in origin, but it was kept separate from the regular series of letterbooks of the postmaster general and apparently did not remain in official custody.

Levi Pease Contracts for Carrying the Mail. New England Historic Genealogical Society Library, Boston, Mass.

Because the Post Office records no longer contain the official copies of the mail contracts, these two documents covering the routes between Boston and New York and between Springfield, Massachusetts, and Hanover, New Hampshire, both in 1794, are of interest as illustrations of the forms and conditions of early postal contracts.

John Stevens Papers. Library of Stevens Institute of Technology, Hoboken, N.J.

These are the records of a family of inventors and businessmen and are especially valuable for studying the early history of steamboating. There are forty or fifty letters and agreements relating to the Stevens steamboat enterprises and connecting stage lines, chiefly for the period 1809–15. They illustrate the development of arrangements between steamboat and stage companies from the very beginning.

Woolfolk Papers. William and Mary College Library, Williamsburg, Va.

John G. Woolfolk and his son Jourdan, both of Bowling Green, were concerned with staging from 1787 to 1838 in Virginia, chiefly between Alexandria and Richmond. The papers consist of account books, pocket memorandum books, packages of bills and vouchers, agreements, mail contracts, and some correspondence (the last of these, however, is mostly post-1830). One folder relates to the settling of the estate of Col. John Hoomes, pioneer Virginia Stage proprietor, also of Bowling Green. "Ledger A" contains accounts of the Petersburg and Portsmouth Stage, 1787–93; the Richmond and Petersburg Stage, 1790–93; and the Edenton Stage, 1788–93, the earliest stagecoach accounts located by this book's authors.

Unpublished Stage Company Records

Book of Records Belonging to the Proprietors of the Boston and New York Mail
Stages by the Way of Worcester, Brookfield, Suffield, Hartford, New
Haven, 1800–14. American Antiquarian Society, Worcester, Mass.

This volume provides a detailed inside picture of an early association of partners
operating on an important road.

Lewis Collins's Stage Book for a stage-house opposite City Tavern, Philadelphia,
September–December 1795. Pennsylvania Historical Society, Philadelphia.

This is an example of the books kept at stage taverns or offices in which all travelers
registered their names upon applying for passage and paying their fares. Each
coach's name, destination, and leaving time were written at the top of a page, and
underneath the passengers signed their names and wrote the addresses where they
were to be picked up. After each name, the clerk entered the passage money paid.

Eastern Stage Company Records. Essex Institute, Salem, Mass.

This very complete set of records details the history of an important, profitable New
England company, though most of the documents are post-1820. This company was
an outgrowth of an association of eleven persons who united in 1803 to run a daily
stage from Boston to Portsmouth, New Hampshire. They were reorganized in April
1814 into the Eastern Stage Company, taking in wider interests, but conducted their
affairs without a charter until July 27, 1818, when they became a "body corporate"
under New Hampshire law. This charter ran for twenty years. The minutes of
stockholders' and directors' meetings for the full period 1818–38 give a more com-
prehensive picture of the inside operations of a large staging business than does any
other source known to this book's authors. There is also a cash book covering 1808 to
1814 for the association that preceded the Eastern Stage Company. The records of
the Boston and Salem Stage Company, which was closely associated with the Eastern, are also at the Essex Institute, but they are dated from 1829 to 1837.

Cash Books of Philadelphia and Lancaster Stage Dispatch. Pennsylvania Historical Society, Philadelphia.

The first of these books contains records of cash paid out from 1792 to 1800 (pp.
19–38) and of cash received from 1792 to 1797 (pp. 51–233). The second book lists
cash received from July 1799 through 1800. (The entries between April 1798 and July
1799 have apparently been cut out.) The total number of trips and number of
passengers carried month-by-month can be calculated using the records in the cash-
received portions

Portland to Kittery Stage Account Book. Manuscript Division, Library of Congress, Washington, D.C.

Since Kittery, Maine, was across the Piscataqua River from Portsmouth, New Hampshire, this is really a record of the Portland-Portsmouth service. The first 50 pages are
accounts of the line's triweekly operation from July 1797 through September 1800.
The next 150 pages are a monthly record of the number of passengers and receipts
both ways between July 1816 and October 1822.

Published Federal Records

*American State Papers: Documents, Legislative and Executive, of the Congress
of the United States.* 38 vols. Washington, D.C., 1832–61.

This series covers the first twenty-five Congresses, 1789–1838. For this book, the
most use has been made of volume 27, which includes documents related to the Post
Office Department.

Annals of Congress: Debates and Proceedings in the Congress of the United States, 1789–1824. 42 vols. Washington, D.C., 1834–56.

Carter, Clarence E., ed. *The Territorial Papers of the United States.* Washington, D.C., 1931–.

> These volumes provide useful information about the extension of horse-and-rider mail routes between the Alleghenies and the Mississippi but not about stage lines, since no stages were found in the territories before 1820.

Executive Papers No. 64. 17th Cong., 1st sess., serial 67. 1821.

> This small document lists mail contracts made in October 1820.

Executive Papers No. 87. 16th Cong., 2d sess., serial 53. 1820.

> This record includes a list of mail contracts made in 1818 and a smaller list of contracts that were to go into effect in 1820.

Ford, Worthington C.; Hunt, Gaillard; Fitzpatrick, John Clement; and Hill, Roscoe R., eds. *Journals of the Continental Congress, 1774–1789.* 34 vols. Washington, D.C., 1904–37.

House Document No. 85. 15th Cong., 1st sess., serial 8. 1817.

> This paper lists mail contracts made in 1817. Earlier lists of contracts are found only in the Postmaster General's Letterbooks (listed here under Unpublished Official Records).

Statutes at Large of the United States of America, 1789–1873. 17 vols. Boston, 1850–73.

Published State Records

Hening, William W., ed. *The Statutes at Large, Being a Collection of All the Laws of Virginia, 1619–1792.* 13 vols. Philadelphia and New York, 1823.

Laws of the State of New York...from the First to the Twentieth Session, Exclusive. 3 vols. 2d ed. New York, 1798.

Laws of the State of New York Passed at the Twenty-Eighth Session. Albany, 1805.

New Hampshire State Papers, vol. 22, *1790–1793.* Concord, 1893. Patterson, William, ed. *Laws of the State of New Jersey.* Newark, 1800.

Private or Special Laws of the State of Maine. vol. 1. *1820–1828.* Portland, 1828.

Walton, E. P., ed. *Records of the Governor and Council of the State of Vermont.* 8 vols. Montpelier, 1873–80.

Almanacs and Directories

City directories, and before them almanacs, usually contained, as a service to the public, a list of stages setting out from the city together with the places and times of their departure. By studying the changes in these lists from year to year, a researcher can obtain an indication of the development of a city's transportation facilities, as well as an index for comparison between cities. Not all of these can or need be listed, since they are easily found in any good reference library catalog. The following examples (arranged alphabetically by city) have been used the most in preparing this book.

ALBANY, New York
   Albany Register and Albany Directory for the Year 1815.

BALTIMORE, Maryland
   The Baltimore Directory for 1799... By John Mullin.
   The New Baltimore Directory and Annual Register; for 1800 and 1801.
   The Baltimore Directory for 1803... By Cornelius W. Stafford.
   The Baltimore Directory for 1810... By William Fry.
   The Baltimore Directory and Register for the Year 1816... By Edward
      Matchett.
   The Baltimore Directory Corrected up to June, 1819. Compiled by Samuel
      Jackson.

BOSTON, Massachusetts
   New England Town and County Almanack for 1769.
   The Boston Directory (1800).
   The Boston Directory (1805).
   The Boston Directory (1810).
   The Boston Directory (1820).
   The Massachusetts Register and United States Calendar...for...1824.

NEW YORK, New York
   Hutchin's Improved: Being an Almanack and Ephemeris...for...1760.
   Longworth's American Almanack, New-York Register, and City Directory
      (1797).

PHILADELPHIA, Pennsylvania
   The Philadelphia Directory for 1810... By James Robinson.
   The Philadelphia Directory and Register for 1819. By John Adams Paxton.
   Philadelphia in 1824.

PORTSMOUTH, New Hampshire
   The Portsmouth Directory (1800).

RICHMOND, Virginia
   The Richmond Directory, Register and Almanac for the Year 1819.

WORCESTER, Massachusetts
   *Isaiah Thomas Juniors, Massachusetts, Connecticut, Rhode Island, New
      Hampshire and Vermont Almanack for 1801.*

Newspapers

As the endnotes reveal, contemporary newspapers were major sources of information for this study. Newspapers sometimes carried news items concerning stage accidents or delays caused by weather conditions or special circumstances. On rare occasions, editors commented on the quality of stage service or mail arrangements. But newspapers were valuable chiefly for their public notices and advertisements of stagecoach service, which not only show the existence of certain lines but also reveal detailed arrangements, such as schedules, connecting lines, stopping places, and rates, and indicate where competition existed. In general, advertisements were more frequent when the service was new or there was competition. Larger newspaper advertisements with pictures at their heads of stages and flying horses were often the same as handbills that were plastered on tavern walls and at other public places. (A few of these are occasionally found in library broadside collections.) The newspapers for the period covered by this study are well categorized by place of issue, files preserved, and libraries and archives where they can be found in Clarence S. Brigham's admirable *History and Bibliography of American Newspapers, 1690–1820* (2 vols., Worcester, Mass., 1947). The newspapers listed below are chiefly those of staging centers, and they are listed alphabetically by state and city.

ALABAMA	Huntsville	*Alabama Republican*, 1821–24
CONNECTICUT	Hartford	*Connecticut Courant*, 1783–93
DELAWARE	Wilmington	*Delaware and Eastern-Shore Advertiser*, 1795
DISTRICT OF COLUMBIA	Georgetown	*Centinel of Liberty*, 1796–1801
		Columbia Chronicle, 1793–96
		Federal Republican, 1812–16
		George-Town Weekly Ledger, 1790–93
		Independent American, 1809–11
		Messenger, 1816–18
		Museum and Washington and George-Town Advertiser, 1801–02
		Times and Potomack Packet, 1789–91
		Washington Federalist, 1800–07
	Washington	*City of Washington Gazette*, 1817–19
		National Intelligencer, 1800–22
		Niles' Weekly Register, 1815–32
		Washington Gazette, 1796–98
GEORGIA	Augusta	*Augusta Herald*, 1800
		Augusta Chronicle and Georgia Gazette, 1819–30
	Milledgeville	*Georgia Journal*, 1819–30
	Savannah	*Columbian Museum and Savannah Advertiser*, 1798–1800
		Savannah Republican, 1820
KENTUCKY	Frankfort	*Argus of Western America*, 1819–27
	Lexington	*Kentucky Gazette*, 1821–30
MAINE	Portland	*Eastern Argus*, 1805–10
MARYLAND	Annapolis	*Maryland Gazette*, 1745–77, 1780–99
	Baltimore	*Baltimore American*, 1808–09, 1815, 1821–22
		Baltimore Daily Repository, 1791–94
		Baltimore Patriot, 1813, 1815–20
		Federal Gazette, 1796–1812
		Federal Intelligencer and Baltimore Daily Gazette, 1795
		Maryland Gazette, 1783–92
		Maryland Journal and Baltimore Advertiser, 1773–93
	Hagerstown	*Maryland Herald*, 1802–05, 1807, 1810–23

MASSACHUSETTS	Boston	*Boston News-Letter*, 1712–63
		Boston Gazette, 1773–75, 1782–92
		Columbian Centinel, 1791–1801
		Massachusetts Centinel, 1784–88
		Massachusetts Gazette, 1766–73
	Salem	*Salem Gazette*, 1785–87
	Worcester	*Massachusetts Spy*, 1784–98, 1810–12
NEW HAMPSHIRE	Concord	*Courier of New Hampshire*, 1794–1805
		New Hampshire Patriot, 1808–24
NEW JERSEY	Morristown	*Genius of Liberty*, 1798–1801
	Mount Holly	*Burlington Mirror*, 1819–20
	Newark	*Centinel of Freedom*, 1801–09
	Trenton	*Trenton Federalist*, 1803
NEW YORK	Albany	*Albany Argus, 1813–19*
		Albany Gazette, 1792–1800, 1807–13
		Albany Register, 1801–13, 1816
	Buffalo	*Buffalo Gazette*, 1816–18
		Niagara Patriot, 1820–21
	Canandaigua	*Ontario Repository*, 1817–18
	New York	*Commercial Advertiser*, 1798–1803, 1808–13
		Evening Post, 1804–12, 1814–25
		Independent New-York Gazette, 1783
		Loudon's Diary, 1792–93
		New-York Daily Advertiser, 1785–89
		New-York Gazette, 1764–71
		New-York Journal, 1768–72, 1787–96
		New-York Packet, 1785–89
	Whitestown	*Whitestown Gazette*, 1796–98
NORTH CAROLINA	Raleigh	*Raleigh Register*, 1818–21
OHIO	Columbus	*Columbus Gazette*, 1818–19, 1823–25
PENNSYLVANIA	Lancaster	*Intelligence and Weekly Advertiser*, 1799–1802
		Lancaster Journal, 1799–1801
	Philadelphia	(Dunlop & Claypool's) *American Daily Advertiser*, 1794–98
		(Poulson's) *American Daily Advertiser*, 1815–21
		(Bache's) *General Advertiser* (later *Aurora and General Advertiser*), 1792–93, 1795–97, 1799, 1801–16
		Independent Gazatteer, 1784–88
		Pennsylvania Gazette, 1761–69, 1781–85, 1790
		Pennsylvania Journal, 1757–73, 1782–84
		Pennsylvania Packet, 1772–76, 1781–84, 1788–90
		(Relf's) *Philadelphia Gazette and Daily Advertiser*, 1804–10

	Pittsburgh	*Commonwealth*, 1805, 1812–13
		Pittsburgh Gazette, 1812–21
	Wilkes-Barre	*The Gleaner*, 1815
SOUTH CAROLINA	Charleston	*City Gazette*, 1798–1803
TENNESSEE	Knoxville	*Knoxville Register*, 1818–21, 1824–30
	Nashville	*Clarion and Tennessee State Gazette*, 1817–19
VIRGINIA	Alexandria	*Alexandria Advertiser*, 1801–03
		Columbian Mirror and Alexandria Gazette, 1792–93
		Times and Alexandria Advertiser, 1797–98
		Virginia Gazette, 1791
		Virginia Journal and Alexandria Advertiser, 1784–91
	Norfolk	*American Beacon*, 1815–22
		Norfolk and Portsmouth Herald, 1820
	Richmond	*Richmond Enquirer*, 1808–14, 1819–22
		Virginia Gazette and General Advertiser, 1791–92

Guidebooks and Gazatteers

The second quarter of the nineteenth century saw the publication of a great number of travelers' guides to the United States or portions of it. Because many of these guides were issued in successive editions, in which the changes in transportation facilities can be traced, they are an important source for plotting the growth of stage lines and competing facilities. These books often contained excellent maps. Even the best libraries usually do not have all editions of these titles, however, and there is no bibliographical guide that can be used as a reference to check them. Moreover, relatively few of these guides exist for the period before 1820. When carefully used, some of the books issued in the 1820s can be of value for studying the earlier period, and they are listed here. Gazatteers are of less value than guidebooks for studying routes, but they are useful for checking old place names and are invaluable if a researcher is attempting detailed local studies.

Amphlett, William. *The Emigrant's Directory to the Western States of North America*. London, 1819.

Brown, Samuel R. *The Western Gazetteer, or Emigrant's Directory*. Auburn, New York, 1817.

Colles, Christopher. *A Survey of the Roads of the United States of America, 1789*. New York 1789.

Dana, Edmund. *Geographical Sketches on the Western Country: Designed for Emigrants and Settlers*. Cincinnati, 1819.

Darby, William. *The Emigrant's Guide to the Western and Southwestern States and Territories*. New York, 1818.

[Dwight, Theodore.] *The Northern Traveller and Northern Tour.* New York, 1825. Reprinted in later editions.

[Elliot, William.] *The Washington Guide.* Washington, D.C., 1822.

Hewett, Daniel. *The American Traveller.* Washington, D.C., 1825.

Melish, John. *Geographical Description of the United States.* Philadelphia, 1822.

——.*The Traveller's Directory through the United States.* Philadelphia, 1815. 5th ed., 1819.

>Includes *A Description of Roads in the United States* (first published separately, Philadelphia, 1814).

Moore, S. S., and Jones, T. W. *The Traveller's Directory: Or, A Pocket Companion Showing the Course of the Main Road from Philadelphia to New York; and from Philadelphia to Washington.* 2d ed. Philadelphia, 1804.

>This guidebook is especially interesting because of its detailed strip maps.

Morse, Jedidiah. *The American Gazetteer.* Boston, 1797. 2d ed., 1804. 3d ed., 1810.

——. *The Traveller's Guide.* Philadelphia, 1815.

Pease, John C. and Niles, John M. *A Gazetteer of the States of Connecticut and Rhode-Island.* Hartford, 1819.

Sherwood, Adiel. *A Gazetteer of the State of Georgia.* 2d ed., Philadelphia, 1829.

Temple, George. *The American Tourist's Pocket Companion; A Guide to the Springs, and Trip to the Lakes.* New York, 1812.

Maps

Many of the more useful maps are found in guidebooks and gazetteers. Two important bibliographical guides are P. Lee Phillips, *A List of Maps of America in the Library of Congress* (Washington, 1901) and C. H. Le Gear, *United States Atlases* (Washington, 1950). The latter covers both contemporary atlases and more recent state and country atlases, which often contain helpful local details. The following maps are of outstanding importance; a complete list of useful contemporary maps would be far too long for inclusion here.

The United States

Bradley, Abraham, Jr. "Map of the United States Exhibiting the Post Roads, Situations, Connections & Distances of the Post-offices, Stage-roads, Counties, Ports of Entry, and Delivery for Foreign Vessels, and the Principal Rivers." W. Barker, Sculp. 35 x 37 in., Philadelphia, 1796.

>Although published privately, this map may be thought of as the first official map of the Post Office Department inasmuch as it was distributed to all postmasters to aid them in their duties. Especially valuable for this study was its separate designation of mail stage routes by a Post Office official.

Bradley, Abraham, Jr. "Map of the United States Exhibiting the Post Roads, the Situations, Connections & Distances of the Post-Offices, Stage Roads, Counties, & Principal Rivers." Engraved by Francis Shallus. 38 x 53½ in. Philadelphia, 1804.

>A detail of this map is reprinted in this book's photo essay.

Carey, Mathew. *Carey's American Atlas*. Philadelphia, 1795.

——— and Son. *Carey's General Atlas*. Philadelphia, 1814, 1818.

Carey, H. C., and I. Lea. *Complete Historical, Chronological, and Geographical American Atlas*. Philadelphia, 1822.

Lewis, Samuel, "A New and Correct Map of the United States of America; Exhibiting the Counties, Towns, Roads, etc., in Each State." 67 x 73½ in. Philadelphia, 1819.

Melish, John. "United States of North America." 19 x 19½ in. Philadelphia, 1818.

Individual States

Carleton, Osgood. "Map of Massachusetts Proper. Compiled from Actual Surveys Made by Order of the General Court...." 32 x 47 in. Boston, 1802. Rev. ed., 1822.

Carrigain, Philip. "New Hampshire by Recent Survey." 46 x 60 in. Concord, 1816. This map shows turnpikes, roads, and villages in great detail.

Eddy, J. H. "The State of New York, with Part of the Adjacent States." 38 x 43 in. New York, 1818.

Greenleaf, Moses. "Map of the District of Maine from the Latest and Best Authorities." 40 x 26 in. Boston, 1815, 1820.

Griffith, Denis. "Map of Maryland." 30 x 50 in. Philadelphia, 1795.

Howell, Reading. "A Map of the State of Pennsylvania." 21 x 33 in. Philadelphia, 1811, 1817.

Kilbourne, John. "Map of Ohio." 25 x 23¾ in. Columbus, 1822.

Lay, Amos. "Map of the State of New York with Part of the States of Pennsylvania, New Jersey, &c." 40 x 50¾ in. 2d ed. rev. New York, 1820.

Madison, James. "A Map of Virginia Formed from Actual Surveys...." 45 x 68 in. Richmond, 1818.

Melish, John. "Map of Pennsylvania." 50 x 74 in. Philadelphia, 1822.

Tanner, H. S. "The Traveller's Pocket Map of Georgia with Its Roads and Distances." 10 x 12½ in. Philadelphia, 1831.

———. "The Traveller's Pocket Map of Tennessee with Its Roads and Distances from Place to Place Along the Stage and Steam Boat Routes." 10¼ 14 in. Philadelphia, 1830.

Warren, Moses, and Gillet, George. "Connecticut from Actual Survey...." 35 x 44 in. Hartford, Conn., 1812.

Whitelaw, James. "Vermont from Actual Survey...." 45 x 30 in. Hartford, Vt., 1821.

Young, J. H. "Map of North and South Carolina and Georgia." 16 x 21 in. Philadelphia, 1832.

Autobiographies, Diaries, and Reminiscences

Bentley, William. *The Diary of William Bentley, D.D.* 4 vols. Salem, Mass., 1905–14.

Breck, Samuel. *Recollections of Samuel Breck, With Passages from His Note-books.* Edited by H. E. Scudder, Philadelphia, 1877.

Davis, Matthew L. *Memoirs of Aaron Burr with Miscellaneous Selections from His Correspondence.* 2 vols. New York, 1836–37.

Everett, Edward. "Eighteen Hundred Fourteen," *Old and New,* 7 (1873): 47–54.
An account of a trip by stage from Boston to Washington.

———. *The Mount Vernon Papers.* New York, 1860.

Latrobe, Benjamin H. *The Journal of Latrobe.* New York, 1905.

Quincy, Josiah. *Figures of the Past from the Leaves of Old Journals.* New edition. Edited by M. A. De Wolfe Howe. Boston, 1926.
An account of a stage trip from Boston to Washington with Joseph Story.

Worth, Gorham A. "Recollections of Cincinnati." Albany, 1851. Reprinted in *Quarterly Publication of the Historical and Philosophical Society of Ohio.* 11 (1916): 8–25.

Travellers' Narratives

The observations of foreign travelers on American travel conditions and facilities were perhaps more accurate than their observations on other aspects of American life. In addition, the foreigners had the advantage of perspective since they could make comparisons with their home country or other countries in which they had traveled. At the end of their journeys, most foreign travelers had had more experience within America than all but a few Americans of the day. Few extensive travel narratives of this period were written by Americans for publication. Researchers must go to diaries, letters, and memoirs for the picture as it was seen by Americans, who were more likely to mention the exceptional than to describe the normal.

There are excellent lists of British travel narratives in Allan Nevins, *Social History as Recorded by British Travellers* (rev. ed., New York, 1931) and Jane Merick, *The English Traveller in America, 1785–1835* (New York, 1922), and of French travel narratives in Charles H. Sherrill, *French Memories of Eighteenth-Century America, 1775–1800* (New York, 1915) and Frank Monaghan, *French Travellers in the United States, 1765–1932* (New York, 1932). These books also provide wise counsel in using and interpreting the observations of foreign travelers. Other lists, which include published narratives by Americans as well as foreigners, can be found in W. P. Trent et al., *Cambridge History of American Literature* (4 vols., New York, 1917–21), 1:468–90; Ralph L. Rusk, *Literature of the Middle Western Frontier* (2 vols., New York, 1925), 2:101–36; and in Oscar Handlin et al., *Harvard Guide to American History* (Cambridge, Mass., 1954), pp. 150–61.

[Anonymous.] *A Summer Month: or, Recollections of a Visit to the Falls of Niagara and the Lakes.* Philadelphia, 1823.

Baily, Francis. *Journal of a Tour in the Unsettled Parts of North America in 1796 and 1797.* London, 1841.

Bernard, John. *Retrospections of America 1797–1811.* New York, 1877.

Bernhard, Karl, Duke of Saxe-Weimar-Eisinach. *Travels through North America during the Years 1825 and 1826.* 2 vols. Philadelphia, 1828.

Bigelow, Timothy. *Journal of a Tour to Niagara Falls in the Year 1805.* Boston, 1876.

Blane, William N. *An Excursion through the United States and Canada during the Years 1822–23.* London, 1824.

Brissot de Warville, Jean Pierre. *New Travels in the United States of America Performed in 1788.* London, 1792.

Buckingham, James S. *The Slave States of America.* 2 vols. London, 1842.

———. *America, Historical, Statistic and Descriptive.* 3 vols. London, 1843.

Coke, Edward Thomas. *A Subaltern's Furlough.* 2 vols. New York, 1833.

Dalton, William. *Travels in the United States and Upper Canada.* Appleby, England, 1821.

Darby, William. *A Tour from the City of New York to Detroit, in the Michigan Territory.* New York, 1819.

Davis, John. *Travels of Four Years and a Half in the United States of America During 1798, 1799, 1800, 1801, 1802.* London, 1803.

Dickens, Charles. *American Notes.* London, 1842.

Duncan, John M. *Travels through Part of the United States and Canada in 1818 and 1819.* 2 vols. New York, 1823.

Dwight, Timothy. *Travels in New England and New York.* 4 vols. New Haven, 1821–22.

Fearon, Henry B. *Sketches of America.* 2nd ed. London, 1818.

Fowler, John. *Journal of a Tour in the State of New York in the Year 1830.* London, 1831.

Hall, Basil. *Travels in America.* 3 vols. Edinburgh, 1829.

Hall, Francis. *Travels in Canada and the United States in 1816 and 1817.* London, 1818.

Hamilton, Thomas. *Men and Mariners in America.* 2 vols. Edinburg, 1834.

Harris, William Tell. *Remarks Made during a Tour through the United States of America in the Years 1817, 1818, and 1819.* London, 1821.

Hoffman, Charles Fenno. *A Winter in the West.* 2 vols. New York, 1835.

Hodgson, Adam. *Letters from North America.* 2 vols. London, 1824.

Howitt, Emmanuel. *Selections from Letters Written during a Tour through the United States.* Nottingham, 1819.

Janson, Charles W. *The Stranger in America.* London, 1807.

Lambert, John. *Travels through Canada and the United States in the Years 1806, 1807, and 1808.* 2nd ed. London, 1814.

La Rochefoucauld-Liancourt, Francois, duc de. *Travels through the United States of America and Upper Canada in the Years 1795, 1796, and 1797.* 2 vols. London, 1799.

Latrobe, Charles J. *The Rambler in North America.* 2 vols. Philadelphia, 1835.

Lyell, Charles. *Travels in North America.* 2 vols. New York, 1845.

Mackey, Alexander. *The Western World.* 3 vols. London, 1849.

Marryat, Frederick. *A Diary in America*. 3 vols. London, 1839.

Martineau, Harriet. *Retrospect of Western Travel*. 3 vols. London, 1838.

Maude, John. *Visit to the Falls of Niagara in 1800*. London, 1826.

Melish, John. *Travels in the United States of America in the Years 1806, and 1807, and 1809, 1810, and 1811*. 2 vols. Philadelphia, 1812.

Montule, Edouard de. *A Voyage to North America and the West Indies in 1817*. London, 1821.

Murray, Amelia. *Letters from the United States, Cuba, and Canada*. 2 vols. London, 1856.

Palmer, John. *Journals of Travels in the United States of North America and in Lower Canada Performed in the Year 1817*. London, 1818.

Parkinson, Richard. *A Tour in America in 1798, 1799, and 1800*. 2 vols. London, 1805.

Power, Tyrone. *Impressions of America*. 2 vols. London, 1836.

Schoepf, Johann David. *Travels in the Confederation*. Translated and edited by A. J. Morrison. 2 vols. Philadelphia, 1911.

Shirreff, Patrick. *A Tour through North America*. Edinburgh, 1835.

Stuart, James. *Three Years in America*. 2 vols. New York, 1833.

Sutcliff, Robert. *Travels in Some Parts of North America in the Years 1804, 1805, and 1806*. 2nd ed. York, 1815.

Tudor, Henry. *Narrative of a Tour in North America*. 2 vols. Philadelphia, 1836.

Twining, Thomas. *Travels in America 100 Years Ago*. New York, 1894.

Wansey, Henry. *An Excursion to the United States of North America in the Summer of 1794*. 2nd ed. Salisbury, 1798.

Weld, Isaac. *Travels through the States of North America and the Provinces of Upper and Lower Canada during the Years 1795, 1796, and 1797*. 4th ed. 2 vols. London, 1807.

Index